Taylor's Guides to Gardening

Judy White

Frances Tenenbaum, Series Editor

HOUGHTON MIFFLIN COMPANY

Boston • New York

Taylor's Guide to Orchids

For information about this and other Houghton Mifflin trade
and reference books and multimedia products, visit The
Bookstore at Houghton Mifflin on the World Wide Web at
http://www.hmco.com/trade/.

Taylor's Guide is a registered trademark
of Houghton Mifflin Company.

Library of Congress Cataloging-in-Publication Data

Taylor's guide to orchids / Judy White.
        p. cm. — (Taylor's guides to gardening)
    Includes index.
    ISBN 0-395-67726-2
    1. Orchid culture. 2. Orchids. I. White, Judy. II. Series.
SB409.T38 1996
635.9'3415 — dc20   95-44963
                                                 CIP

Printed in Hong Kong

DNP 10 9 8 7 6

Cover photograph *Phalaenopsis*, Brazilian Legend,
© by judywhite/New Leaf Images

Contents

For my mother

Ermalinda Russo White

who quietly and with great steadfastness

has helped make many things possible

including this book.

Foreword

Somehow, the word seems to have gotten around that orchids are difficult to grow. Fortunately, this book is here to help set the record straight.

I'm not sure how orchids gained such an undeserved reputation. Perhaps it's because they're so beautiful and people assume that anything so beautiful has to be difficult. Perhaps it's because of all those Rex Stout detective novels in which the world's greatest and huskiest fictional detective, Nero Wolfe, devoted the better part of every morning to the potting bench in his rooftop greenhouse. Perhaps it's simply that the orchid suggests something exotic and is usually thought of as a tropical plant, and everybody feels that exotic, tropical plants are delicate and fussy.

No matter. Whatever the origin of this canard, I can think of no one better qualified to guide you through the world of orchids than the author of this book. Whatever your skill level and knowledge base — whether you are a green beginner or a longtime veteran of what the Victorians called Orchidelirium — you'll find the *Taylor's Guide to Orchids* wonderfully useful. The fact is, orchids are easy to grow, but they also reward greater knowledge and skill. It doesn't take a lot of knowledge to grow orchids, but growing orchids gets better the more knowledge you acquire.

In my position as Executive Director of the American Orchid Society (AOS), I've had many opportunities to rely on Judy's knowledge and skill. In fact, this book began as an extraordinary seven-part series for beginners written by her for the American Orchid Society's magazine, and it immediately became the most popular and most widely acclaimed series in the 75-year history of our publication. She is also the recipient of the society's highest journalistic prize, the Dillon/Peterson Award, for an article on orchid potting materials that is still regarded as the definitive text on the subject.

A nationally recognized writer, photographer, and lecturer on orchids and many other gardening subjects, Judy has also been the orchid columnist for *HousePlant* magazine, and orchid/garden consultant on CompuServe's online Garden Forum. Her photography has graced the covers of many magazines and books, and her articles are standouts for their lively text and common sense.

It is from long years of personal experience, as much as from her impressive résumé, that I commend you to her capable words and beautiful orchid photography. I can tell you she is generous, good-natured, and articulate — the characteristics of most of the world's best teachers.

So if you've thought it might be fun to try your hand with orchids, or if you're already an aficionado and hope to acquire more information, or if you're simply enthralled by the gorgeous photography of the world's most seductive flower, I recommend this book to you without reservation. Consume its easy-reading, educational text and glorious pictures. And when you can no longer resist the temptation, go buy your first orchid, or add yet another to your collection.

Take it from me — you're in good hands.

— *Lee S. Cooke*
Executive Director
American Orchid Society

Introduction: The Misunderstood Orchid

No flower is as misunderstood as the orchid. Although many orchids are indisputably gorgeous, the reigning royalty of all flowers, people are afraid to try to grow them. No plant is more intimidating than the orchid, but its reputation is quite undeserved. Orchids are not difficult; they are simply different.

When it comes to orchids, most people are still in the Victorian ages, still mistakenly believing that hothouses, steamy conditions, and a fistful of dollars are necessary to grow them. Yet many orchids can be grown in any home. By and large, orchids are rugged and adaptable and don't need a jungle or a greenhouse. Many novices find to their delight that they can bloom orchids successfully even while their African violets sulk in another window. And, given a number of recent laboratory developments, particularly those that make it possible to clone thousands of plants from a small piece of one, it no longer costs a fortune to buy them, either.

Orchids are so different from other plants, and often so different from one another, that visitors to orchid shows find it hard to believe that every flower displayed is an orchid. Practically anyone can recognize a classic corsage orchid, but when confronted with flowers that resemble elbow macaroni spray-painted neon orange, or female bees, or Puck-faced laughing gnomes, few people could immediately say, "Aha, an orchid." But yes, they are *all* orchids.

Orchids are the most diversified and successful flowers on Earth. Unlike the rose, for example, which is simply a single group (or genus) of about 100 natural species within a larger family of flowers, orchids make up an entire family all by themselves. That family is huge, with an estimated 25,000 wild species of orchids and 1,400 groups (or genera), more than any other family of flowers. In a world of perhaps a quarter million flowering plant species, more than one out of every ten species is an orchid.

Orchids grow nearly everywhere in the world, in swamps and deserts, in deeply shaded woodlands, in the broad burning sun of a lava flow site, from sea level to 14,000 feet, even as far north as the Arctic Circle. The only place it seems they don't grow is in the ocean. The vast majority and greatest diversity can be found on the sides of trees in tropical forests, particularly of the South American Andes and Himalayan mountains. Orchids prefer these cool, mid-mountain (or montane) forest or cloud-forest regions to the lowland tropical rain forests. Most can be found at elevations between 3,000 and 7,000 feet, where the rainfall exceeds 100 inches a year, with at least 2 to 3 inches each month, and temperatures typically range from 50° to 90°F. The Neotropical South American country of Colombia, which runs a gamut of habitats in a small area, is home to 10 percent or more of all orchids, with a conservatively estimated 3,000 species. In the Old World tropics, the island of New Guinea, with its vast mountain ranges and forests, may boast an even greater diversity.

Orchids span just about the entire color range, even to coveted shades of blue, and come in every color combination, often with spots, stripes, "warts," and other striking patterns. While horticulturally there is no real color "black," some orchids, particularly some of the newest *Paphiopedilum* "vinicolored" hybrids, are of such deep maroon and brown that they look black. Orchids range in size from minuscule *Platystele* plants that fit neatly inside a thimble to monstrous *Grammatophyllum* growths weighing as much as a bull elephant, from flowers the size of a flea to 8-inch dinner-plate specials. And to quote orchid scientist Dr. Alec Pridgeon, orchids resemble their nearest relative, the iris, about as much as whales resemble their nearest relative, the hippopotamus. Furthermore, these extraordinarily common flowers are so highly developed and unique that orchids are to the plant kingdom what humans are to the animal kingdom, both at the top of their evolutionary heaps.

What Makes Orchids Different?

Peer inside an orchid corsage or a lady's slipper orchid and the immediate effect is that of a painting by Georgia O'Keeffe, with heightened realities and definite sexual overtones. Many people would be hard pressed to put names to the various parts of an orchid flower, which aren't as distinctly obvious as in a daisy or even a rose.

But orchid flowers, although they often look very different from one another, have one thing in common. If you draw a line from top to bottom through the center of the flower, it will be identical on either side. All orchids have six symmetrical parts that most people would be tempted to call petals. Actually, it's not six; it's two sets of three. The first three are known as sepals, one on top (the dorsal) and two at either lower side (laterals), and the other three are technically the petals. Yet even in this simple anatomy orchids can seem baffling, for, in typical orchid exceptions, the various parts can be outlandishly exaggerated, or the two lateral sepals can fuse together (such as in *Paphiopedilum*), or all three can even fuse into a cup (such as in *Masdevallia*), with the petals almost disappearing altogether. All this can be very confusing to someone trying to decipher the parts.

One of the petals, however, is very often spectacular in shape, color, pattern, and/or size. That petal, located almost always at the bottom of the flower, is called the lip, or labellum. Orchid buds actually twist around 180° during development to ensure that the lip is lowermost (or resupinate). Since most other types of flowers don't perform this twist, orchids are frequently mistakenly displayed in vases and in pictures upside down, with the conspicuous lip at top. But, in fact, all the designations for orientation used in describing orchid flowers (dorsal, lateral, and so forth) are in relation to this bottommost lip. The lip, in its cleverly twisted lower location, is often ingeniously designed to attract pollinators, with the sexual organ usually located conveniently just above this bottommost lip.

The single best identifiable feature that makes orchids different from just about all other flowers is the sexual organ. In orchids, the male part of the orchid flower (stamen) and the female part (pistil) are so advanced that instead of being separate, as in most flowers, the two have been incorporated into one structure, a unique orchid feature known as the column.

At the top of the column sits the male part, where, depending on the species, two to eight rather large knoblike packets of pollen are kept. Orchids don't produce wind-dispersible pollen like so many other flowers do, and only a small amount of pollen is made at all. Orchids seduce insects and birds instead to carry off the entire pollen bundles (or pollinia) intact. After the pollen clump has been deposited on a receptive column, masses of dustlike seed are produced, the tiniest and most numerous seed of all flowering plants, with as many as five million in each ripened seed capsule. This vast amount of seed carries far more genetic diversity than pollen could, an important reason why orchids have evolved into the largest flowering plant family. That genetic diversity means orchids can afford to produce such fascinating species, from the classic beautiful corsage to the ones that look like rotting meat complete with maggots to attract the species' pollinator, the carrion fly.

Delightful Seduction

Orchids have made thousands of such bizarre adaptations in order to seduce specific pollinators, giving some of the most potent and compelling demonstrations of the theory of evolution. Some (*Ophrys*) have even evolved into uncannily accurate reproductions of female bees, complete with female bee texture and perfume, so that the male bee will try to mate with the flower. He winds up instead hauling away the orchid pollen, which then gets deposited in a second "mating" frenzy (scientifically known as pseudocopulation) onto another attractive-looking, "musky"-smelling yet totally bogus paramour.

Many orchids attract pollinators to their beautifully patterned or flamboyant lips that act as irresistible landing platforms. Still others are equipped with ingenious Rube Goldberg–type traps, buckets, and/or hinges to force the pollinator through mazes to first deposit pollen from another flower and then pick up the new pollen, thus ensuring that the flower doesn't pollinate itself and guaranteeing greatest genetic diversity. Some even shoot the pollinator in the head with sticky pollen, in something very much like a child's rubber-tipped dart gun.

Fragrance is another seductive device. People familiar with orchids only as corsages or cut flowers are unaware of how wonderfully scented orchids can be, since fragrance usually fades after the flower is picked, but a goodly proportion have some sort of scent. Besides the obvious allure of rotting liver, some orchids (*Stanhopea,* for example) use fragrance as an intoxicant, causing the bee to fall drunkenly into an orchid tank of liquid, where it is rudely awakened into recovery. With wings soaked and the option of simply flying away now gone, the insect must instead crawl and climb to escape and, naturally, must pass by the pollinia on the way out.

Orchid fragrances range from cinnamon to jasmine, lemon, baby powder, hyacinth, orange, coconut, chocolate, wintergreen, and even watermelon and menthol. In fact, vanilla is an orchid. Others are decidedly unpleasant.

Orchids have no peer at seducing insects and birds into landing on and pollinating their flowers. They are so good at their deceptions that Charles Darwin wrote an entire book about this fascinating and diverse process. The book, *On the Various Contrivances by which Orchids Are Fertilised by Insects,* appeared in 1862, three years after his famous *Origin of Species.*

Seeds of Success

Yet despite our fascination with orchid pollination, for almost a hundred years humans had a terrible time trying to get orchid seeds to grow. Unlike many flowering plants, orchids don't provide their seeds with any internal food while the embryos are developing, and the seeds therefore can't grow on their own. This seemed strangely counterproductive, especially for such an advanced flower family, but in the late 1800s several scientists, working separately, discovered that in nature, orchid seeds had to be invaded by a specific fungus that would convert complex starches into sugars and thus provide the seedlings with food while the fungus was provided with a home. This symbiotic (of benefit to both parties) relationship explained why seeds in cultivation grew only when scattered around the potting medium of the parent orchid. Successful germination, however, occurred only occasionally, obviously whenever the particular fungus for that species happened to be present. Still, even armed with this information, growing orchids from seed continued to be a haphazard and frustrating undertaking.

But in 1922 a true revolution occurred, when American scientist Lewis Knudsen, working at Cornell University, discovered that orchid seeds didn't need the fungal relationship in order to germinate. They simply needed the right proportions of carbohydrates and mineral nutrients the fungi gave them. Knudsen successfully germinated seeds in a laboratory environment, in flasks on sterile agar jelly with a nutrient solution. By 1930 those seeds had grown to flowers, and in one fell swoop, a new industry was born. Anyone and everyone with a toothpick and two compatible orchids in bloom at the same time began creating hybrids.

With this orchid flasking under way, prices became more reasonable and orchids more accessible. But it wasn't until 1956 that another revolution helped to change the orchid world even more dramatically. French plant physiologist Georges Morel was engrossed in work to produce a virus-free potato when he realized that the growing tip of new shoots did not contain the virus. Based in part on Knudsen's work, Morel successfully grew those potato growing tips (known technically as apical meristematic tissue) on constantly agitated nutrient agar. Since Morel was an orchid hobbyist, he decided to experiment with *Cymbidium* orchids, and he found that he could create from just a few cells thousands of virtually identical copies — or "clones" — of the parent plant with this new tissue culture method, called meristemming (from the Greek for "divisible").

With those two laboratory developments, interest in orchids skyrocketed. Orchids went from the greenhouse provinces of kings and the superwealthy to the windowsills and plant lights in suburbia and city apartments. Even the U.S. government has gotten on the orchid bandwagon, for the USDA recently developed *Phalaenopsis* varieties geared to withstand the most atrocious houseplant abuse, even the tortures of potting soil. The American Orchid Society, which was founded the year before Dr. Knudsen made his germination discoveries, went from 100 charter members in 1921 to more than 30,000 by the 1990s, becoming the largest horticultural society in the world devoted to a single subject.

Growing Orchids at Home

Cattleya

Modern man first tried to grow orchids in the mid-1700s, when plants began to arrive in Europe from the Central and South American tropics, bedraggled and dried out after months of sea voyaging. These sorry-looking specimens were plunked into soggy mixes and placed in airtight, dripping wet greenhouses heated enough to satisfy any Satan, which was the environment mistakenly thought to most resemble a tropical rain forest. When the orchids died, instead of blaming the conditions, growers blamed the orchids.

But, in fact, those conditions are nothing like the tropics, and nothing like what orchids want. Regardless of location, tropical habitats — even the jungles — are fresh and airy, full of breezes. Far from being constantly hot and steamy, the temperature in tropical habitats varies dramatically depending on elevation. The higher orchids live, the cooler the temperatures. *Pleione* orchids, for example, break through Himalayan snowtops in subtropical Tibet to bloom, and even at the equator, a 12,000-foot cloud forest can have frost at night. Orchids in the warmest, lowest environments do not have to endure daytime highs above 90°F for very long. Nowhere do orchids suffer in nature through hot, steamy, stagnant, airtight conditions. The temperature in orchid habitats in the same location also changes radically from day to night, dropping at least 15°F but sometimes as much as 40°F from the daytime high.

Most tropical orchids do not live in the ground, or in anything resembling potting soil, and herein lies a big difference between orchids and other houseplants. The vast majority — 75 percent or more — live on the sides of trees or even on rocks, using the tree bark or rock simply as anchor. These are known as epiphytes (Greek for "air plants"), or lithophytes, which is a subset of epiphytic life if they grow atop rock. Terrestrial orchids that do live in the ground usually do not grow in the tropics; they are found in more temperate regions.

Orchids are not parasites and do not sap life from the plant on which they may be anchored. They thrive because they can exist in nutrient-poor habitats, such as the top of a tree, that would quickly kill many other types of plants. Most orchids have thickened roots that run along the bark or wave in the air, catching whatever water and nutrients pass by, getting wet, quickly drying out, getting wet, then quickly drying out again. Because of the paucity of nutrients and the quick-drying microclimate, living in a tree is very much like living in a desert, and cactuslike plants are often found growing in the same habitat as epiphytic orchids.

Orchids possess other physical features with a lot of water-storage capability, such as thick leaves and/or swollen stems known as pseudobulbs. Camellike, such orchids are much better able to withstand periods of drought and dry seasons than an environment that constantly keeps their roots sopping wet, subject to rot and disease. Even terrestrial orchids usually sink their roots into a very loose and quick-to-drain nutrient-poor flooring, for they too do not like environments that are rich or continually sopping wet.

Orchid Environments in the Home

How do we go about simulating an orchid habitat in homes devoid of trees, tropical mists, and breezes? Fortunately, this is simpler than it seems, mostly because orchids are so adaptable.

Any well-lit, well-ventilated, indoor spot will suit many orchids nicely. It's possible to grow a number of types in typical home humidity, although spots that can receive extra humidity from a humidifier or extra misting or other means are always preferred. Some terrestrial orchids are even hardy enough to withstand winters outdoors in the garden under snow, and in frost-free climates such as southern California, many orchids can live year-round outdoors in pots and mounted on trees. The vast bulk of cultivated orchids, however, enjoy life inside the average home, whether on windowsills, under skylights, in sunrooms, in a greenhouse, even under a couple of fluorescent shop lights, or any combination thereof.

If the spot is not well lit, well ventilated, humid, or even the right temperature, it's possible to make it so, or find another that is. Orchidists with an ever-expanding collection have adapted and invented many interior and exterior environments, from the sills of living-room picture windows, to damp basements full of light carts, to linen closets rigged with air vents, to outdoor bogs lined with plastic.

Fortunately for the beginning orchidist, there's no need to go to extremes in growing orchids. Any sunny windowsill will do fine for many popular orchids, without much more fuss or bother than periodic watering.

Plant lights are eminently suitable for growing orchids. Two shop-light fixtures with four fluorescent tubes placed 8 inches above the orchids will bloom many low-light orchids. Virtually all other higher-light plants bloom wonderfully with high-intensity-discharge lamps (sodium vapor or metal halide) placed several feet away. An excellent orchid environment is in a basement, on plant light carts in an area enclosed by clear plastic draping.

Windowsill greenhouses also are excellent, as long as they are well caulked and tightly fit. Southern exposures are best, then southeast, then southwest. Make sure the glass is insulated and well ventilated with screens, since windowsill greenhouses can get very hot in summer and very cold in winter.

Orchid growers always lust after a real greenhouse, and these are more affordable than ever. One of the best organizations for information about creating one is the Hobby Greenhouse Association (8 Glen Terrace, Bedford, MA 01730, 617-275-0377).

Growers are divided in opinion about whether the benefits of a summer outdoors outweigh the disadvantages. The higher light, airy fresh environment, and ease in watering are offset by insects and other pests, the prospect of too much sunlight burning leaves, rots caused by too much rain, and plant resentment when they are put back in the house, particularly if you do so after the heat is turned back on. Higher-light orchids such as *Cattleya, Oncidium, Vanda,* and *Cymbidium* really seem to benefit from the summer outdoors. Orchids brought outdoors need an acclimation period, a "hardening-off" adjustment. Don't put them out until night temperatures are 60°F, and bring them back inside at night for the first few days. Initially, keep them very sheltered from the sun. Gradually let them get more light, but be careful of hot noon and afternoon sun, which can cause the leaves to sunburn and turn black. Choose a permanent spot with filtered light; a slatted-roof lath house is ideal. Reverse the hardening-off procedure when you bring them back indoors in fall to allow them to adjust to lower light and humidity. Wash pots and leaves to minimize tag-along pests.

Hardy orchids are those that can withstand outdoor temperatures, often even below freezing. Some, such as *Bletilla,* often sold as a bulb plant, are truly garden plants, overwintering in the ground and reappearing to bloom every year without much care.

The Most Popular Orchids for the Home

Ease of growth and showy blooms are the two main reasons why certain orchids have become especially popular, dominating the number of hybrid cross registrations and American Orchid Society awards.

Cattleyas

At the top of the list is the group of orchids that belong to the Cattleya Alliance. Cattleya types are among the showiest and most rewarding orchids to grow in the home, ranging in color from classic orchid lavender to white, red, yellow, orange, green, and blue. Many are very fragrant. Intergeneric hybridizing trends in the past decade have produced compact and miniature "catts" that greatly reduce the space needed for traditionally big and gawky cattleya plants, yet still produce nice-sized flowers.

Several related genera make up the Cattleya Alliance of orchids, which can cause beginners some confusion in names. *Cattleya, Laelia, Sophronitis, Brassavola, Broughtonia, Epidendrum,* and *Rhyncholaelia* are the main genera that are interbred. Whatever the combination of genera, cattleyas are all grown in a fairly similar manner. Native from Mexico to Brazil, these are epiphytes, usually growing on sides of trees. In the home, they prefer intermediate home temperatures with winter nights of 55°F. To flower well, medium-bright light is essential. Cattleyas can grow well for years without giving a bloom, frustrating many a grower, but the reason is almost sure to be too little light. A southern or southeastern exposure with 2,000 to 3,000 footcandles is excellent, and the higher the light in this range, the more blooms. A dilute

20-10-10 weekly fertilizer will also mean more flowers. Cattleyas are "camels" in the orchid world, possessing pseudobulbs that store water, and must have a well-drained mix, such as one of 80 percent fir bark or stone, with 20 percent perlite. Water thoroughly only when the mix has dried out to an inch below the surface.

Phalaenopsis

Next most popular, possibly the best beginner's plants, are the *Phalaenopsis* orchids and the virtually indistinguishable man-made genus of *Doritaenopsis* (*Doritis* × *Phalaenopsis*), which are both called phals for short. Phals are among the easiest orchids to grow at home, preferring lower light and warm home temperatures where winter nights do not drop below 60°F. Give an eastern exposure with 1,000 to 1,500 footcandles of light, just enough to cast a soft shadow when a hand is held between the sun and the plant. If windowsill light is not adequate, phals do fine under four fluorescent light tubes, about 8 inches away, on a timer for 14 hours a day.

Known as the tropical Moth Orchids, from their resemblance to wide-winged moths in flight, phalaenopsis send up long arching sprays of flowers up to 6 inches across, in colors from basic white to pink, yellow, peach, red, and green, with any combination of stripes, spots, and colored lips. It's not unusual to have breathtaking clouds of sprays with 20 to 30 blooms that can last four months. They make excellent cut flowers as well, lasting a good week in water. When bloom is over, the inflorescence (spike) can be cut down to just above the second or third node, enticing the node to send up another spray.

Pot the epiphytic phalaenopsis in well-drained potting material, such as a mix of medium-size fir bark, coarse perlite, and chopped sphagnum moss (6/2/2 ratio). If home humidity is less than 30 percent, use plastic pots instead of clay, to keep more moisture around the roots. Low humidity can cause buds to "blast" and fall onto the floor before blooming, so use a humidifier near the plants or set them on plastic egg crate grids in trays filled with water to raise humidity. Phals don't like to dry out completely, but they need a rest between waterings, so water thoroughly once a week on average. Fertilize weekly with a quarter-strength 20-10-10 fertilizer.

Paphiopedilums

Excellent to grow side by side with phalaenopsis are plants of the genus *Paphiopedilum*, known as paphs. Paphs are trop-

ical Indo-Asian orchids related to North
American lady's slippers. The tropical paphs
make excellent houseplants, particularly
because of low light needs (1,500 footcandles) and warm/intermediate temperature preference. Paphs are unique in
appearance, so different in structure
that some scientists would like to
reclassify them altogether into a new
category of flowers. The sophisticated, waxy pouch and striking top sepal, combined with a variety of spots, stripes, hairs,
twists, and even "warts," on green, brown, red, yellow, pink,
and white (even approaching the elusive black) flowers, make
these a connoiseur's choice. Some have beautiful mottled foliage as well.

Grow paphiopedilums in deep, narrow plastic pots in a
semiterrestrial mix of 50 percent medium to fine fir bark and
25 percent coarse quartz sand, with an equal blend of coarse
perlite and milled leaf mold or chopped sphagnum moss.
Repot yearly, using plastic pots. Paphs do not like to dry out
completely between waterings, so water thoroughly every
three to four days, or when the mix feels dry ½ inch down.
Fertilize lightly with 20-20-20 (¼ strength) weekly, flushing
with plain water every month.

Cymbidiums

The oldest cultivated orchids
are plants of the floriferous genus
Cymbidium. These Asian natives
have become the orchid mainstay
of the cut-flower industry, beloved
for spikes of white, green, yellow, rose,
and red flowers that sometimes last two
months or more in water. These
big plants are very easy to grow,
given very high light (3,500 footcandles or higher) and very
cool temperatures; they need 45°F autumn nights to set buds.
They often are grown outdoors in warmer climates. Indoors,
a humid sun porch or greenhouse suits them best. Smaller-
growing, warmer species are being hybridized to create more
temperature-tolerant plants that can grow on more windowsills.

Coupled with high light is a need for regular fertilizer.
While most orchids are not heavy feeders, cymbidiums benefit
from 20-20-20 fertilizer applied at ¾ strength with each watering. Humidity of 50 percent or more also helps, as does an
extremely well drained semiterrestrial potting medium of 50
percent medium fir bark, 30 percent chopped sphagnum

moss, and 20 percent perlite, with a layer of stones or styrene foam on the bottom of a deep pot. Keep evenly moist.

Dendrobiums

Dendrobium is a hugely diverse genus with some of the most spectacularly beautiful flowers. Its more than 1,000 species span a large range of types, sizes, colors, shapes, and cultural requirements. Most are profuse-blooming epiphytes from Asian and South Pacific tropics and subtropics. Dendrobium culture can be confusing because some types are deciduous, dropping their leaves in early winter, while others are evergreen.

Home growers typically encounter two types of dendrobiums, both with tall canes. Hybridizers have created an industry of readily available, brilliantly colored "Yamamoto" (or *nobile*) dendrobiums. These are deciduous; they need a dormant, cool, low-water rest beginning in autumn, and intermediate temperatures the rest of the year. The other common type is the phalaenopsis dendrobium, an evergreen warm grower (with no relation to *Phalaenopsis* orchids except that its white to deep purple blooms resemble them). This tropical plant needs warm (60° to 65°F) winter nights.

Most dendrobiums, regardless of type, want bright light (2,500 to 3,000 footcandles), small pots, well-drained mixes (rock often works well, as does medium bark with coarse perlite), good air movement, and humidity between 50 and 70 percent.

Oncidiums

For sheer number of brilliant yellow blooms, few orchid groups rival the dancing sprays of the delightful plants of the genus *Oncidium*. Just about any branched shower of little yellow flowers in an elegant florist's bouquet is bound to belong to this relatively easy-to-grow group. *Oncidium* is closely related to quite a number of other orchid genera, including *Odontoglossum, Miltonia, Brassia, Comparettia,* and *Cochlioda*. Thousands of intergeneric hybrids have been made between them to create a large group of more than 50 new genera called the Oncidium Alliance. In general, however, straight oncidiums are among the easiest of all to grow, with the most temperature tolerance, particularly for heat.

All oncidiums like lots of light (2,500+ footcandles) for

best bloom, and a bright southern windowsill often works well. Most prefer intermediate temperatures (55°F minimum winter nights). Oncidiums grow best in clay pots filled with a coarse, well-drained mix, or mounted on clay slabs. Good air movement — fresh breezes and fans — along with humidity above 50 percent keeps oncidiums happy. They prefer lots of water and regular quarter-strength 20-20-20 fertilizer, but they need a decided drying out between watering.

Vandas

Gloriously brilliant *Vanda* orchids have long enjoyed popularity, especially in high-light (4,000 footcandles and higher), high-temperature areas such as Florida and Hawaii. Their colors include spectacular blue, and the full, round flowers can reach 5 inches wide on long, profuse spikes. Most orchids bloom in winter, but vandas dominate the summer months. Vandas, with lots of aerial roots, grow exceptionally well undisturbed in baskets. They are interbred often with *Ascocentrum* orchids, to make the very popular genus *Ascocenda*, which helps to downsize the otherwise often ungainly vanda (which can climb 10 feet high), as well as giving a broader color range, especially in scarlet and orange. Many other related genera are also hybridized with vandas; all are called vandaceous orchids. Bright, hot southern window exposures are perfect, and a spot where the plants can be watered and fertilized freely and abundantly is ideal.

Temperature and Light Growing Groups

As houseplants, orchids are commonly classified into several growing groups based on what temperatures they prefer and how much light they want. The essay "Light and Other Bloom Factors" will go into more detail with both these topics, but an overview is useful now.

Temperature

The higher the elevation of an orchid's native habitat, the cooler the plant's preferred temperature. As a rough rule of thumb, there are four orchid temperature groupings. "Warm"-growing orchids are typically from lowland regions; they like their winter nights (that is, coldest temperatures) to go no lower than 60°F. "Intermediate"-growing orchids prefer winter nights no colder than 50° to 55°F. "Cool"-growing orchids, those that live at the highest elevations or most temperate zones, generally like winter nights of 45° to 50°F; some even withstand frost. "Hardy" orchids are terrestrial plants from temperate regions that can grow outdoors year-round, sometimes even where there is snow in winter.

Cool-growing plants may perish in hot daytime temperatures. Most orchids, even the warmest growing, don't like temperatures much above 90°F for very long, although some notable exceptions (vandas, for example) get through blazing Florida summer heats with no real problems.

While these temperature groupings are common, there are no hard and fast lines. So-called intermediate growers will often tolerate temperatures that are a bit higher or lower; many warm growers will thrive below the temperatures recommended; some cool growers may be fine alongside intermediates. This is especially true with hybrid orchids interbred between different growing groups, such as when an intermediate-temperature *Cattleya* is hybridized with a cool-growing *Sophronitis* to make *Sophrocattleya.*

However, some orchids do not adapt as well to crossing temperature lines. These are "narrow-temperature" growers, such as *Miltoniopsis* and *Odontoglossum,* which do not fare well with large fluctuations from their preferred temperatures in winter nights and summer days. For example, both cattleyas and miltoniopsis are classified as intermediate growers, but while cattleyas do fine with day temperatures in the 80s, Miltoniopsis must stay in the 70s. They are "narrow-intermediate" growers.

This narrow-temperature concept is one often overlooked, but it is essential in learning how to grow all sorts of orchids. The classic temperature groupings are useful as a general guide in many respects, but they are neither infallible nor all-descriptive.

If your growing area is too cold for warm orchids, bottom heat can solve the problem. The temperature of the root zone, rather than the leaves, is what really needs to be kept warm. If you place 70°F plant heating coils or pads, such as those used to germinate seedlings, under pots of phalaenopsis, for example, they will grow even where the air temperature is 10° to 15°F lower than their preferred night minimums of 60°F.

Another often overlooked and even more important aspect of home orchid growing is getting the temperature to drop at least 10°F at night, as it would in orchid habitats. A clock setback thermostat on the heating system works well in winter. In summer, if you keep the house constantly air conditioned to an even temperature, put orchids outside, where nature will drop the night temperatures.

Light

Orchids are often classified as "low-light," "medium-light," and "high-light" growers. Again, these are artificial classifications that orchids often easily will cross. As a general rule, however, the higher the light levels an orchid gets, usually touching the upper limit of the light grouping, the better it will flower.

Low-light orchids generally grow either on lower parts of trees or even in the shaded ground underneath them, frequently not receiving direct sunlight. Since so many homes are low on available light, this grouping of orchids makes for some of the easiest to grow. Low light is classified as 1,200 to 2,000 footcandles of light intensity, found in an eastern window or even under fluorescent lights. Classic low-light orchids are *Phalaenopsis* plants.

Medium-light orchids often grow at the tops of tree canopies, with less competition for light than ones below, and they prefer 2,000 to 3,000 footcandles. Southern-facing windows can be excellent spots for them. *Cattleya* and related genera and hybrids fall into this category.

High-light growers are typically found in full sun habitats and need 3,000 footcandles or more to bloom well. They can be more difficult in the home environment, unless extremely well-lit windows or sunrooms, skylights, or greenhouses are available. Often the trick with high-light orchids is to make sure they're getting enough light while making sure they're not burning up from the high temperatures that commonly can accompany such light. *Cymbidium* and vandaceous plants like high light to bloom well.

Making the Environment as Good as Possible

Few things help orchids more than good air movement, for natural environments are full of continual breezes. Little "muffin" fans sold for computers work well, as do variable-speed fans that oscillate, or ceiling-mounted paddle fans. Let them run 24 hours a day all year long, and move them periodically, or change their direction, just as in nature breezes come from constantly changing directions. Fans blowing directly on any one area will dry it out.

Air movement is tremendous preventive medicine for many potential evils lurking around orchids. Stale, stagnant air breeds fungi and bacteria, encourages rot, makes potting mixes stay wet too long, causes leaves in high light to stay too hot, and allows the air to layer into hot high areas and cold lower regions instead of mixing freely and evenly. Fresh moving air offers a continual source of carbon dioxide for photosynthesis.

Orchids grow and bloom best if humidity can be kept near 50 to 60 percent, which can be measured with a hygrometer. Ways to increase humidity include adding a small humidifier, additional hand misting, draping the area with plastic, and keeping groups of orchids together rather than growing one or two. If the growing area is "buoyant" and feels comfortable and fresh to you, you're on the right track. If it feels stale and dry, the orchids won't like it either.

Grouping orchids together enhances better overall growth. Orchids like to grow with other orchids. Fortunately, this is ridiculously easy to accomplish. Orchids are like potato chips, impossible to have just one.

What Do You Have to Offer?

Probably the simplest way to approach growing orchids at home is to look at what environments already exist there, and then choose orchids that fit those environments. "Right place, right plant" is an axiom especially suited to orchids.

This sounds like a good idea, but orchids have a way of seducing would-be owners into losing this well-intentioned, common-sense approach. More typically, a novice grower falls in love with a particular orchid flower (or two, or three, or ten) and totes the plant home, without regard to whether it will do well there. In that case, you'll have to adapt the growing area to the needs of the orchid.

There are usually a multitude of microclimates present in any possible orchid-growing spots. In a bay window, for example, the area closest to the window pane will not only have much greater light intensity than a spot a few inches back but also will have the coldest winter temperatures and probably the warmest summer ones. A spot next to a heat vent will be much warmer in winter than one a couple of feet away, but it will also be much drier, affecting not only how fast the pot dries out but likewise humidity in the air. These microclimates mean it's possible to grow different types of orchids in relatively close proximity. This is especially true of greenhouse settings.

Answer a few questions about your own potential orchid environments, in various spots, to get a feel for what you have available:

1. What is the range of maximum daytime highs throughout the year, and the minimum low during winter nights? The range for orchid growing runs from 45° to 90°F, depending on type. An inexpensive maximum/minimum thermometer is invaluable for accurate information, and it will often yield surprising figures.

2. How much light intensity, in footcandles, does the area

receive? This will vary throughout the year as the sun slants during different seasons. Footcandles can be measured or estimated. Orchid footcandle needs start as low as 1,200 footcandles and rise to 4,000 or more, depending on type.

3. What kind of humidity is present? Orchids (and humans) do best with at least 40 percent humidity. In winter the humidity is often drastically lower than it is in summer, but air conditioners also dry the air excessively.

4. Is the air stagnant, or are breezes or fans (not drafts) available? Orchids want a buoyant, fresh atmosphere.

Thus begins the process of taking a look at the total environment, gathering information so the orchids put into those environments will not only grow but will bloom and thrive as well. Based on this information, you can choose what to grow, or see what needs to be modified.

I Had an Orchid, and I Killed It

For most hobbyists, trial and error is still the greatest teacher. All orchid growers send their share of plants to orchid heaven, especially when they first start out. Sometimes it takes a little while to get used to orchids. Each grower's environment is different in some way than every other grower's environment, and what works for one may not work for another. Some orchids will grow much better for some people, while others will grow better for others. Each environment is individual. If you are having success with an orchid, then continue doing what you are doing. If you are having failures, then take a look at what those failures are telling you.

When today's greatest orchid growers are interviewed about their successes, one "secret" is common to nearly all of them: Try to find out as much as possible about each particular orchid's habitat in the wild (if it is a species), especially noting the elevation for temperature clues, and then try to approximate that habitat artificially. For hybrids, these good growers say, it usually helps to discover what species are in the background pedigree, and again, try to approximate what those species want. It's simple advice, a learning process that requires a little reading, but a powerful key to success.

It's also important to learn what works for you and what doesn't. Thomas Edison was famous for trying one unsuccessful item after another in his experiments to find electric light filaments and a host of other inventions. He was asked more than once if he'd gotten discouraged by lack of results. "No results?" he answered with a laugh. "Why, I got a lot of results. I know several thousand things that *won't* work." For as Edison well understood, learning what *doesn't* work is as important as learning what does.

Pots and Potting Materials

Cymbidium

Orchids can grow in almost anything if they are matched with the right type of watering, fertilizing, and surrounding conditions. The trick is in knowing how to put it all together.

In nature, orchids generally grow *on* things, rather than *in* them. Pots solve many orchid-growing problems, but they also create some.

Orchid pots are made of clay or plastic. Most commercial growers use plastic pots, primarily because of lower cost. Virtually any orchid you buy will arrive inside a plastic pot. But just because an orchid comes in plastic doesn't mean you must automatically keep using plastic. There are decided differences between clay and plastic, advantages and disadvantages to both.

The most important difference is air. Clay pots breathe and plastic pots do not. Any plant potted in plastic is more confined than in nature or even in a clay pot. Plants in plastic have to be treated differently to avoid overwatering and to ensure that air is abundantly available to roots. Orchids resent sitting with wet roots, and clay pots help them dry out between waterings. It's more difficult to overwater a plant in a clay pot, and since more orchids are killed by overwatering than anything else, the appeal of clay goes up.

But this porous nature has its disadvantages, because pots can dry too quickly, particularly in a typical house where humidity is low. Orchids prefer 50 percent relative humidity or higher, and heated houses in midwinter can fall to a desertlike 20 percent. In low-humidity conditions, plastics keep the environment around orchid roots much wetter. Plants need less attention, require less watering, and are stronger than ones desiccated by root drying. Orchids that need to stay wetter than others can suffer in a clay pot. Heavy-handed waterers may do better with clay pots, whereas those with a tendency to neglect may find plastic pots keep orchids better supplied with water. On average, orchids in plastic should be watered half as often as those in clay. One way to avoid overwatering evils is to adapt plastic pots by adding more holes at the bottom and along the sides, punching from inside out. A soldering iron is handy for this task. Even clay pots benefit from enlargement of center holes.

There are other differences. Roots can't attach well to plastic's smooth walls, making plants easier to remove without breaking roots when repotting. Plastic doesn't absorb minerals from water or fertilizers, while salts and other elements sink easily into clay pots and can burn roots, especially with hard water.

Clay gives cultural clues: Algae growing on the pot sides is a sign of high humidity and good fertilizing. If clay is tapped, it makes a thud when filled with wet medium, and the sound gets higher in pitch as the medium dries out, a helpful hint in learning when to water.

One way to make life easier is to use the same potting mix (see below) for the bulk of the collection while mixing plastic and clay pots. Watering is simpler, because that same mix will tend to dry out at the same rate. This solution may not be ideal, but by using both clay and plastic, individual plant needs for drier or wetter environments can be met without a lot of effort.

Pot Shapes

A standard round horticultural pot is about twice as wide at the top as at the base, and as deep as the top is wide. With some exceptions, orchids do better in pots that aren't quite so deep, because their roots are less likely to rot if less mix surrounds them. "Azalea" pots are a good alternative because they are only three-quarters the regulation depth. Especially good are azalea pots with extra drainage slashes and holes, known in the horticultural world as "cyclamen" pots.

Terrestrial and semiterrestrial plants such as *Paphiopedilum* and *Cymbidium* tend to do better in deep pots, if the pots are narrower than they are deep. "Cymbidium" pots are specially designed in this configuration.

Square pots can be placed much closer together than round ones for greater insulation to reduce heat loss in winter, and they are easier to fit together on shelves. Orchid plants as a rule like to be near one another, which helps create a microclimate higher in humidity. But keeping pots too close together can cut down on airflow between them, aggravating rot and allowing pests to climb easily between. With square shapes, make sure there's enough space for air to move freely around them.

The Beauty of Pots

Orchid growers get so caught up in the utilitarian aspect of the pot that the total picture of pot and plant gets lost. There is an art to matching a pot to a plant, creating a picture much in the same way bonsai artists do. One new trend is using unusual and beautiful containers to create plant/pot harmonies. Hand-thrown ceramic planters in neoclassic designs, complete with good drainage holes, are now made by potters specifically for orchids. This is truly the Zen of orchid growing, a passion for pots and everything in them.

Baskets

Baskets are natural containers for many orchids, especially ones with pendent flower spikes (*Stanhopea*) or long dangling roots (*Vanda*). They are better drained and airier than any pot, but they dry very quickly. Anything in a basket will require more watering than anything in a pot. Wood and tree fern are two of the most popular orchid baskets, with tree fern the more durable. Don't line orchid baskets with plastic. Sheet moss can be used instead to keep the baskets from leaking excessively or the mix from falling out.

Slab Culture

Plants mounted on slabs need at least 60 percent humidity, and often daily watering, to survive. If these conditions can be met, many epiphytic and lithophytic orchids grow exceedingly well. Terrestrial and semiterrestrial orchids generally do not like slab culture. Deeply furrowed materials hold the most moisture and allow roots to grab on. Durability is also important because it delays the time between remounting, frequently traumatic for the plant.

The most popular slab materials are cork bark and tree fern, both very durable. Cork is strong and lightweight, while tree fern holds more water. Tree-dwelling orchids are generally specific about which types of trees they prefer, so if an orchid doesn't grow well on one mount, try another type. Good mounting woods include sassafras, black locust, cottonwood, tupelo, white and black oaks, rock chestnut oak, driftwood, cypress, sweet gum, metasequoia, redwood, persimmon, mock orange, lilac, cholla, and cactuslike ocotillo. Branches less than 2 inches in diameter can be used in the round; otherwise saw them in half to make flat slabs.

Other successful mounts include fir bark slabs with fiberglass applied to the backs to reduce decay, grapestocks, large limestone rocks (for lithophytes), and plastic rain-gutter screening folded and filled with sphagnum moss or rockwool.

Slab culture can be used to grow cool-growing orchids in climates normally too warm for them. Hollow pipes made of cured cement or clay are plugged at the bottom to hold water. Orchids such as odontoglossums are mounted on the pipe over a small pad of moss. If the pipe is kept full, the evaporating water provides a cool microclimate around the roots.

Taking the Mystery Out of Potting Materials

There are many types of potting materials available for potting orchids. Fortunately, there are some easy ones you can use without much need for sophisticated knowledge.

Many growers choose a basic main ingredient and stick with that — fir bark is a standard potting medium by itself, particularly in a plastic pot. But making a media mix of potting materials is very much like making spaghetti sauce; everyone has a favorite blend of ingredients. To simplify things, supply houses offer a number of premixed potting materials made from barks, tree fern, moss, rocks, rockwool, fern roots, coconut fiber, even plastics and ceramics, just to name a few.

Orchid growers are constantly on the lookout for the so-called perfect potting medium. However, because there are so many individual growing conditions, in different geographic locations, with varying water quality and habits, there is no single magic mix.

At some point, almost every grower is seized with a desire to try an amazing new potting product. But don't repot everything at once into a new mix. Too many collections have been murdered by mass transplantations into something that worked for someone else's conditions. Experiment with a few victims, then assess results after six months, through winter's low light, even better with a full year's use, before making judgments. See "Orchid Potting Materials" in the appendices for specific materials.

What Do Potting Materials Do?

A potting medium is basically just a way to get an orchid plant to stand upright in a pot so that it can be grown in the house or greenhouse. Simply, it is a support system. But besides support, a potting medium must also let plenty of air get to the roots and let water run freely past the roots so they don't rot, while retaining moisture for the plant's needs.

Because of their different physical makeups, potting materials give different amounts of drainage and air movement. Some absorb water; others don't hold any. Some deteriorate; others do not. Orchidists therefore tend to fiddle with mixes. The amount of room humidity, light, watering likely, type of orchid, size of pot, how often the grower likes or doesn't like to repot, even the material the pot is made of — all make a difference as to which medium will give the best results in a particular environment.

Orchids in a commercial nursery often enjoy optimum growth environments. When they are brought home, their environmental balance changes. The original potting materials may not suit the new surroundings, and beginners find it all too easy to overwater such mixes, turning roots to mush.

Understanding various potting materials and pots helps hobbyists choose and use potting media logically, instead of blindly copying other growers' mixes.

Potting Materials: The Breakdown Factor

The best way to divide potting materials into categories is by whether they deteriorate. Materials originating from something living — trees, ferns, moss (typically some sort of plant) — usually deteriorate. Those made of materials such as rocks, minerals, or man-manipulated substances do not deteriorate.

Potting materials that were once living things break down and release nutrients to the plant. In addition, their cation exchange capability is good, meaning that they help plants take up nutrients and are better able to buffer plants from rapid chemical changes, such as in pH.

Nondeteriorating potting materials don't release anything of nutritional value, nor do they buffer. Orchids potted in a nondegrading material such as rock, shale, rockwool, plastic, or charcoal are grown almost hydroponically and must be supplied with all necessary nutrients, requiring full, balanced fertilizer with trace elements and minerals. Neglectful growers may be better off with a material that deteriorates, ensuring that nutrients reach the orchids even when not fertilized regularly.

However, nondeteriorating materials are a real bonus because they don't break down into bits, so the mix stays open, airy, and well drained and the plants only need repotting when they outgrow the pot. Deteriorating media pieces get smaller and smaller, closing out air and holding too much water, with more danger of root rot, and frequent repotting is critical with these.

Often the solution is to add steadfast materials to an otherwise deteriorating mix — chunky perlite to fir bark, for instance — to get the best of both worlds.

Ingredient Size

Root thickness can guide potting material size. Generally, the thicker the root, the larger the particle size of potting material. For seedlings and thin-rooted orchids, use "seedling grade" or "fine" (¼-inch-diameter) particle sizes. For plants with medium-size roots (the vast majority), select ½-inch ("medium grade") particles. Thick-root orchids get ¾-inch-size ("coarse" or "large") potting materials.

Media pH

Most orchids grow naturally in a somewhat acidic environment, with pH below 7.0, although there are exceptions that grow, for example, atop alkaline limestone deposits. In general, orchid roots are most efficient when grown in a medium with pH between 5.2 and 6.5.

Deteriorating organic materials such as bark, sphagnum, and osmunda are naturally acidic, and they have good buffering capacities; they are able to maintain their pH via microbial activity and chemical reactions even when they are watered and fertilized with material with a different pH. Nondeteriorating media don't have much (or any) buffering capacity, so if the water source pH is high, avoid using such media.

To measure the pH of a particular blend of ingredients, use kits of plastic strips with pH-sensitive dyes, which yield results close to those obtained via digital pH meters. Use distilled water to make readings.

If necessary, small amounts of dolomitic limestone or soil sulfur can (respectively) raise or lower media pH of organic mixes. It takes about a week to measure change.

Terrestrial versus Epiphytic Mixes

Ingredients for potting orchids generally stay the same but are combined differently, with different particle sizes used to accommodate orchids that grow naturally on trees (epiphytes) and rocks (lithophytes) and those in a more decayed substrate (semiterrestrial and terrestrial). Materials that hold more water are more necessary in terrestrial-type mixes.

Quick Guide to Choosing Potting Materials and Pots

Take a look at your surrounding environmental conditions or problems, then adjust your potting materials and/or pots to suit them. Here are some suggestions for the following situations:

Humidity

- Where humidity is low (below 30 percent), as is common in houses, use plastic pots with a mix of bark/perlite/sphagnum moss, or osmunda.
- If humidity is better than average (35 to 50 percent), use plastic pots with a bark and perlite mix, or sphagnum moss.
- Excellent humidity (55 percent and up) means that you can use clay pots with bark, stone culture, charcoal, or tree fern. Slab culture and baskets are also possible.

Watering

- If you are an excessive (heavy-handed) waterer, use clay pots with tree fern, stone culture, charcoal, or cork.
- Once weekly watering is fine with plastic pots with a bark and perlite mix.
- Neglectful watering tendencies are offset by using plastic pots with a bark/perlite/sphagnum moss mix.
- If you like to water everything at once, use the same mix for everything, potting the more camellike orchid types in clay and the ones that like to stay wetter in plastic pots.

Water quality

- If rainwater is available, you are free to use sphagnum moss, gravel culture, or rockwool.
- Where water is high in salts, use charcoal as a filter on top of the mix, or use bark or tree fern.
- An extreme pH (high or low) of a water supply can be counteracted by using a deteriorating organic mix such as bark for buffer capability.

Repotting

- If you like to repot every year, use plastic pots with medium or fine bark or soilless mixes.

- Where repotting is undertaken only as necessary, generally every two years, use coarse fir or redwood bark, or tree fern.
- For those who repot rarely, use stone, lava rock, or expanded shale (any of which can be added to a fir bark mix); rockwool; osmunda; or charcoal.

Fertilizing

- If you tend to apply heavy doses of fertilizer (whether frequently or infrequently), buffer the effect by using plastic pots with tree fern, or use baskets.
- Where fertilizing is dilute and regular, you can use any medium.
- If you rarely or never fertilize, use osmunda or sphagnum moss.

Miscellaneous considerations

- In high light and heat (high-decay-prone situation), use tree fern, stone culture, or redwood.
- For seedlings or ailing plants, use sphagnum moss.
- If cost is not a factor, try sphagnum moss, tree fern, redwood, or osmunda.
- If you prefer to be cost-effective, use plastic pots with fir bark and additives of perlite or polystyrene peanuts, or stones.
- For top-heavy plants, use clay pots, or else try plastic pots with stones or expanded shale.
- If you prefer a mix that stays put, even when the pot overturns, use sphagnum moss, rockwool, or osmunda.
- If you can devote much time and attention, use rockwool or stone culture.
- Hobbyists with little time and attention should use bark.

Light and Other Bloom Factors

Dendrobium

"I can get my orchids to grow," begins a common complaint. "I just can't get them to *bloom*."

Even with a healthy plant, the right pot, good potting materials, correct water and fertilizing, and well-timed repotting, an orchid still may not bloom. An orchid can grow in the house for years, looking healthy and content, yet never send up even a trace of a flower. Sometimes it may produce a flower sheath, but with nothing inside.

So why won't it bloom?

The most likely reason is that it isn't getting enough light. A secondary reason may be that the temperature at night doesn't drop. In their natural habitat, most orchids experience a 15° to 40°F difference between day temperatures and night temperatures. Plants that stay at the same temperature around the clock have their natural rhythms disrupted and don't send signals to make flowers.

Therefore, if plants aren't blooming, more than likely they

are not in the right place. They're not getting enough light and/or not getting a drop in temperature at night.

There are other reasons why an orchid won't flower. The plant may not be mature enough. Many orchids must be at least four years old before flowering, and sometimes as old as twelve in the case of orchids such as the notoriously reluctant *Paphiopedilum rothschildianum*. Plants may not be receiving enough hours of light. Another cause can be the setback a plant experiences when moved from a seller's greenhouse to home conditions. In that case, give the plant a year to adjust, for it may skip a cycle and flower the following year.

What's Enough Light?

Plants that flower need more light than plants grown simply for their foliage, because of the extra energy and materials needed to create a bloom. This is why it's quite possible to grow orchids that look fine but don't flower. They're getting enough light to survive, but not to bloom.

Plants give the best clues as to proper light, for no light meter will be a better guide than actually looking at the leaves. Orchids in the proper amount of light usually have leaves that appear a moderate to light grassy green in color. If the level of light is too low, the leaves and growths appear deeper and greener. They may look healthy, but they're not getting enough light to bloom.

In lower light, the leaves also get less shiny, so less light will be reflected. Very low light will make the plant softer, with stunted foliage, elongated stems, and greater distances between the stems.

Too Much Light

Orchids generally do not receive too much light when grown indoors, but they can be subjected to excesses when put outdoors for the summer. If heat builds up too much, particularly in direct sunlight, the leaves can burn and blacken in a form of "sunburn." Even if the plant doesn't actually sunburn, high light can deplete food reserves so that the plant actually starves, which shows up as yellowing in the leaves. Orchids at their very highest light-level tolerance will often become red-tinged.

Measuring Horticultural Light

Light for growing orchids is often expressed in terms of foot-candles of light. Footcandles (abbreviated fc) simply measure the intensity of light, the amount that actually falls on a surface, or its illumination. A footcandle is the density of an amount of light. As described in the essay "Growing Orchids at Home," orchids are classified into three basic light groups: high (3,000+ fc), medium (2,000 to 3,000 fc), and low (1,200 to 2,000 fc).

Footcandles do not, however, measure the quality of light or its duration, and both are horticulturally important. But footcandles do give a guide to the relative needs of different orchids, to help gauge certain categories of light requirements.

Measuring light intensity by footcandles is useful when assessing actual sunlight, which consists of the full range of the light spectrum, perfect for orchids. If you are growing orchids in sunlight, the quality of light does not have to be of much concern. It's the best there is. The intensity of that sunlight is of interest, and it can be measured in footcandles, using a photometer.

Another way to gauge relative intensity is with a hand/eye test. Put your hand between the light source and the plant, with the hand 6 inches above the leaves, and look at the shadow cast. A sharp-edged shadow means the light is high, a soft-edged shadow is probably good for medium- to low-light orchids, and no shadow cast means the light is not strong enough for an orchid to flower.

Outside, in full sun on a bright summer day, the amount of footcandles illuminating a surface is about 10,000. An overcast day yields about 1,000 footcandles of light. The indoor light near a window can be as low as 100 footcandles, or as much as 5,000 if the plant is right up against the window on a clear day at noon at standard time on June 21, which is when the amount of light falling on the Northern Hemisphere is greatest. Measure light intensity on that date at noon to determine the maximum footcandles that reach the orchids growing there.

Light Duration

Orchids need a certain duration of light intensity. Those with highest light needs bloom best with a full day of light of at least six hours. Even the lowest-light orchids need their light for as long as possible during the day.

Manipulating Natural Light

Light varies considerably throughout the year everywhere except at the equator. It is high in summer, low in winter, often differing by a factor of five to ten times as much. Light also varies a great deal during the day. Take several readings at different hours on a single day to gauge the difference.

Many windows are perfectly suitable or can be adapted nicely for growing orchids, especially if the plants are kept close to the glass. Windowsill orientation makes a difference in the intensity and duration of light received. A south-facing window generally works best for orchids, then east (which gets mostly morning sun), then west (though westerly windows can get excessively hot since they get much afternoon sun), then north. North windows are touted as being no good for growing orchids, but that may not be true if they face reflective walls, or can be made more reflective, or can be more illuminated by the addition of artificial light.

Keep sunlight-transmitting glass clean, push plants closer to windows, buy plants that best suit the light available, keep plant leaves clean so they can utilize light absorption to capacity, and space plants so that no leaves are blocked by leaves of other plants.

When necessary, add artificial light, and increase the amount of time the artificial lights are on to compensate for what they lack in sunlight power. Make the environment around the plants as light-reflective as possible. Use matte-white walls, aluminum foil, mirror tiles, or, best of all, Mylar lining, which can reflect up to 98 percent of light available.

The Trick of Duplicating Light

Artificial light varies greatly in light quality, and there is large difference in the spectrum of light that various types of light bulbs emit. If you are simply adding more light to an environment that is already receiving natural sunlight, light quality doesn't matter significantly. But if you grow orchids completely under lights, quality of light becomes critical.

The best growth in completely artificial light is through a combination of light sources that complement one another to produce a spectrum closer to sunlight than any type does separately. To help make up for what artificial lights lack in sun power, keep them on for 14 to 16 hours per day. One advantage to growing completely under lights is that there are never any cloudy days, and so watering and culture techniques remain more constant.

Fluorescent Light

Regular incandescent bulbs are not good for growing orchids because they give off enormous amounts of heat and because they must be too close to the plant to be useful, burning it. Fluorescent tubes work much better. They cover a wide area, provide even illumination, give off relatively small amounts of heat compared with the amount of light they produce, and are inexpensive and efficient. They are best for low-light orchids. Those that require more than about 1,800 fc probably won't bloom well under fluorescent lighting.

All fluorescents are deficient in some portion of the visible spectrum. The standard "cool white" bulbs are much higher in blue and green wavelengths but are deficient in the photosynthetically important orange-red spectrum. "Warm white" fluorescents are deficient in the blue portion of visible light, leaning more toward the yellow region. A good, inexpensive solution is to mix standard cool white and warm white bulbs together for growing orchids, which seems to give enough of all the wavelengths to satisfy the plants.

"Grow light" fluorescent bulbs are horticulturally designed. They come in a wide variety of types (GroLux, Wide Spectrum, Vita-Lite, Agro-Lite, TruBloom, to name a few), with spectral peaks in the areas needed in photosynthesis. Grow lights can cost fifteen times as much as cool white fluorescent, yet there is no definitive evidence proving orchids grow or bloom any better. Many growers, however, swear by them.

Fluorescent tubes will last a long time before burning out. Cool whites are rated at 20,000 hours if left on continuously. But for horticultural purposes, their useful life span is considerably less than burnout time. Replace fluorescent tubes in orchid use every year, certainly not more than every two years, even though they still light.

Light is highest in the middle of a fluorescent tube, where higher-light plants should be placed. Light drops off dramatically at the ends of the tubes, and short tubes, such as 2-foot ones, are virtually useless for growing orchids. "Power-twist" fluorescents, which have more surface area, emit 15 percent more light than standard ones.

For orchids, you need a minimum of four 40-watt tubes, spaced 6 inches apart. The closer the tops of the plants are to the tubes, the higher the light. Place plants within 8 inches of the tubes, or closer to get more light, especially at the ends where the light is less intense. If heat from ballasts becomes a problem for cooler orchids, buy fixtures that have removable ballasts, so they can be wired to another area.

To avoid searing off the ends of elongating flower inflorescences, try hanging fluorescent fixtures on chains, so they can be moved higher as spikes grow.

High-Intensity-Discharge Lamps

High-intensity-discharge (HID) lamps are the best artificial lights for orchid growing, although the most expensive. These include high-pressure sodium lamps and metal halide ones, quartz tubes filled with sodium or mercury vapors under pressure and surrounded by an ultraviolet-absorbent envelope coated with phosphors. HID lamps are very efficient and give excellent-quality spectral light, but their special fixtures drive up cost. Over long-term use, however, the low cost of running can offset the initial outlay. Virtually any type of orchid will bloom under HID light, since, for example, a 1,000-watt lamp can emit as much as 12,000 footcandles. A 400-watt lamp typically illuminates a $6' \times 8'$ area with 1,000 to 2,000 fc.

Metal halide fixtures cost less initially than sodium ones, and they can be converted easily to hold sodium lamps if desired later. But halide lamps deteriorate much more rapidly than sodium. At burnout they've lost half their power, whereas sodium have lost only 20 percent. Sodium lamps should be replaced every two years; metal halide need yearly replacement. High-pressure sodium lamps are higher in the red-orange-yellow spectrum, the preferred choice in commercial greenhouses. But sodium lamps give off a yellowish, very unattractive light that makes the plants appear an awful pink-gray while under them. Metal halide light is more balanced and natural looking, higher in blue than standard sodium. "Agro"-designated sodium vapor lamps have been specially designed for horticultural use, adding 30 percent more blue as well as more overall light. Metal halide emit roughly 125 lumens/watt (lumens are the measure of brightness available per watt), while sodium vapor can be as high as 140 lumens/watt.

If you want to add light to a window or greenhouse, any HID lamp is a good choice since it can be positioned much farther away than can a fluorescent, as far as 5 feet for high-output HID lamps versus 6 inches for fluorescent. While this can be an advantage with tall plants, far more plants can be put in the same area in a tiered fluorescent light setup.

Be careful when using water near HID lamps, for droplets on hot bulbs can sometimes cause breakage. Use a reflector to keep very intense HID light from shining directly in the eyes. A rotator can continuously move the lamp over the plants, ensuring even lighting and avoiding hot spots.

Other Flowering Factors

Day length and temperature are two other factors that can help convince orchids to bloom, especially at the crucial time of year when the buds or spikes start to form. For orchids that bloom during peak season, between February and April, bud initiation is in late summer and early fall, as the day length begins to get shorter and the temperature begins to drop naturally.

Day/Night Temperature Differentials

Even with shortened day length, a temperature drop at night is still crucial. The good effect brought on by the shortening day can be obliterated by high temperatures at night, marring or even eliminating chances of bud initiation. Plants grown under uniformly even temperatures will not grow or flower as well as those grown under fluctuating night and day temperatures. For some orchids, particularly those that initiate buds at very low temperatures (*Cymbidium*), day length has no real effect, for it is the drop in temperature that causes flower formation. Some orchids need high light along with those lowered temperatures; low light in fall and winter can mean that cymbidiums won't form buds even if the temperature drops.

If dropping the temperature is difficult to achieve regularly, then at least concentrate on the six weeks when bud and spike initiation is supposed to begin. One easy way is to allow plants to summer outdoors, leaving them there in late summer and early fall, where they will get a natural drop. For plants kept indoors, if windows are kept open, even just a smidgeon, night differentials happen fairly easily. Under lights, there's a drop because the heat from the light ballasts stops when the lights go off, which helps drop temperatures at least 5°F; an open window can do the rest. If heat is on in the house, a thermostat with a setback thermometer can be the answer. Some growers even place ice cubes atop the potting mix at night, or water the mix (not the leaves) with cold water at night from late August through mid-October to encourage a cool root zone, especially when trying to encourage spike formation. Temperatures can also be reduced by adding fans.

A maximum/minimum thermometer will measure on a daily basis the highest and lowest temperatures reached that day in the growing environment. As with light, it's surprising to see how much individual areas can vary. Near the floor or closest to the windows there can be decidedly marked differences, particularly in the extreme seasons. Keep the coolest growers there.

If a plant does not do well in one spot, try it in another. Don't be afraid to experiment. Many growers have had great success with orchids in areas purportedly unsuited for them.

Air conditioning is not suitable for cooling orchid environments, because it creates a very dry atmosphere, robbing the air of humidity. An evaporative cooler, also known as a wet-pad "swamp" cooler, is far better for keeping air cool for orchids, while keeping it rich in vapor, although if outdoor humidity is very high during high summer temperatures, evaporative coolers become very inefficient.

Bud Blast

Few things are more maddening than buds that appear and grow larger and larger, and then suddenly wilt and shrink and fall on the floor in a sodden little heap. This is bud blast. Some orchids, such as *Phalaenopsis* and *Dendrobium,* seem particularly sensitive.

Unfortunately, there are lots of reasons why buds fall off before flowering. Bud blast can result from (1) extremes of temperature near the buds, (2) low humidity, (3) excessive fluctuations in humidity, (4) too much sunlight hitting the buds, (5) lack of water or watering with cold water, (6) water standing on the buds or in the sheaths (this is more bud blight than bud blast), (7) air conditioning, 8) heating vents that blow directly on buds, (9) bringing the plants back into the heated house from a summer outdoors, (10) genetic aberrancy, (11) smog and/or pollution, (12) gas leaks or inefficient burning of gas stoves or heaters, and (13) ethylene.

But the most likely causes are the lack of sufficient humidity and ethylene gas. Watch humidity carefully when orchids are starting to bud. If there's only one time of year when you really try to keep moisture in the air high, it should be when buds are forming.

Ethylene is a plant regulatory hormone produced in gas form in large amounts by certain types of fruit, and orchids are among the most susceptible flowers to even low levels (three parts per million). Ethylene can cause flowers to not open, make them age faster and fall off, blast buds, distort flowers, prevent budding, and shorten distances between nodes on inflorescences. High ethylene producers are apple, avocado, papaya, peach, pear, plum, and passion fruit; moderate producers are banana, fig, melon, and tomato. So keep bowls of any of these away from orchid buds and flowers. Nonplant sources of ethylene are also fairly abundant: furnaces, stoves and engines with incomplete combustion; smoke from cigarettes, cigars, and pipes; open fires; even poorly performing fluorescent light ballast transformers.

It's not necessary to have maximum light while buds develop, just enough to let the color develop. After the flowers are open, they'll last far longer if kept in dim light and cooler temperatures. The drop in light at this point won't hurt the plant at all. Some orchids develop different-colored flowers depending on the time of year. Reddish flowers can bloom as yellow/orange in the heat of summer, then rebloom in the cool of winter as brilliant scarlet, testament to the power of horticultural temperature.

Other Tips on Flowering

Is it possible to know *when* a specific plant is supposed to bloom? Orchid species are fairly easy to predict, because they are very regular and time-specific in their flowering times. Hybrids can be more unpredictable, although generally they will bloom at the same times every year. Bloom times are also included in the encyclopedia section of this book.

When conditions are difficult for an orchid, the plant may decide that the vegetative state may not be the best route for survival, and it will flower instead to try to produce seed. This is why sometimes very stressed, even dying, plants will send up buds. Such last-ditch efforts should be pinched off, to avoid sapping strength, and the plant nursed back to health. Any orchid plant in less than good health should never be allowed to bloom.

For additional urging of bud initiation, switch to a "blossom booster" fertilizer formula at the time when buds will be forming. Blossom booster (i.e., 10-30-20) is a fertilizer that is lower in nitrogen (the first number on the product's label) and higher in phosphorus and potassium, both of which are needed more for flowers. At the very least, cut back on a high-nitrogen formula at this crucial time.

If All Else Fails

No matter what, there will always be some orchids that simply refuse to bloom in a particular environment. Give such plants away, although try threats first. Just about every orchidist has tales about plants that suddenly decided to bloom as they were moved closer and closer to the garbage pail.

Water and Fertilizer

Oncidium

Orchids are more camellike than most people realize. Hence orchids are killed by the "kindness" of overwatering more than any other reason. In a similar way, overfertilizing also causes many common problems, since orchids normally live in nutrient-poor environments.

Quick Guide to Water and Fertilizer

Orchids can get by with a lot less water, and a lot less fertilizer, than is generally assumed. They're made with a variety of water-storing pseudobulbs, fleshy leaves, and thick roots that evolved because they endure periods of drought in nutrient-poor habitats in nature. Virtually all orchids need to dry out somewhat between watering. The top part of the plant should dry within an hour of watering, the roots more slowly. Plants with the thickest roots, juiciest leaves, and fattest pseudobulbs need the least water of all. Those with finer roots, thin leaves, and no pseudobulbs will need more water.

Orchids usually grow on trees or on rocks and attach their roots to the surface. When it rains, water runs off freely and quickly past their roots and leaves. Therefore orchids prefer to be drenched with water that runs quickly through the pot, rather than light applications of water. Bring pots to the sink and run them under the faucet for a few minutes. Don't just moisten the top of the medium every day. You can't overwater an orchid by pouring too much water on the plant at one time. You can kill it by watering too frequently.

Orchids that don't normally grow on trees but grow more in the ground (terrestrials and semiterrestrials such as paphiopedilums, cymbidiums, and phragmipediums) need to stay wetter than epiphytic orchids. This does not mean they relish light applications of water. They require a somewhat denser medium in which to grow, to hold the water. Thus water all orchids the same way, by soaking them thoroughly. The difference in the amount of water needed will be adjusted by the mix (and perhaps by watering a bit more frequently), not by the way water is applied.

There are several ways to estimate when plants want water. Stick your finger (or a dry, thin stick) about an inch down into the medium, near the center. The trick is to catch the mix just as it's beginning to dry out. If it's wet, don't water. If it's dry, water. When in doubt, don't water. Another way to gauge is to pick the pots up often to learn the difference in weight between a newly watered pot and one that is dry.

Orchids in big pots don't need to be watered as frequently as orchids in little pots. Group pots of similar size together, since they will generally dry out at the same time if the mix is the same composition and age.

An orchid in a clay pot will need to be watered twice as often as the same orchid in a plastic pot. Orchids on slab mounts or in open baskets demand more frequent, even daily, watering. Orchids growing in hot temperatures need more water than orchids in cooler temperatures. Orchids will also require water more often on sunny days than on cloudy ones.

Resist the temptation to overfertilize. Orchids can go for years potted in bark without added fertilizer, and still grow and bloom. Because of their evolutionary ability to store water and the nutrients carried by water, orchids need much less feeding than other plants.

It is not necessary to use a fertilizer that officially says "orchids" on it, for any general water-soluble houseplant fertilizer with a ratio close to 10-10-10 or 20-20-20 is fine. The difference with specially formulated orchid fertilizer is that it can be used at the rates recommended on the label. For all other types, use half the recommended doses, preferably quarter strength.

To flush out any possible accumulated fertilizer salts, water once a month with plain water, preferably with rainwater. This process is known as "leaching." Too much fertilizer in general will show up often as "burned" leaf tips — tips that turn brown or black. Never apply fertilizer to a dry plant. Water it first, then apply the fertilizer diluted in water. Also avoid fertilizing plants that look sickly, since salts can further stress them.

Orchids in brighter light will need more water and more fertilizer than orchids in dim light. Orchids that are fertilized regularly will need more water than orchids that are not.

If watering and fertilizing still seem bewildering, use the most basic and simplistic rules of all. Water plants in 2-inch pots every three days. Water plants in 4-inch pots every five days. Water plants in 6-inch pots every week. If even that's too hard, water them all once a week, with dilute fertilizer added every other week. The ones that live are the perfect orchids for the environment.

Overwatering

What happens when you overwater a plant is that there will not be enough oxygen around the roots. Roots take in oxygen in order to convert the stored sugars made by photosynthesis to a usable energy form, in a process called respiration. In respiration, the oxygen taken in by roots produces carbon dioxide, which is given off by the roots. A lack of oxygen around the roots combined with carbon dioxide that can't be carried away means root rot, which eventually means a dead plant.

Watering too often can also cause plant leaves to yellow and shrivel due to starvation because stored sugars aren't being released. Beginners tend to panic at this sight and think that the shriveling is a sign of insufficient water, so they compound the error by pouring on more water. A look at the roots, however, will reveal rot in the form of mushy brown or black roots. Stop watering until the plant can dry out.

Overwatered organic potting mixes break down much more quickly, exacerbating the problem by retaining even more water around the roots. Orchidists with a heavy hand in watering can adjust their mix to accommodate the tendency. Clay pots also help.

Watering from above the plant, such as with a hand-held watering can or overhead sprinkler, can likewise damage orchids. Water-soaked plant leaves can lead to several problems. Water standing in the crown of plants such as phalaenopsis or in the new, softer growths or leaves of many plants will cause rot. Overhead watering can also deposit calcium, magnesium, or iron residues on the foliage, reducing leaf photo-synthetic ability. Direct the water to the potting mix rather than the leaves. Permanently tip forward the pots of plants that tend to collect water in the crowns, to allow water to run off. Slightly tipped is how the plant would grow in nature.

Underwatering

Underwatering can result in problems too, usually less severe than those caused by overwatering. There are two kinds of underwatering. The worst is just sprinkling the top of the mix. Such watering destroys the plant's incentive to grow deep roots, since water never reaches deep enough in the pot. Likewise, because water never drains completely through the pot, salts in the water and in fertilizer settle around the roots and cling to the mix, which is ultimately toxic. Letting water — particularly pure rainwater — drain fully and thoroughly through the pot on a monthly basis allows harmful salts to be leached out in a beneficial flushing process.

The second method of underwatering is by watering correctly (deeply and thoroughly) but not often enough. Underwatered roots shrivel, turning gray and brittle. The potting mix can be fine-tuned with the addition of more water-retentive materials. Plastic pots also aid the infrequent waterer, for they hold twice as much water as clay ones will.

Rescuing Overwatered and Underwatered Orchids

Overwatered plants can be rescued if the problem is discovered in time. If the mix is badly deteriorated, repot into something coarser. Plants with destroyed roots will recover better if misted and given high humidity rather than watered, regenerating new roots. If there are no viable roots left, there's real difficulty in saving the plant. Cut the rotted parts off and dust with sulfur. A clear, covered, plastic sweater box with moist sphagnum moss in the bottom is an excellent place to put any damaged plant for a few weeks, until roots appear. Mist occasionally to maintain humidity, with the lid slightly vented, and keep out of bright sun.

Desiccated, underwatered plants with destroyed roots can be revived with similar high-humidity treatment in a clear plastic box for several weeks.

Water Temperature and Timing

Cold water, below 50°F, can damage roots, kill root hairs, and also cause cell collapse on leaves if splashed on top, particularly in warm-loving plants such as phalaenopsis. Cold roots don't take up water and nutrients well. Use room-temperature water.

Water as early in the day as possible, to help the leaves dry and the root ball to return to ambient temperatures before the cold damp night can bring fungal and bacterial disease.

Water Quality

In general, most tap water is fine to use to water orchids. Don't be overly concerned about water quality unless plants seem to be languishing for no other apparent reasons.

Orchids grow better when they receive water with small amounts of dissolved salts in it, such as those found in good-quality tap water, rather than distilled water. Water quality, however, does differ from place to place in chlorine, pH, mineral salts, and other solids. If dissolved salts (TDS) exceed 300, use another water source.

An excellent solution is rainwater, which normally contains very low levels of mineral salts. Many growers swear by the good results, especially for orchids particularly sensitive to salts, such as masdevallias and phragmipediums. However, using rainwater can lead to deficiencies of calcium, magnesium, and iron, even if supplemented with fertilizers, for most fertilizers don't contain these since manufacturers assume the water supply will provide sufficient amounts. One way around this is to water with tap water every fourth watering or to mix some tap water with the rainwater.

Softened Water

Do not use "softened" water on orchids. Standard water softeners in the home use a process that removes calcium and magnesium ions and replaces them with sodium, a salt far more toxic to plants than the original ones. If possible, tap into the water line with a "T" spout to obtain water for orchids before it enters the water softener.

If this is impractical, look into "deionizing" methods such as a "weak acid" ion-exchange resin water softener, or "reverse osmosis," which is more water-wasting but which easily removes up to 99 percent of dissolved ions, minerals, hardness, and contaminants.

Water pH

Generally, the pH of water for orchid growing can range from 4.0 to 7.5, with optimum between 5.5 and 6.5, although growers have used water with pH as high as 9.0, which is very alkaline, without too much problem. A pH of

7.0 is neutral; anything below 7.0 is acidic, anything above it is alkaline.

Optimum pH increases the availability of beneficial fertilizer elements and reduces adsorption of harmful elements. Extremes of pH (below 4.0, above 7.5) can inactivate many nutrients. One reason orchids tend to withstand extremes of pH better than many houseplants is because orchids have evolved in nutrient-poor environments. Thus, even when fertilizer becomes unavailable at extreme pH, orchids survive.

Rainwater pH is generally fine for orchids. Rainwater is usually acidic, with a pH around 5.6.

If pH needs to be lowered, use citric acid (grapefruit juice works safely). Adjusting pH too much can add ions that may burn plants. Hard water, however, is difficult to adjust, since pH buffers are commonly added by municipalities.

Humidity

Without question, orchids love humidity, preferably 50 percent or more. They'll grow with far less, but blooms and growth will be much better if humidity is in the 50 to 70 percent range. Relative humidity can be measured with a hygrometer.

Air can be made more humid by growing plants together, rather than scattering one or two here and there. A humidifier also helps. Ultrasonic types emit a finer mist that stays in the air longer, and they have a cartridge to filter out salt deposits. Another method is to mist the air around plants several times a day with a fine mister/sprayer.

One of the best ways to raise humidity is to place plants over trays of water. Never stand pots directly in water, however, or roots will rot. "Pebble trays," water-filled trays of stones with pots on top of the stones, are often recommended, but pots tend to wobble. Better still is "egg crate," the rigid latticelike panel covering used in dropped ceilings over light fixtures. Placed over trays of standing water with pots of orchids on top, egg crate is sturdier and convenient. It can be cut to size by snipping lattice joints with a wire cutter.

Air conditioners excessively dry the air, so avoid keeping orchids near them.

Fertilizing

Fertilizer applied at very low rates, much lower than usually recommended on fertilizer labels, and given at regular intervals will help plants more than not fertilizing. A heavy hand at fertilizing, especially at odd intervals, is worse than not fertilizing orchids at all.

What Do Orchids Need?

There are nine major nutrients required by orchids (and all other plants as well). The most important by weight are hydrogen, carbon, and oxygen, available from air and water. The next six are known as "macronutrients," and three are needed in large enough amounts to warrant that fertilizers are based on them. The primary three are nitrogen, phosphorus, and potassium (N-P-K). The other three macronutrients are calcium (Ca), sulfur (S), and magnesium (Mg).

Another seven mineral elements have been found to be necessary to plants. Once called "trace" or "minor" elements because they are needed in exceedingly small amounts, these are now technically termed "micronutrients" because the terms "trace" and "minor" seemed to minimize their importance. These seven are iron (Fe), manganese (Mn), zinc (Zn), copper (Cu), boron (B), molybdenum (Mo), and chlorine (Cl). Thus, in total, sixteen nutrients have been found to be vital to healthy plants.

Fertilizer is given to make sure the plants are receiving sufficient amounts of nitrogen, phosphorus, and potassium. Unless you are using rainwater or an inorganic potting mix that does not break down, don't worry about adding other macro- and micronutrients, for they will generally be made available to the plants through water and the organic mix. Adding micronutrients when not really necessary runs the risk of severe root damage due to salt buildups.

Growing orchids in an inorganic mix is like growing them hydroponically. Under those conditions, use a fertilizer that contains macronutrients and micronutrients.

Fertilizer Ratios

Nitrogen, phosphorus, and potassium (N-P-K) are so important that it is their ratio, expressed in percentages, that is indicated by the numbers on fertilizer labels. (As a way to remember whether P stands for phosphorus or potassium, these primary macronutrients are always listed in alphabetical order — phosphorus comes before potassium. The chemical symbol K for potassium comes from the German word for potassium, *Kalium*.) Unless they are potted in bark, orchids generally prefer a "balanced" formula of N-P-K; a common formula on the market is 20-20-20. If bark is used, normally a higher-nitrogen fertilizer such as 20-10-10 (not 30-10-10) is preferred (see "Orchid Potting Materials" in the appendices for details on the special fertilizing needs of fir and redwood bark).

Any fertilizer that is termed "complete" does not necessarily contain micronutrients or even all the macronutrients.

"Complete" simply means the fertilizer has significant amounts of nitrogen, phosphorus, and potassium. Most other nutrients are not included in fertilizers because they are often available to plants via other ordinary sources.

Organic versus Inorganic Fertilizer

The basic difference between organic and inorganic fertilizers is that organic fertilizers are more complex and must be broken down by bacterial processes in order to be utilized by the plant. They are very slowly released sources of nutrients. The most popular organic fertilizer for orchids is fish emulsion, a liquefied fish by-product with an N-P-K ratio of 5-1-1.

Inorganic sources are almost immediately available to the plant, with less lost by leaching. Nutrients from inorganic fertilizers typically show up in a plant's system within an hour or less.

Studies routinely associate significantly smaller pest populations when organic fertilizers are used, compared with plants fertilized with highly soluble (inorganic) N-P-K materials. Plants stay healthier and better able to withstand stress. Organic fertilizers are generally more expensive, and they encourage rapid breakdown of organic potting mixes owing to the increased microbial activity needed to break down the fertilizer. They tend to leach out of epiphytic mixes quickly.

An especially effective home-brewed organic fertilizer is made from steeping aged cow manure in water and using the diluted resulting "tea" to fertilize orchids. Put 20 tablespoons of aged 4-4-2 manure into 1 gallon of water, shake it, then allow it to sit for 24 hours. Then decant the tea from the residue at the bottom into a 5-gallon bucket, with enough water added to fill the container. Dilute this mixture further upon use to 1:16. "Teas" are not robust fertilizers; they're more like a general tonic.

Timing, Timing, Timing

As you become a more sophisticated orchid grower, you can become more sophisticated about when and what to fertilize. Because there are so many different types of orchids, individual fertilizing requirements can vary greatly.

Orchids need fertilizer, particularly nitrogen, most from the time they begin new growth until it is about two-thirds complete. Then, as the plants go into a slower phase of growth, they require less fertilizer. Orchids at rest (not in active growth) need virtually no fertilizer, so when the lead growth or new flush of leaves is mature, reduce water and fertilizer until new growths or flower inflorescences appear.

Buying and Caring for New Orchids

Paphliopedilum

Orchids are priced by plant maturity, which is often measured by the size of the pot in which the plant is growing. When starting a collection, buy the most mature plants you can afford. If you buy a seedling plant, the wait for bloom can be too long, with a much greater chance of things going wrong. Mature plants are stronger, more established, and less sensitive to environmental change and grower goofs.

A standard-size cattleya in a 2-inch pot is seedling size, three to four years away from blooming, while one in a 5-inch pot will be close to blooming. Pot size won't, however, help you judge the age of "miniature" or "compact" growers, which will bloom in small pots; you'll have to rely on representations by the seller. (True "miniature" orchids are classified as those with plant height that does not exceed 6 inches.)

Monopodial-growth orchids such as phalaenopsis are

typically sold by "leaf span" instead of pot size. A standard-size phalaenopsis must be 6 to 8 inches across to be blooming size.

Unless a mail-order buyer specifies otherwise, orchids are usually sent "out of pot," arriving bare-root, much like a dormant shrub or rosebush. Many buyers prefer this, so they can check the plants for health and pests and then pot them in their own choice of mix and pot. If you don't want to have to pot up your new orchids, ask to have them sent in pots. It will cost a little more because of extra shipping weight.

Determining Plant Health

Check the health of any new plant before bringing it into a home collection. Examine the whole plant, not just the seductive flowers, and send back any plant that arrives in less than good condition. As a precaution, isolate all newly received plants from the rest of your orchids for at least a week and observe them carefully to be sure they aren't carrying insects or diseases that can infect your other plants. Some growers automatically unpot any newly received potted plant, to check roots and search for pests.

Healthy plants have medium-green leaves and pseudobulbs, showing no signs of shriveling or wrinkling on new growths, with vigorous-looking roots, preferably white with green tips, some of which may stick out of the pot. Orchid plants frequently have some dead or dying roots, but the majority should be strong live ones. If not, reject that plant.

When an orchid is moved to a new environment, some leaves may yellow and fall off. Plants adapt to changes in climate and environment by dropping a leaf or two, usually in response to lesser light. This is nothing to be alarmed about if it is one of the lower leaves. If top leaves start to fall off, then there is cause for worry, because something other than adaptation may be going on, and fungal and bacterial rot can be suspected. But the yellowing and discarding of bottom leaves or backbulb leaves (not the newer growing points) usually is natural.

Initial Care of Transported Plants

The more similar your growing conditions are to those in which a plant has been grown, the better it will survive once home. Plants from Hawaii, for example, are grown outdoors in tremendously bright conditions and may suffer when brought to dimmer situations such as a windowsill in Maine. Orchids often experience "setback shock" when moved from one place to another. Hardier, bigger plants survive best.

Plants shipped through the mail may spend a week in a box in total darkness, without water, subjected to cold or heat stress, although most nurseries have a policy not to ship during freezing months. Remove all wrapping materials and tape around the orchids as soon as possible. Place mail-order plants in a dimmer spot than where they will eventually go, to help them harden off for a few days and get used to light again. Keep the humidity as high as possible during this time. High humidity always helps stressed plants recover far better than drenching their pots with water does.

Orchids transported in person also require extra care, especially during extreme weather. A large picnic cooler with room-temperature interior is a perfect solution to protect plants from cold or heat. Leaving unprotected plants in a closed car quickly reduces orchids to slush during summer, or to frozen black messes during winter. Buds are particularly susceptible to extremes of weather.

Seedling Care

High humidity coupled with good air movement keeps young seedlings healthiest. If the humidity in the general environment is less than 60 percent, you can easily improve seedling growing conditions. One method is to create a humidity dome over the seedling pots for the first few weeks by placing them under plastic germination covers such as those sold with garden-seed germination kits. Another option is to pot directly into the cut-off bottom of a large plastic soda bottle, with the top part used as the removable dome; the bottle cap can be put on or off as needed to allow fresh air into the enclosed environment. Another solution is to keep pots in a clear plastic sweater box lined with damp sphagnum moss, with cover slightly ajar.

Keep seedlings moist, misting when possible and never allow them to dry out completely. Set them in areas where temperatures range from 60°F nights to daytime highs of not over 80°F; cooler-growing orchids need even lower daytime maximums. Start with lower light levels, such as under four fluorescent tubes, gradually increasing to higher natural light as seedlings establish. Seedlings grow best with long-light days.

If seedlings become infected with damping-off fungi or bacterial disease, isolate them and wash with mild fungicide. Step up the air movement around them, and make sure night temperatures don't go below 60°F.

Seedlings will grow at different rates, and some may need to spend up to a year in a community pot (commonly called a compot), where they grow together with a group of other seedlings. Faster-growing individuals can be pricked out of the compot into single pots whenever they seem large enough.

Orchids Bought in Bud or Flower

That tempting first orchid is commonly purchased in bloom or with buds evident. As flower inflorescences and sheaths and buds develop, try not to move the plant, watering it in place rather than shifting it so it then tries to reorient to the light. This reorientation skews the natural way the plant would have presented the flowers, twisting them instead on the stem. If you grow under lights, arrange the lights so either they can be raised or the plant shelf lowered when the flower spikes elongate. If the pot must be moved in order to water it, mark the pot and its location with tape on three spots at the bottom of the pot corresponding to three tapes on the plant shelf to aid you in placing it back in precisely the same position and orientation.

Staking the flower stem while it develops will help show off the blooms to best advantage, especially on plants with long inflorescences such as phalaenopsis and cymbidiums. Staking after the entire inflorescence is developed gives too artificial a look. To stake properly, once the inflorescence reaches about 3 inches long, place a flower stake (wood or metal) deep into the mix and loosely tie the inflorescence to it. As the inflorescence grows, tie again near the first flower bud, loosely, then allow the natural arc to develop as buds enlarge. Work with inflorescences after putting the plants in a warm place for a while, since cold spikes may break.

On some orchid types (*Cattleya*) the buds may be enclosed in a sheath. Usually the sheath will open by itself to allow the buds to bloom, but sometimes it is too dry and reluctant to part. Gently slit the top with a sharp blade, taking care not to slice the buds. Keep water from sitting inside a sheath, and from sitting on buds in general, and keep air moving and fresh, for *Botrytis* fungi are ever present and waiting to disfigure flowers with spots.

How Long Blooms Last

It's often quite dismaying for a beginner to watch as flowers lose clarity and substance, wilt, and fall to the floor in a sodden heap. Flowers do that, regardless of how good their care. At some point, usually after a month or so of prime flowering for each phalaenopsis flower, or two to three weeks for each cattleya, sometimes a month or two for a paphiopedilum, the flowers fall off and die. It is a function of senescence, of nature.

The time each flower will last depends on when it first opened. Phalaenopsis flowers open one at a time on the flower spike, and each flower will fall off at a different time than the rest. The blooms on a cattleya inflorescence, on the other hand, may open together and fall off together.

Many orchids are excellent as cut flowers. Generally the sturdier the flower substance, or the thicker the spike, the better. When an orchid flower is picked and placed in water, it will last only one-half to one-third the time it would have on the plant itself. Prolong this by using warm (100°F) water in the vase, plunging the stems in immediately after cutting with a sharp instrument, and then putting the vase in a cool spot for several hours to allow warm water uptake. Change the water daily.

Some orchid types make terrible cut flowers, wilting immediately. Miltonias are a classic example.

Encouraging Rebloom

Once finished blooming, many orchids will not bloom again until the same time the following year. Some types continue to bloom in succession. If the tip of any flower inflorescence stays green, don't cut it, for the end may develop further with more buds.

It is possible to get a phalaenopsis in particular to rebloom off the same inflorescence. If the plant seems healthy, cut the inflorescence to just above the second node, or notch, from the bottom of the inflorescence. (Cut about ¼ inch above that node.) Often a secondary spike will arise from the node. Once blooms are obviously over, cut the inflorescence off completely.

Coping with Repotting

Phalaenopsis

There are two main reasons to repot orchids, and they often, but not always, occur at the same time.

first, an orchid needs to be repotted if it gets too big for its pot. Orchids can have an extensive root system inside the pot and the potting mix, but they also typically have roots that extend out of the mix into the air, and this normal behavior is not usually a clue for repotting. But when the pseudobulbs hang over the pot side or new roots can't find their way into the pot at all, then that orchid needs repotting.

The second reason to repot is because the mix has decomposed. If they're made from natural materials, most potting mixes deteriorate with time, breaking down into a fine, tightly packed mix that closes out air. With no air, roots die, and the plant is doomed unless it is released from that compacted environment.

Recognizing deterioration

To tell if an orchid needs to be repotted, brush away the top of the potting mix and look at the materials underneath for signs of decomposition. Generally, if you can sink your finger in easily to the second joint, the orchid needs repotting. Signs of decomposed roots — blackening and mushiness or graying and brittleness — are more potent evidence.

Different potting media in different conditions deteriorate at different rates. A mix of medium-size bark pieces will last about two years, while finer pieces may break down in half that time. Tree fern may last two to three years; rock doesn't deteriorate at all. Using a mix that combines both decomposing and nondecomposing materials helps lengthen the time between repotting.

Some types of orchids particularly resent having their roots disturbed by the ordeal of transplanting, and one way to put off repotting is to eliminate one of the reasons to repot. If the mix doesn't deteriorate, then repotting is necessary only when the plant outgrows the pot.

Timing, Timing, Timing

Repotting gets its reputation for being difficult because people classically repot at the wrong times, and orchids are quick to show their resentment of bad timing. *Timing is the most crucial part of good repotting.* Orchids go through cycles of growth. New pseudobulbs, leaves, and roots appear and elongate. After the leading growth or leaf is mature, there is generally a rest period. Afterward, flower spikes and sheaths typically begin, followed by buds and flowers. Most orchids initiate new growth in late winter and spring.

Each time an orchid is repotted, its growth is disturbed. Orchids are more forgiving of other potting mistakes if they are at least repotted at the correct time. *In general, the best time to repot an orchid is when new growths and new roots are just beginning to form, before those new roots reach even ½ inch long. For most plants, this occurs right after flowering.* This means that nearly all repotting should take place between February and June.

Orchidists often complain, "Repot this year, get no bloom the next." If the plant is left too long after the growth cycle begins before repotting, it must struggle to reestablish itself. If the roots get broken or damaged by repotting, they don't make the branches necessary for a healthy and extensive root system. Energy expended to make replacement root tips is energy taken from flowering. But if plants are repotted at proper times, orchids *do* bloom on schedule the next year.

Handling new roots when they are tiny means minimum plant setback. New roots are exceedingly brittle, and there's less chance of breakage if the roots are less than 1 inch long. Repotting at this time gives new roots the longest time to grow before the next repotting disturbance, and they'll be growing into fresh mix. The plant will stay healthier if its roots are well established before it enters the rest period, when no active plant growth is going on. (Of course, since there are lots of exceptions with orchids, there are types that grow actively year-round. These can be repotted anytime.)

What If Timing Is Bad, But Repotting Is a Must?

Sometimes an orchid desperately needs repotting because the mix is so deteriorated or the plant is badly overgrown. Waiting until the proper cycle to repot may mean that the resulting root damage could hurt the plant more than repotting could. Be as gentle as possible with plants potted out of time, watching them carefully afterward.

If you find that the roots are rotten, clean the roots and pot the plant into a very small pot, and wait until the regular repotting time to repot as usual. Don't overdo the watering, but provide as much humidity as possible.

If the plant is overgrown but the mix is still acceptable, a procedure called "dropping on" is useful. Remove the plant from its overgrown pot and place it, mix and all, into a larger pot. Then add fresh mix to fill gaps. Dropping on disturbs roots very little and is an acceptable way to repot even at proper times if the mix is still good. Orchids that prefer a somewhat decayed mix (such as *Cymbidium*) do better being dropped on, with a full repotting only every other time.

Another useful trick for overgrown sympodial plants climbing over the side of the pot is to place another same-height pot next to it to accommodate the overhanging pseudobulbs and roots. The second pot should be plastic, so that you can cut away a U-shaped section of the rim so it will fit better under the overhanging growths. Position the second pot under the new growths and roots hanging over the side of the other pot, and fill it with new mix. Then tape the two side-by-side pots together around both rims, to prevent the new pot from moving. The overgrown parts can establish in the new pot without too much disturbance. When the proper time arrives, the entire plant can be repotted into a larger pot, or easily divided, with a natural break at the point between the two pots.

Another time you should avoid repotting a plant is when it is in bud or flower. Wait until flowering is over, because repotting can cause enough trauma to make the flowers or buds drop off. If the plant has a flower sheath with no buds evident inside, or if the spike is still short and budless, feel free to go ahead if necessary.

Newly acquired plants may require repotting if the mix is

obviously deteriorated or the plant is overgrown. However, give new plants at least a month to acclimate themselves to their new growing conditions before repotting, to allow recovery from the trauma of a new environment without the added trauma of repotting.

Spreading Virus, Disease, and Pests

Because of all the handling and cutting that goes on during repotting, and because people usually repot more than one plant at a time, the probability of passing virus, disease, and pests between plants is very high. You need to take great precautions. (See "A New Look at Pests and Diseases.")

The wisest course of action is simply to assume that every plant is virused. With such a blanket assumption, orchidists will be inordinately careful between each plant, trying not to infect one from the other.

Use plastic disposable gloves, changing them between plants or at least washing them. Don't use your bare hands. Repotting is a sloppy operation; fingers tear away rotten roots or break off old pseudobulbs, and even with washing, plant pieces can remain under your fingernails, ready to infect. Gloves eliminate many variables, and they protect hands from splinters or possible pathogens in the medium.

The other primary source of infection during repotting is the cutting instruments. Never use a cutting instrument on one plant and then reuse it on another without first sterilizing it between plants. Sterilize tools by using a propane torch flame or by soaking the tools in trisodium phosphate solution. Dipping tools in chlorine or alcohol will *not* sterilize them enough to kill viruses. An easier solution is to buy packs of single-edged razor blades, and use one for each plant. Blades can be cleaned and oven-baked at 375°F for an hour to sterilize.

If you suspect a plant of carrying virus, or being full of pests, repot it last.

Reusing Potting Materials

If a material is still in good shape, you can reuse it with no problem for the *same* plant in a different pot. But never transfer a used potting material from one plant to a pot of another orchid. This is sure to transfer pestilences. The best recourse with old organic mix is to resign it to the compost heap.

New clay pots have been oven-dried, so presoak them in water for half a day to fill pores. Older clay pots that have been washed and dishwasher-dried also need presoaking.

To clean clay pots encrusted with leached salts and algae,

soak them in hot water for several days, changing the water a few times. Then scrub with steel wool in warm water with dish detergent added. Adding a little vinegar to the soak water helps loosen salt deposits. Resoak if necessary.

In order to kill any virus present on clay and polypropylene pots, pots must be subjected to a temperature of 180°F for 30 minutes. Some high-temperature dishwashers get this high, but most don't. A safer way is to soak the pots overnight in a 9:1 water/bleach solution. Then rinse and soak them in plain water for 15 minutes, rinsing again before using. (Don't mix bleach with vinegar; a chlorine gas is produced.) Baking in a 200°F oven is also possible; polypropylene pots have a melting point of 250°F.

Nuts and Bolts of Repotting

When you're ready to repot, first choose a convenient workspace. A spot near a sink and a trash basket is ideal. If there's no counter space, place a piece of board across the sink. Put lots of layers of newspaper down on the workspace, especially if you are repotting more than a couple of plants at a time. In between each plant, the mess can be bundled up in some of the newspaper and neatly disposed of, leaving a clean layer on which to proceed.

Have on hand new or sterilized single-edged razor blades, a box of disposable plastic gloves, a knife, plant labels, a waterproof marking pen or pencil, various sizes of clean pots, plant stakes and ties, rhizome clips, and some way to clean the knife in between plants (trisodium phosphate solution or propane flame). A toothbrush is also handy for ridding plants of insect pests. On the floor have a bucket of potting mix soaking in warm water, preferably overnight.

Soak each plant and pot in a bucket of water for a few minutes; this makes it much easier to convince the plant to leave the pot. Also, the roots will be softer — more pliable and less apt to break — and will release somewhat their often tenacious grip on the inside of the pot. Roots and plant are likewise more pliable when repotted after time in a warm rather than cold environment.

Remove the plant label and put it somewhere safe, preferably not on the work area where it can too easily get wrapped up with debris and thrown away.

Hold one hand over the top of the mix and turn the pot upside down. Some plants slip out easily onto the newspaper layers. If the plant resists, tap the pot sides and bottom, or gently squeeze a plastic pot in various places. If the plant really clings to the inside of a plastic pot, take a sharp sterile knife and run it around the inside wall of the pot. If the roots are stubbornly clinging to a clay pot, you may have to break the pot by turning it on its side and tapping gently with a hammer. If bits of clay hang on the roots, don't remove them, as that will break the root.

If the plant is being repotted because of a deteriorated mix rather than overgrowth, you can reuse the same pot. Otherwise, set the used pot away and don't use it for another plant until it has been sterilized.

Taking a Look at the Roots

Now is an excellent time to pause and take a good look at the potting material, to glean invaluable information about how well it has responded to watering techniques and environment. What shape is it in? Has it decomposed more than expected, or less?

Even more important, take a look at the roots. Let them be the guide to how well a potting material is working. Live roots are usually white, glistening, sometimes green-tipped, and firm to the touch; these are indications of an excellent mix for the conditions. Dead roots are gray, brown, or black and soft, mushy, or dry to the touch. Decaying roots can be something in between.

If the roots are soggy, mushy, or black, the mix is not draining well enough, nor is it aerated enough for the watering technique and environmental conditions. The time between repotting may have been too long. If the center portion of the root ball is dead but roots at the edge of the pot seem fine, then too much water is staying in the mix. Either the potting material itself holds too much water, or you are watering too often.

Desiccated gray roots point to an overdry mix. Roots with black tips can be an indication of too many salts, often caused by overfertilizing or softened water, or even snail damage.

Remedy the errors by fine-tuning the mix. To make the mix drain better, add materials with less moisture retention, such as charcoal, rocks of some sort, tree fern, coarser bark, perlite, a clay pot. To retain more water, add sphagnum moss, rockwool, finer bark, a plastic pot.

While the Plant's Out of the Pot

Clean away all of the old potting material, but try not to break any good roots. The center of the root ball often will be the most decayed. Shake off the mix, pull the root ball gently, and run the plant under tepid water. (Put something over the sink drain to catch bits of bark.) It's not necessary to remove every last bit of clinging mix.

Cut away dead roots up to the base of the plant. To confirm which roots are dead, hold them one at a time and pull gently; if the outer portion slips off easily and a wiry core thread is left, or if the root is brown all the way through the center, the root is dead. Partially decayed roots should also be cut away to a place where fresh tissue starts. If the roots are dead, soft, and mushy, suspect a root-rotting fungus in the mix, and after cutting away rotted parts, treat what's left with powdered sulfur. Try to keep as much of the good root system as possible.

If some roots are extremely long and difficult to get into a proper-size pot, trim them. Trim only thick roots that are covered with white velamen. Don't cut away thin, wiry live roots, for these won't form branches like the thick ones can if cut.

Trim off dead or yellowed leaves, old flower spikes and sheaths, and dried-up or rotten pseudobulbs. If an otherwise live-looking pseudobulb has no leaf, don't remove it, particularly if good roots are attached, for it still stores some reserves of food for the plant. When cutting away rot, dust the remaining part of the pseudobulb or the leaf with sulfur fungicide to help keep rot from spreading or recurring.

Search the plant for insect infestation such as scale or mealybug, which can hide on roots, under sheaths on pseudobulbs, and in the crown of the plant. A toothpick can be useful in searching down leaf sheaths. If pests are discovered, use a soft toothbrush and tepid water with insecticidal soap to very gently clean the plant.

Pot Choice and Size

Next, choose the pot. An easy way to address root problems is simply to change the pot type. A mushy mix with mushy roots in plastic might do better in clay. A shriveled, desiccated root mass in clay may perk up in plastic. In general, use clay for plants that need to dry out. Those that like to be wetter will grow best in plastic.

Beginners often go wrong by selecting a pot that's too large. Plants in the home grow better in small pots, surrounded by less mix, with less chance of staying too wet. If you're going to err on pot size, go smaller rather than larger.

Some growers prefer more room for root growth over potbound plants, especially for orchids that make lots of root growth compared with the size of the plant. If a pot bigger than classically advised is to be used, use a mix coarser than normal, and modify the pot (add more holes, or place a smaller, inverted clay or net pot inside). This allows plants the area they need to grow without also giving too much volume in which to rot.

Choose a pot with room for two years' worth of growth. If the plant grows along a rhizome (sympodial), each growth appearing in front of the last one, like a *Cattleya,* then select a pot that will allow for two new growths, since these plants usually make one new growth a year. To gauge how much room will be needed, look at the space between previous growths for clues. Often a pot 2 inches wider than the previous one will suffice. If a plant grows upward from a single point (monopodial), like a *Phalaenopsis,* then choose a pot that will hold the roots yet provide an extra ½ to ¾ inch around the outside of the root ball for future growth. For younger plants and others that will be repotted every year, adjust the pot size down accordingly, for just one year's growth.

For extra drainage, if desired, add crockery, polystyrene foam, or stones at the bottom of the pot. Arched pieces of crockery should curve down, forming a bridge over the drainage holes so they are not blocked. Another useful drainage trick is to enlarge the hole in the center of the bottom of a plastic pot, and then invert a small clay pot over it. The breathable clay pot will help the center of the root ball, which often sits in the worst wet conditions, stay well drained and airy even in a plastic pot.

Positioning the Plant

Positioning depends on the type of growth an orchid makes. Horizontal growers need to be placed so that the back end of the plant touches the wall of the pot, with the space in front of the newest growth for future spread. If such a plant has symmetrical growth, with no back end apparent, leave the same amount of room all the way around the plant.

Monopodial orchids that grow upward should be set right in the center of the pot. Position the plant in the pot before adding mix so that the rhizome or crown will eventually sit about ½ inch below the pot rim.

It's not necessary to stuff all the aerial roots back into the pot, but spread out the pot roots in the pot as much as possible. Hold the plant in place with one hand, and start adding mix. Always stir the mix before using it, for the various ingredients will settle differently over time, depending on weight and volume.

Pourable mixes such as bark-based or tree fern can simply be filled in about a third at a time; tap the pot gently on the work surface with each addition, so that mix can settle without huge gaps. Materials such as sphagnum moss and rockwool don't settle and must be arranged in the pot, so use gloved fingers to push the medium around. Make sure not to pack either one of these too tightly. Osmunda can be packed tightly. The way the "grain" of osmunda or sphagnum moss lies will also affect how much water the medium will hold (horizontal lay, more; vertical grain, less).

The horizontal plant rhizome of a sympodial orchid is part of the stem rather than a root, so it should not be covered by the mix. Allow it to lie half in and half out of the mix. The monopodial basal crown of leaves in plants such as *Phalaenopsis* should also not be covered but should lie instead just on the mix. Positioning the crown too low, below the mix, will invite rot, and positioning it too far above the mix will cause the plant to overdry.

Once the plant is potted, it may need stabilizing to prevent wobbling, when new root tips can be damaged or broken off. One way to add steadiness is by placing stones on top of the mix. Even better is to stake the plants upright. Any number of traditional plant stakes are available, wood or metal. A good staking material is a bamboo shish kebab skewer. These come in packs in different diameters and lengths, with pointed tips that can be inserted through the mix and into a bottom layer of polystyrene peanuts, an excellent combination for providing good support.

Whatever the stake, insert it through the mix, being careful not to skewer roots, down as far as possible. Several stakes on either side of a growth may be needed to keep it upright, in which case the tie can be looped around the stakes rather than tied to the plant. Single stakes should be tied to the plant with something that won't damage the growth. Avoid using wire. A soft material such as corsage wrapping tape, soft cord, or pieces of pantyhose fare much better. Plant clips are also available.

Another way to keep the plant steady is with a rhizome clip. These special wire clips attach to one end of the pot rim and lie across the top of the medium, on top of the rhizome, holding it down. There are rhizome clips that accommodate the thick rims of clay pots, as well as thinner ones specifically designed for plastic pots. Hobbyists who are good with wire benders can make their own. A good precaution to take with a rhizome clip is to cut a plastic straw to length and slip it over, protecting the growth from clip abrasion.

Labels

Before putting the plant aside, put the label back into the pot, or make a new one if the old one is broken or faded. Plant labels can be made of styrene or vinyl (vinyl lasts longer and costs more), wood, or engravable metal. The plastic types work fine, but write on them with a waterproof marker. A soft graphite pencil actually works best. It doesn't wash off, and it can be erased when needed. Paper labels generated via computer can be attached to plastic ones and then sprayed with plastic varnish for durability.

Write on the label the month and year the plant was repotted. Some labels are sold with lines for record markings printed on them.

Repotting Aftercare

Growers often disagree as to whether a plant should be watered immediately after repotting. Some recommend just light misting. Watering the plant immediately after repotting does help settle and firm the mix. And while there is no hard evidence as to its real benefit, many orchidists swear by the addition of a few drops of vitamin/hormonal additives such as SuperThrive to the water at this time to help give plants a good start.

If the environment is very humid, simply misting at repotting is fine. If you have a relatively dry situation, water. After that, do not water the plant thoroughly for several weeks. Instead, give it light misting every day, just to stimulate root growth. Plants with root systems that have been badly decayed or damaged won't be able to take up much water through the roots, so they are dependent on what the leaves can gather, and light misting helps them immeasurably. The larger pot with more mix will be holding more water than usual anyway, so it's better to keep the plant on the dry side for a while to avoid rot and to allow cut edges to heal. As the roots get longer, eventually going into the mix, begin regular thorough watering again.

It's often beneficial to put the plant in a slightly more shaded place for the first week after repotting, although opinion differs as to whether this is really necessary. In any event, it probably helps to keep the plant out of direct sunlight at first, moving it back gradually. Also avoid putting a newly repotted plant in a cold damp place, especially one with bad air movement.

Dividing an Orchid

Orchids don't have to be divided, but sometimes division is desirable. There are usually two reasons to divide an orchid: to make more plants, or to keep a bushy plant to a reasonable size. If division is desired, do it during repotting.

Sympodial orchids that grow along rhizomes are excellent candidates for division. The plant has to be large enough for division, with at least six pseudobulbs or leads so that each new piece will have at least three for best growth. The piece with the newer and larger growths will bloom before the piece with the old growths (the latter may take two years or more to rebloom).

After unpotting the plant and cleaning off mix and dead roots, look to see where a natural break may want to occur. This is generally the best place for dividing if it leaves the plant with enough pseudobulbs or leads for each new piece. Use a sharp, sterile knife or razor to make the division, then continue as usual with repotting.

Even better for the plant is to initiate the division while the plant is still potted in the pot, preferably six months before repotting, usually in the autumn, although this can take place only four weeks ahead if necessary. Take a knife and cut through the rhizome at the proper place, but then just leave the entire plant in the pot while it gets used to the surgery. Sometimes the back part of the plant will start new growths after this severing. At regular repotting time, the plant can be easily divided, each of the pieces stronger than if repotting and cutting took place together.

Specimen Plants versus Division

The biggest and most abundant flowers will be found on a plant that is allowed to keep on growing, being moved to a larger and larger pot with each repotting. Such "specimen plants" often win cultural awards from the American Orchid Society.

Another cultural trick for growing a specimen plant is to rotate the pot or mount every few days, so that all sides of the plant continually receive equal amounts of light. This helps develop growths and flowers all over the plant, rather than in a single orientation.

Keiki Offshoots

Some orchids are not divisible. Monopodial orchids such as *Phalaenopsis* can't be cut into pieces unless the plant cooperates first by sending out an offshoot, or "keiki" (a Hawaiian word pronounced "kay key"). Keikis usually grow off the flower spike, or sometimes at the base of the original plant. Leaves grow first. Wrap damp sphagnum moss around the keiki's base to encourage roots to grow. Once the roots are 1 to 2 inches long, the keiki can be removed and potted.

To artificially encourage keiki formation, commercially available keiki paste such as KeikiGrow can be applied to a spike node on *Phalaenopsis*. If a keiki forms, the grow paste is removed, since it is a root inhibitor, and a rooting compound such as KeikiRoot (indolebutyric acid) is then applied.

Often, however, keikis will form without any chemical intervention.

A higher-nitrogen fertilizer will help during keiki growth to aid leaf formation.

Orchids on Slab Mounts or Trees

Mounting epiphytic orchids on slabs, or outdoors on trees in frost-free climates, or even in a greenhouse on a small tree is fairly easy. See "Orchid Potting Materials" in the appendices for best mounts to use.

It is very important that the roots are put in direct contact with the mount or tree and then held steady until they've grabbed on for themselves. First, soak the plant in room-temperature water for 15 minutes so roots are pliable. To remove orchids from preexisting mounts, soak the mount and plant first and cut away any tie. Many plants will release their grip, but if not, the mount may have to be crumbled away.

Hold the plant in place with its roots directly against the mount or tree. Position the plant so that there is room for direction of growth. Place a layer of very damp sheet sphagnum moss or osmunda on top of the roots. (Moss under the roots instead of on top tends to defeat the purpose of encouraging the plant to attach to its new home.) Moss or osmunda helps provide the moisture for root growth and also protects the roots from the plant tie.

Wrap strong nylon fishline or strips of pantyhose firmly around the plant, roots, and mount or tree so the plant will not wobble, threading the label through the tie to the back of the mount or tree, then knotting. Alternatively, orchids can be attached to mounts with nontoxic glue such as Liquid Nails or Plumber's Goop. If a tie is used, remove it when the plant has firmly attached itself to the mount or tree, usually within three months, to prevent the tie from cutting into either the orchid or the host tree.

If the mount is to be hung, attach a wire hook or loop to the back.

A small mount can be mounted atop another larger one if desired, to give the plant more room and yet disturb it least. Long branches can even be used for mounting many small epiphytic orchids together, for an interesting and naturalistic effect.

To keep a mounted orchid happier in a low-humidity environment, place the entire thing in a suitable small clay pot in which the mount doesn't reach the bottom, and then put the pot in a saucer of water, watering daily. Water will be absorbed by the porous pot, keeping the microclimate around the mounted plant nicely humid.

A New Look at Pests and Diseases

Vanda

When something goes wrong with orchids, the knee-jerk reaction is to pick up the most potent weapon and spray everything in sight. Don't. There is a systematic way to get rid of unwanted visitors, and it pays to start at the bottom of the ladder. Why use an atom bomb when a Q-Tip will do?

The presence of pests and diseases means that something is wrong with the orchid growing environment. Pay attention to the underlying reasons, instead of just treating the result.

Is the environment really clean, free from faded flowers, dead leaves, and other debris? Is air movement good, allowing water to dry quickly rather than inviting rot, fungal infection, and slugs? Are your plants stressed from lack of water, low humidity, or extremes of temperature? Stressed plants are especially susceptible to pest and disease attack. Overfertilized plants are also prime targets for pests. Are new plants isolated for a week and then inspected for pest and disease? All of these factors and more can mean the difference between healthy and sick plants.

Fungal and Bacterial Diseases

While pests cause great concern, orchid disease can be a faster killer. Yet fungal and bacterial diseases are easier to prevent.

The presence of fungal or bacterial disease announces stale air, an overly cold and damp environment, overcrowded plants, or too many places for fungal spores and bacteria to hide. Treat the disease, but more important, treat the environment so that the condition won't recur.

Destroy infected cuttings and keep the area debris-free and clean. Add more fans and a source of fresh air. Avoid careless watering. Don't let water stand in leaf crowns and crevices; keep pots tipped forward if necessary. Overhead watering systems can spread disease by splashing water from infected plants; isolate infected plants to minimize spread. Plants with newly opened flowers can be protected from ever-present *Botrytis* fungi by bringing them into lower humidity to prevent spotting.

More than 100 fungal and bacterial diseases can affect orchids. Some of the worst are black rot fungi (*Phytophthora* and *Pythium*) and bacterial brown spot (*Pseudomonas*), which kill quickly, especially in plants with central growing leaf crowns, such as *Phalaenopsis*. Diseases that simply cause flower or leaf spotting and rust are less cause for concern. Sooty molds on healthy plants are secondary fungi that signal the presence of aphids, mealybugs, and other pests. Pest damage and fungal infections often go hand in hand.

The worst disease symptoms include soft, water-soaked markings, perhaps with blackened or purple coloration. When these attack, act quickly. To treat, cut away infections by slicing back to healthy tissue, then dust the cut surfaces with powdered sulfur, copper dust, or (for fungus) cinnamon, all of which dry and inhibit disease spots by surface protection. Other fungicides and bactericides include topical quaternary ammonium salts (Physan, RD-20). To wash the environment, 10 percent chlorine bleach is effective.

More potent complex chemicals include systemics, which are taken up by plant tissue and act against established infections that have spread below the surface. Subdue (metalaxyl) and triforene (Funginex) are examples. Overuse of fungicides sometimes causes plant problems, as well as risk to humans. If fungicides are being used too regularly on a preventive basis, stop to assess what's wrong with the environment.

If It's Virus, Say Goodbye

The worst orchid disease is virus. Virtually every orchid collection has virus-infected plants. Orchids can live for years with viral infections, but they cannot be cured. Virused orchids must be destroyed.

There are at least 25 viruses that strike orchids. Most predominant are orchid strains of cymbidium mosaic virus (CyMV), found in 20 percent of cultivated orchids, and odontoglossum ringspot virus (ORSV, also known as tobacco mosaic virus, or TMV-O), found in 2 percent. Both affect a wide range of orchid genera. Another virus, bean yellow mosaic virus (BYMV), is increasing rapidly, especially in *Masdevallia*.

Virus can be confirmed only by laboratory test. Symptoms vary from genus to genus, even from plant to plant, and can be very confusing. Necrotic streaking of old and new leaves is an especially potent sign, particularly if it occurs in a mosaic pattern or parallel to leaf veining, as are sunken spots or rings leached of chlorophyll. If spots are water-soaked and soft, suspect fungal or bacterial disease instead.

Virus can cause general plant unhealthiness, making the plant susceptible to other infestations. Virus often results in decreased vigor, fewer flowers, odd color breaks, pitting, streaking, spots, patterned leaves, yellowing, weird flower forms, and death.

Sometimes a plant will not exhibit symptoms, an undetected "Typhoid Mary" within the collection. Unfortunately, laboratory testing will reveal only the most well-known viruses. The showiest, oldest orchids are the most likely to be infected. Test those first. Home tests involve "indicator plants," nonorchidaceous plants such as *Cassia occidentalis* (sicklepod) for CyMV and *Gomphrena globosa* (globe amaranth) for ORSV that develop characteristic viral signs when rubbed with a leaf from a virused orchid.

If a suspicious orchid tests negative, and seems generally unsound when treatments for other diseases fail, then assume it is virused with a less prevalent strain, and destroy the plant.

Most virus is spread mechanically through the use of unsterilized cutting instruments, whereby the sap of cut plant parts is transferred to other cut or damaged plant parts. The two main viruses persist for a long time on cutting tools and pots. Although ORSV and CyMV do not appear to be transmitted via insects, the major vector for less well known viruses (including BYMV) is the aphid.

Virus is the most important reason to keep the growing environment clean. Approach all orchids as if each one is virused; sterilize instruments between cutting plants, don't reuse potting mixes, sterilize pots before reuse, and don't let water drain from one pot to another. During repotting, plant juices can get on fingers and under nails, thus transferring viruses to another orchid; wear gloves.

To ensure sterility, flame tools for several seconds in a propane torch, dipping them first in alcohol, or use a different single-edged razor blade for each plant. Tools can also be sterilized via a several-second dip in a 10 percent solution of trisodium phosphate (TSP), which allows a viral transmission rate of only 3 percent. Change the solution when it turns green from plant sap.

Mechanical Plant Damage

Orchids can be affected by physical causes as well as by pestilences. Once a portion is damaged physically, it cannot regenerate, but new growth should be fine unless infection sets in. If damaged leaves still have healthy green areas, leave them on, although blackened areas can be cut away.

A drench of cold water can make leaf cells collapse into pitted streaks. Unsightly white or brown spotting that's difficult to remove is due to hard water or high-iron water, causing decreased leaf efficiency. Blackened leaf tips are often a sign of overfertilizing. Intense direct sun can cause blackened areas known as sunburn.

If orchids freeze, try a systemic bactericide. Most of the plants will be lost, but a few may survive.

A Swarm of Insects

The most common orchid pests are mealybugs, scale, aphids, spider mites, whiteflies, thrips, fungus gnats, snails, and slugs.

The primary danger from insect pests is that they can carry diseases from plant to plant. They also suck plant juices and chew plant parts, stunting and killing the plant. Catch infestation early to minimize pest damage.

Ants

When ants appear, suspect infestation by mealybugs, scale, or aphids. All excrete a sugary honeydew attractive to ants, which then stand guard over the insect "cows." Ants do relatively little damage to orchids.

Treatment: Go after the honeydew cause, not the ants. Ants can be deterred by diatomaceous earth. Fire ants in particular can be controlled by rotenone. A beneficial natural predator, *Pyemotes* mite, will infest ant eggs.

Aphids

Soft-bodied and pear-shaped, aphids are the main virus vector. Typically green, aphids are piercing and sucking insects that also excrete a plant-toxic saliva. Females can reproduce without a mate, and they give live birth. Sooty black mold can grow in the excreted honeydew, covering foliage and reducing photosynthesis. Aphids afflict new growing tips, flower inflorescences, and roots. Plants that have been over-fertilized with high nitrogen are often attacked. Damage includes leaf curl, yellowing, and stunted leaf and stem growth.

Treatment: Remove and crush, or spray off with a strong stream of water. Reduce nitrogen fertilizer or try a less soluble source, increasing phosphorus. Use sprays of insecticidal soap or horticultural oil, or 70 percent isopropyl alcohol on swabs. The latter also removes sooty mold. Natural predators are *Aphidoletes* and green lacewing, and fungal and bacterial pathogens such as *Verticillium lecanii*.

Fungus gnats

These common little flies are mostly a nuisance. The more damaging larvae live within pots, particularly in organic mixes, where they lay eggs, feed on roots, and break down mix too quickly. Fungus gnats bring bacterial and fungal root rots. Plants may wilt, show root rot with maggots, and have distorted leaves. Overly wet mix and shady conditions encourage fungus gnats, often introduced via peat.

Treatment: Make sure the potting mix is intact. Keep the area debris-free. Lay yellow sticky traps horizontally on the lip of the pot, with another near the base. Horticultural oil kills adults. To kill larval worms and eggs, use pot drenches of either insecticidal soap or *Bacillus thuringiensis* (Bt) strain H-14.

Mealybugs

Mealybugs are white cottony masses that suck leaf, stem, root, and flower juices. Soft-bodied, waxy, and wingless, mealybugs can crawl from plant to plant. Eggs hatch on the underside of leaves, and the larvae feed in concealed spots; probe a toothpick into leaf junctures and sheaths when monitoring. Sticky honeydew is secreted over the leaves, with subsequent black sooty mold. Heavy infestations cause yellow leaves, stunted growth, and smaller, fewer flowers.

Treatment: Use sprays of insecticidal soap or horticultural oil, or 70 percent isopropyl alcohol on swabs. Avoid over-fertilizing. Keep plants from touching each other. The beneficial beetle *Cryptolaemus* attacks all stages of mealybugs; smaller infestations are treatable with *Leptomastix* wasp.

Scale

These small round insects crawl when young, then attach for life underneath edges and midribs of tough leaves. Scale is a sucking insect, sapping juices. There are many species, but only two basic types. Hard scale is brownish, coated with a protective waxy armor under which eggs are laid or live birth given. Soft scale can look like cottony masses of mealybugs and secrete sticky honeydew. Damage includes yellow spotting. Scale also infests roots, sometimes with no symptoms other than decreased vigor.

Treatment: Clean plants with a soft toothbrush dipped in insecticidal soap or 70 percent isopropyl alcohol. Use sprays of insecticidal soap or horticultural oil, or alcohol on swabs. Avoid overfertilizing. Lacewing is a natural predator.

Slugs and snails

Large holes and silvery trails indicate night-foraging slugs. Snail root damage can be evidenced by blackened tips, especially on new roots, leading to wilted-looking leaves and stunted growth. Flowers and buds are also prime targets. Tiny bush snails can live within the pot undetected. Eggs hatch in four to six weeks, when reinfestation can occur.

Treatment: Moist bark-based mixes tend to harbor these pests, while osmunda and tree fern deter them. Most slug/snail pesticides (metaldehydes) are acutely toxic to humans and animals and should be avoided. Snails and sowbugs will float to the top of a bucket of water when infested pots are submerged for several minutes. Place preferred slug food (lettuce or banana) atop the pots and handpick foragers at night with flashlight illumination. A spray of vinegar and water kills slugs. Affix comblike copper strips around pots or around bench legs. Dust the area and pots with horticultural diatomaceous earth. Cotton puffs wrapped at the base of flower stems thwart bloom eaters. Beer or malt barley traps are more effective outdoors than in, working by scent lure, then by drowning. Decollate snail (*Rumina*) is a natural slug predator.

Spider mites

Mites are hard-to-detect piercing and sucking insects. They appear when plants are stressed by low humidity or water and/or high temperatures, attaching to leaf undersides. Leaves appear pin-poked, with tiny yellow dots that give a silvery stippled appearance. A hand lens will reveal tiny webbing. After leaves stipple, spots become sunken and rusty, and leaves yellow, sometimes falling off. Mites especially affect new growth and thin-leaved plants. Mites are not insects, since they belong to the spider family, so standard chemical insecticides are not effective.

Treatment: Increase humidity. Destroy infected plant debris, removing badly infested leaves. Isolate infected plants, cleaning off webbing with insecticidal soap. To kill, use horticultural oil, insecticidal soap, sulfur dust, pyrethrum, or miticide. Many kinds of predatory mites are commercially available; two or more mite species control better than one.

Thrips
A hand lens is needed to see thrips, which scrape tissue surfaces and suck juices, usually attacking flowers, causing a streaked pitting easily mistaken for virus. Leaf damage is silvery scarred flecks, with thrips feeding on the underside. Adults fly, carrying disease and virus. Dry conditions favor thrips.

Treatment: Increase humidity. Pick and destroy badly infested flowers. Sprays are generally useless for flowers. On infested leaves, use horticultural oil, isopropyl alcohol, or insecticidal soap. Predatory mites (*Phytoseiulus* and *Amblyseius*) and lacewings are natural controls.

Whiteflies
Whiteflies are not flies but are related to mealybugs and scale, secreting honeydew. Adults are white waxy fliers; the more damaging greenish yellow nymphs have sucking mouthparts and feed heavily. Nymphs attach to the underside of leaves, with eggs laid in a small circle. Whiteflies are most active in warm environments. Damage includes wilted leaves with sooty mold or sticky leaf residue, leaf and plant death.

Treatment: Hang yellow sticky traps vertically a few inches above plants. Reduce nitrogen fertilizer. Drop temperatures to decrease activity. Spray with insecticidal soap, horticultural oil, or pyrethrin. A natural enemy is *Encarsia formosa,* a minuscule parasitic wasp not dangerous to humans; *Encarsia* work best under warm, humid conditions.

Pest Control

More than a billion pounds of a vast number of pesticides are used in this country annually. There are so many pesticides not because there are so many types of pests, but because insects quickly become immune. Every time insects are sprayed, most die, but a few survive. Those tough survivors live to breed, creating dominant generations that carry pesticide-resistant genes.

As pesticide resistance develops in the population, growers try higher doses applied more frequently, causing greater speedup in the genetic resistance. Result: New and more pesticides are needed to fight an enemy now tougher to control.

Besides the pressing environmental reasons to stop such massive pesticide application, it doesn't make sense to keep creating more resistant pests. Today there is a better choice of alternative controls to which pests don't become resistant.

Integrated Pest Management (IPM) incorporates careful monitoring of the plants. IPM advocates using pesticides when necessary, but the emphasis is on learning when it's necessary. The core is to look at plants, discover when infestation is present, then think out controls systematically. IPM moves from monitoring and discovery, to handpicking controls and traps, to soaps and oils, to natural predators, to botanical pesticides, to chemical controls, in that order.

The first line of defense, if the pests are large enough, is to handpick. Pests never get resistant to being squashed. The next line of defense is to isolate the infested plant and apply something directly to it, never automatically spraying everything in sight.

Pesticides go in and out of orchid fashion. Suddenly a particular one is unavailable, while new ones appear. The Environmental Protection Agency (EPA) regulates pesticides on a national level, but states retain local regulatory rights; availability of different chemicals and trade names can vary throughout the country.

Pesticides are not supposed to be used in any way except as specified on the labels. Many, however, have never been tested for use on orchids, since manufacturers usually don't consider orchid testing economically viable. Orchids often are not listed on a label even when orchid growers have found that product useful. Even with products that have been tested on certain types of orchids, orchid diversity makes it impossible to be certain which may be harmed by a particular treatment. Therefore, test any new product carefully on a few leaves, wait a few days, then observe if there has been any damage to the plant before applying the product to the whole plant.

Ultrafine horticultural oil

One of the most effective treatments for home use to rid plants of soft-bodied sucking insects, particularly hard and soft scale, as well as mealybugs, aphids, spider mites, immature whiteflies, and adult fungus gnats, is lightweight horticultural oil.

Don't confuse this with a related petroleum oil known as "dormant" oil, applied in winter on outdoor plants to kill overwintering pests. Dormant oil is harsh and can't be used for actively growing houseplants. Instead, manufacturers have learned to refine and purify paraffinic oil almost as light and mild as baby oil. These ultrafine oils evaporate within 24 hours or less, degrading rapidly after application.

Horticultural oil works by smothering and suffocating insect pests and eggs. Oil is a contact poison and is ineffective as a preventive. Beneficial insects that wander onto the plants will not be harmed. No resistance has been found.

Growers sometimes report plant damage when using horticultural oil. Any oil will coat plant leaves, interfering with the ability to take in and give off water, oxygen, and carbon dioxide until it evaporates. Use oils correctly.

The most common misuse of horticultural oil is as a dip. When diluted in water, oil rises to the top of the bucket and overcoats the plant at too great a concentration. Instead, use oil as a spray, diluted in water at 2½ tablespoons per gallon (1 percent solution). Constantly agitate during use to keep the spray mixed. Spray when the oil will dry quickly, and never under high temperature, under direct light conditions, in humidity over 70 percent, or on drought- or heat-stressed plants. Spray the top and bottom of leaves thoroughly, in all crevices, so that the spray drips off the plant. Allow a week to pass before spraying a second time to eradicate missed insects and eggs or newly hatched ones.

Insecticidal soap

An environmentally gentle control is insecticidal soap. Soaps are effective against soft-bodied insects: aphids, soft scale, whiteflies, mealybugs, mites, and thrips. Soaps work by contacting the pests and rapidly smothering them.

Many people have tried insecticidal soaps with little success. But soaps often are not used properly. Soaps are effective only while wet. An infested plant has to be absolutely soaked, so that the spray drips off the plant, reaching tops and undersides of leaves. To make sure the drying time is as long as possible, spray early in the morning, preferably when temperatures are coolest and humidity high. Keep shaking the solution as you apply it. Soaps require at least two applications, five days apart (two to three days apart for aphids); three applications may be needed.

Insecticidal soaps don't work well in hard water, which has many dissolved solids; soap is inactivated and precipitates, making it toxic to leaves. Use soft (not softened) water. A good source is rainwater or distilled water. To tell if water is soft or hard, shake the soap solution. If it is clear and sudsy, the water is probably soft, but if it is whitish with few suds, the water is hard. If the water pH is alkaline and leaves a whitish coating on plant leaves when soap is added, add a little lemon juice to the water. Rinse with water any plant that wilts within a few hours of being sprayed with soap.

Studies have shown that mild dishwashing liquid (1 teaspoon per quart of water) is almost as effective as EPA-registered insecticidal soaps, but less plant damage occurs with the specially designed insecticidal soaps.

Pesticides are much more effective when insecticidal soap is added to the solution. Pesticide concentration can be cut in half or even by three-quarters when half the recommended soap concentration is mixed in (add last), with effectiveness higher than if either is used alone at full strength. Combinations of horticultural oil and insecticidal soap also work better together than apart. Do not mix soaps with rotenone.

Isopropyl alcohol
Another alternative being used as a pesticide by orchid growers (although not EPA-approved) is 70 percent isopropyl alcohol (rubbing alcohol). A contact poison, isopropyl spray has been found to control mealybugs, whiteflies, scale, fungus gnats, thrips, and red spider mites.

Alcohol can desiccate plants, so test different dilutions and do not use on sensitive plants. Spray the alcohol solution at intervals of a couple of days until the infestation is over. Rinsing the plant almost immediately with plain water will keep down leaf damage. Even more selective is to soak a cotton swab in alcohol and directly apply it to the infested areas. A gentler alternative is witch hazel.

Botanical pesticides
Insecticides derived from plants break down in the environment quickly. They are more toxic than nonchemical controls but generally less toxic than chemical pesticides.

Pyrethrum is a natural pesticide derived from chrysanthemum. It provides fast knockdown of aphids, whiteflies, mites, and thrips. There is, however, some toxicity to plants, animals, and especially fish. A stomach poison that must be ingested by the pest, pyrethrin is fairly unselective in action, killing beneficial insects such as ladybugs and lacewings as well as unwanted pests.

Rotenone, derived from the roots and stems of tropical shrubs and vines, is also a stomach poison. It is more selective and kills thrips, aphids, red spider mites, and fire ants. Rotenone is very irritating to human breathing passages; use a respirator.

Another botanical insecticide is neem, extracted from the seeds of *Azadirachta indica*. Neem works by disrupting the hormonal balance of juvenile insects, interrupting the feeding of mealybugs, whiteflies, aphids, and thrips, with little harm to beneficial insects, and it repels insects once sprayed. It biodegrades readily.

Diatomaceous earth
When slugs, ants, and cockroaches infest a collection, a dusting of diatomaceous earth (D.E.) kills by absorbing the

outer coat, causing loss of body fluids. When ingested, D.E. interferes with insect respiration, digestion, and reproduction. It kills mechanically, not by poison.

Use only horticultural-grade diatomaceous earth, not swimming pool quality. Both are sharp, silica-based fossils of aquatic plants, but horticultural grade is purer, is less hazardous to the human respiratory system, and comes from freshwater organisms. Reapply after watering.

Beneficial predators

Natural insect predators are excellent ways to control pests in greenhouses. The finest all-purpose predator is the green lacewing, which preys on aphids, mites, spider mites, mealybugs, thrips, immature scale, and whiteflies. *Phytoseiulus* eats red spider mites. Ladybugs eat scale, aphids, mealybugs, spider mites, and thrips.

In order to induce beneficial insects to stay around once released, a small amount of pests must be tolerated. This means creating a natural balance. Pesticides can't be used when trying to encourage beneficial insects.

Another beneficial organism, a bacterium known as *Bacillus thuringiensis* (Bt), can selectively kill many types of pests. It works by ingestion, disrupting digestion. One strain (Bt H-14) has been developed specifically for fungus gnat larvae.

Sticky traps

A mechanical product useful in a confined area is the sticky yellow insect panel that traps whiteflies, aphids, and fungus gnats as they fly. Large greenhouses use them as IPM monitoring devices to inform growers that pests exist. Home growers can use sticky traps for actual control. They're most effective in 1-foot-square sizes, placed 3 feet apart. More whiteflies are trapped by vertical hanging of the trap, while fungus gnats are more drawn to traps placed horizontally across pots.

You can create homemade traps by spreading plastic yellow picnic plates with petroleum jelly or STP oil treatment on both sides, and then hanging them with wire. Simply wipe them clean when they're full of pests, and reapply ointment.

Chemical pesticides

If, despite trying other methods first, you find that pest problems have gotten out of hand, then consider more hardcore pesticides. Many laboratory chemicals have a residual effect on plants, because they do not degrade quickly and remain on the surface, or because they are "systemic," absorbed into the plant and then ingested by the pest. Organic phosphates, malathion and diazinon, are among the least dangerous. They do, however, kill beneficial insects as well, working by contact and as a stomach poison.

To keep plant damage to a minimum, use wettable powder (WP) forms of pesticides rather than oil-based (emulsfiable concentrate, or EC) ones. Pesticide damage can show up as darkly spotted leaf tips or edges (entire leaves may turn black). Young growing points may die, leaves can yellow (a condition known as chlorosis) or distort, and general stunting may occur.

Don't spray when temperatures are above 90°F or in high humidity. Rapid pesticide drying is desired. Apply thoroughly, underneath leaves and in crevices. Don't spray severely stressed plants; they may die.

Since insects quickly become immune, one pesticide treatment will rarely be sufficient. Watch for ineffectiveness and use a different control when needed, alternating pesticide treatments. Apply three or four diligent follow-up treatments a week apart. Intermittent spraying just creates an extra-strong enemy.

Pesticides can build up inside the human body, retained in fatty tissues. People who have used them for years with no ill effects can suddenly be pushed over the body's tolerance level and become extremely sick. New research indicates that much pesticide damage is not immediately seen, showing up in third and fourth generations.

When working with pesticides, wear thick unlined gloves, for a lining would absorb and hold the chemicals. Always use a respirator to protect lungs, not just a dust mask. Apply pesticides outdoors whenever possible for best ventilation. Be aware that the worst exposure will be when you are diluting concentrated chemicals.

Summing Up Pest Controls

Whatever route you choose to combat the dreadful things that sometimes afflict orchids, remember to start with the safest. Don't call out the entire fire brigade just to blow out a match.

When Is the Battle Not Worth the Cure?

Not every afflicted orchid deserves saving. Virused ones should always be destroyed. Those severely infested with insects may require too much time, trouble, and chemicals to be worth the effort of rehabilitating a probably replaceable plant. Assessing whether it's worth it or not is something good orchid growers have to do regularly. Sometimes the best route is simply to throw a plant away.

The Color Plates

Cattleya
Alliance

Barkeria
spectabilis

Plant height: to 10 in.
Flowers: 3 in. wide
Blooms between April and October
Medium to high light
Cool to intermediate temperature
Can grow into a many-flowered plant
p. 239

Brassavola
perrinii

Plant height: to 18 in.
Flowers: 2½ in. wide
Blooms between April and October, with
peak bloom in July
Medium to high light
Intermediate to warm temperature
Very night fragrant
Easy to grow into a many-flowered plant
p. 243

Brassocattleya
Angel Lace

Plant height: to 12 in.
Flowers: 4½ in. wide
Blooms in spring or summer
Medium to high light
Intermediate temperature
Intensely fragrant
Easy
p. 245

Brassocattleya
Binosa

Plant height: to 18 in.
Flowers: 3½ in. wide
Blooms in fall or winter
Medium to high light
Intermediate temperature
Very fragrant
Easy to grow into a many-flowered plant
p. 245

Brassocattleya
Green Dragoon

Plant height: to 2 ft.
Flowers: 4 in. wide
Blooms in fall or
winter
Medium to high
light
Intermediate
temperature
Fragrant
Easy
p. 245

Brassoepidendrum
Peggy Ann

Plant height:
to 30 in.
Flowers: 2 in. wide
Blooms in winter
Medium to high
light
Intermediate to
warm temperature
Easy
p. 246

Brassolaelia
Richard Mueller

Plant height: to 10 in.
Flowers: 2½–3 in. wide
Blooms in summer
Medium light
Intermediate temperature
Easy
p. 247

Brassolaeliocattleya
Mem. Dorothy
Bertsch

Plant height:
to 20 in.
Flowers: 5 in. wide
Blooms in winter
Medium light
Intermediate
temperature
Very fragrant
Easy
p. 247

Brassolaeliocattleya
Port Royal Sound

Plant height: to 22 in.
Flowers: 5 in. wide
Blooms in spring or
summer
Medium light
Intermediate
temperature
Fragrant
Easy
p. 247

Cattleya
amethystoglossa

Plant height: to 3 ft.
Flowers: 3 in. wide
Blooms between
February and April
Medium light
Intermediate to
warm temperature
Fragrant
Easy
p. 253

Cattleya aurantiaca

Plant height: to 18 in.
Flowers: 2 in. long in
clusters
Blooms between
February and May
Medium light
Intermediate to
warm temperature
Blooms while still
young
Easy
p. 253

Cattleya forbesii

Plant height: to 18 in.
Flowers: 4 in. wide
Blooms between May
and October
Medium light
Intermediate to
warm temperature
Fragrant
Easy to grow into a
many-flowered plant
p. 253

**Cattleya
harrisoniana**

Plant height: to 22 in.
Flowers: 4 in. wide
Blooms between July and October
Medium light
Intermediate to warm temperature
Fragrant
Easy
p. 254

**Cattleya
intermedia**

Plant height:
to 20 in.
Flowers: 4 in. wide
Blooms between
March and May
Medium light
Intermediate to
warm temperature
Fragrant
Easy to grow into
a many-flowered
plant
p. 254

Cattleya skinneri

*Plant height:
to 20 in.
Flowers: 3½ in.
wide
Blooms between
February and June,
with peak bloom
in May
Medium light
Intermediate to
warm temperature
Grows well into a
many-flowered
plant
p. 254*

**Cattleya
walkeriana**

*Plant height: to 10 in.
Flowers: 4 in. wide
Blooms between November and May
Medium light
Intermediate to warm temperature
Fragrant
p. 254*

Cattleya
Carla Avila

Plant height: to 20 in.
Flowers: 6 in. wide
Blooms in winter or spring
Medium light
Intermediate temperature
Fragrant
Easy
p. 254

Cattleya
Chocolate Drop

Plant height: to 2 ft.
Flowers: 2½ in. wide in clusters
Blooms in fall
Medium light
Intermediate to warm temperature
Long-lasting waxy flowers
Easy
p. 254

***Cattleya*
Pumpernickel**

Plant height: to 22 in.
Flowers: 5 in. wide
Blooms in spring
Medium light
Intermediate temperature
Fragrant
Easy
p. 255

Cattleya
Sophia Martin

Plant height: to 2 ft.
Flowers: 3½ in.
wide
Blooms in fall
Medium light
Intermediate
temperature
Fragrant
Easy
p. 255

Cattleytonia
Why Not

Plant height:
to 14 in.
Flowers: 3 in. wide
Blooms from
February to April;
may bloom again in
summer
Medium to high
light
Intermediate to
warm temperature
Very crystalline
flowers
p. 255

Dialaelia
Snowflake

Plant height:
to 18 in.
Flowers: 3 in. wide
on long sprays
Blooms from
February to March
Medium to high
light
Intermediate
temperature
Grows well into
a many-flowered
plant
p. 272

**Encyclia
atropurpurea**

*Plant height:
to 22 in.
Flowers: 3 in. long
Blooms from
March to June
Medium to high
light
Intermediate to
warm temperature
Very fragrant long-
lasting flowers
p. 277*

Encyclia cochleata

*Plant height:
to 20 in.
Flowers: 3 in. long
Blooms nearly year-
round
Medium light
Intermediate to
warm temperature
Very easy
p. 277*

Encyclia prismatocarpa

*Plant height:
to 15 in.
Flowers: 2 in. wide
Blooms between
July and October
Medium to high
light
Intermediate to
warm temperature
Fragrant
Can grow into a
many-flowered
plant
p. 278*

Epicattleya
Fireball

*Plant height: to 3 ft.
Flowers: 3 in. wide
in many clusters
Blooms often at
variable times
Medium light
Intermediate
temperature
Easy
p. 278*

**Epidendrum
cinnabarinum**

Plant height: to 4 ft.
Flowers: 1½ in.
wide in clusters
Blooms in summer
High light
Warm temperature
Upside-down
flowers
Very long
successive bloom
p. 279

**Epidendrum
conopseum**

Plant height: to 8 in.
Flowers: ¾ in. wide
Blooms September
to October
Low light
Cool temperature
Northernmost
epiphyte
Many fragrant
flowers
p. 279

Epidendrum ilense

*Plant height:
to 16 in.
Flowers: 2½ in.
long on hanging
spray
Blooms between
June and January
Medium light
Warm temperature
Saved from
extinction when
habitat was
destroyed*
p. 279

**Epidendrum
porpax**

*Plant height: to 4 in.
Flowers: ½ in. wide
Blooms in fall or winter
Medium light
Intermediate temperature
Very waxy flowers
Grows well into a many-flowered plant*
p. 280

**Epidendrum
stamfordianum**

*Plant height:
to 20 in.
Flowers: 2 in. wide
on long spike of
many flowers
Blooms between
January and April
Medium light
Warm temperature
Fragrant
p. 280*

**Epidendrum
Costa Rica**

*Plant height: to 30 in.
Flowers: 1½ in. wide in clusters
Blooms in winter or spring
Medium light
Intermediate temperature
Easy
p. 280*

Isabelia violacea   *Plant height: to 3½ in.*
Flowers: 2 in. wide
Blooms in winter, with peak bloom in
February
Medium light
Intermediate to warm temperature
Flowers last only a week
Easy
p. 286

Iwanagaara   *Plant height: to 18 in.*
Apple Blossom   *Flowers: 3½ in. wide*
Blooms in winter or spring
Medium to high light
Intermediate temperature
Easy
p. 287

Laelia anceps

*Plant height:
to 12 in.
Flowers: 4–5 in.
wide on 3-ft. spike
Blooms between
November and
March
High light
Intermediate
temperature
Easy
p. 288*

**Laelia
harpophylla**

*Plant height:
to 18 in.
Flowers: 2–3 in.
wide, up to 10 on a
spike
Blooms between
February and May
High light
Intermediate to
warm temperature
Many long-lasting
flowers
p. 288*

Laelia jongheana

*Plant height: to 6 in.
Flowers: 5 in. wide
Blooms between
February and May,
with peak bloom
in March
Medium to high
light
Intermediate to
warm temperature
p. 288*

Laelia pumila   *Plant height: to 9 in.
Flowers: 5 in. wide
Blooms in fall; peak bloom in October
Medium light
Cool to intermediate temperature
High humidity
Fragrant
p. 288*

Laelia purpurata   *Plant height: to 2 ft.*
Flowers: 6–8 in. wide
Blooms May to June
Medium light
Intermediate to warm temperature
Fragrant
p. 289

Laeliocattleya   *Plant height: to 20 in.*
Amber Glow   *Flowers: 6 in. wide*
Blooms in summer or fall
Medium to high light
Intermediate temperature
Easy
p. 289

Laeliocattleya
Mary Ellen Carter

*Plant height:
to 20 in.
Flowers: 5 in. wide
Blooms between
summer and
winter, often twice
Medium to high
light
Intermediate
temperature
Easy
p. 289*

Laeliocattleya
Mini Purple

*Plant height: to 8 in.
Flowers: 3 in. wide
Blooms between fall and spring, often
several times
Medium light
Intermediate to warm temperature
Blooms well while very small
Extra humidity
p. 290*

**Laeliocattleya
Platinum Sun**

*Plant height: to 22 in.
Flowers: 7 in. wide
Blooms in winter
Medium light
Intermediate temperature
Fragrant
Easy
p. 290*

*Oerstedella
centradenia*

*Plant height: to 2 ft.
Flowers: 1 in. wide
Blooms January to
March
Medium light
Warm temperature
Grows well into a
many-flowered
plant
Easy
p. 307*

**Potinara
Beaufort Gold**

*Plant height:
to 10 in.
Flowers: 3½ in.
wide
Blooms in winter
or spring
Medium light
Intermediate to
cool temperature
p. 325*

**Rhyncholaelia
digbyana**

*Plant height: to 18 in.
Flowers: 7 in. wide
Blooms between May and July
High light
Intermediate temperature
Strong lemonlike fragrance
p. 330*

Rhyncholaelia glauca

Plant height: to 14 in.
Flowers: 4 in. wide
Blooms between January and March
High light
Intermediate temperature
Gloriously fragrant
p. 330

Sophrocattleya Beaufort

Plant height: to 8 in.
Flowers: 3 in. wide
Blooms in fall or winter
Medium light
Intermediate to cool temperature
Extra humidity
p. 337

Sophrocattleya Seagulls Beaulu Queen

Plant height: to 6 in.
Flowers: 2½ in.
wide
Can bloom several
times from fall to
spring, with peak
bloom in December
Medium light
Intermediate
temperature
p. 337

Sophrolaelio-cattleya Coastal Sunrise

Plant height:
to 20 in.
Flowers: 5 in. wide
on long spray
Blooms in winter
Medium to high
light
Intermediate
temperature
Easy
p. 337

Sophrolaelio-
cattleya
Hazel Boyd

Plant height: to 10 in.
Flowers: 4 in. wide
Blooms in winter or spring, often twice
Medium light
Intermediate temperature
Very vigorous high-quality hybrid
Easy
p. 338

Sophrolaelio-
cattleya
Jewel Box

Plant height: to 16 in.
Flowers: 4 in. wide on arching sprays
Blooms in winter or spring
Medium light
Intermediate temperature
Easy
p. 338

Sophrolaelio-cattleya
Precious Stones

Plant height: 14 in.
Flowers: 3 in. wide
Blooms between
summer and fall
Medium light
Intermediate
temperature
Fragrant waxy
flowers
Easy
p. 338

Sophrolaelio-cattleya hybrid

Plant height: 8 in.
Flowers: 3 in. wide
Blooms in fall or
winter
Medium light
Intermediate to
cool temperature
Fragrant waxy
flowers
p. 338

**Sophronitis
cernua**

Plant height: to 3 in.
Flowers: 1 in. wide
Blooms from October to December
High light
Cool temperature
Extra humidity
Can grow into a many-flowered plant
p. 339

**Sophronitis
coccinea**

Plant height: to 6 in.
Flowers: 3 in. wide
Blooms between
January and April
Medium light
Cool nights
Extra humidity
Can be difficult
p. 339

Dendrobium Tribe

**Bulbophyllum
phalaenopsis**

*Plant height: to 40 in.
Flowers: 2½ in. long
Blooms in winter or spring
Low light
Intermediate to warm temperature
Extra humidity
Unpleasant odor
p. 248*

**Cadetia
chionantha**

*Plant height: to 2 in.
Flowers: ¼ in. wide
Blooms in winter
Medium light
Cool to intermediate temperature
High humidity; best in greenhouse
Fragrant
For collectors
p. 249*

Cirrhopetalum gracillimum

Plant height: to 7 in.
Flowers: 2 in. long
Blooms successively from October to January
Low light
Warm temperature
Extra humidity
Fragrant
p. 257

Cirrhopetalum makoyanum

Plant height: to 3½ in.
Flowers: 1½ in. long
Blooms anytime, in long succession
Low light
Warm temperature
Extra humidity
Musty scent
Grows well into a many-flowered plant
p. 258

Cirrhopetalum medusae

Plant height: to 10 in.
Flowers: 6 in. long
Blooms from October to January
Low light
Warm temperature
Extra humidity
Strong musty odor
p. 258

Dendrobium atroviolaceum

Plant height: to 12 in.
Flowers: 3 in. wide
Blooms nonstop from February to May
High light
Warm temperature
Fragrant long-lasting flowers
Grows well into a many-flowered plant
p. 267

**Dendrobium
chrysotoxum**

*Plant height: to 16 in.
Flowers: 1½ in.
wide
Blooms March to
June
High light
Intermediate
temperature
Many very fragrant
long-lasting flowers
p. 267*

**Dendrobium
cuthbertsonii**

*Plant height: to 2 in.
Flowers: 1 in. wide
Blooms year-round
Low to medium
light
Cool temperature
High humidity
Each flower can
last 9 months or
more
p. 268*

Dendrobium kingianum

Plant height: to 18 in.
Flowers: 1 in. wide
Blooms from February to March
High light
Intermediate temperature
Fragrant
Easy to grow into a many-flowered plant
p. 268

Dendrobium loddigesii

Plant height: to 8 in.
Flowers: 2 in. wide
Blooms in spring
High light
Cool to intermediate temperature
Many fragrant long-lasting flowers
Easy
p. 268

**Dendrobium
nobile**

*Plant height: to 2 ft.
Flowers: 3 in. wide
Blooms between
January and April
High light
Cool to
intermediate
temperature
Fragrant long-
lasting flowers
p. 268*

**Dendrobium
pendulum**

*Plant height: to 2 ft.
Flowers: 2½ in. wide
Blooms between September and May
High light
Intermediate temperature
Fragrant long-lasting flowers
p. 269*

Dendrobium primulinum

*Plant height:
to 14 in.
Flowers: 2½ in.
wide
Blooms between
February and May
High light
Intermediate
temperature
Fragrant long-
lasting flowers
p. 269*

Dendrobium speciosum

*Plant height:
4–40 in.
Flowers: 1 in. wide
Blooms between
December and
May
High light
Cool to
intermediate
temperature
Fragrant
Grows well into a
many-flowered
plant
p. 269*

Dendrobium subacaule

Plant height: to 6 in.
Flowers: 1 in. wide
Blooms in spring or summer
Medium light
Cool temperature
Extra humidity; best in greenhouse
For collectors
p. 269

Dendrobium toressae

Plant height: to 1 in.
Flowers: ¼ in. wide
Blooms intermittently through year
Medium to low light
Cool temperature
Interesting densely matted plant habit
p. 269

Dendrobium victoria-reginae

Plant height: 1–4 ft.
Flowers: 1 in. wide
Can bloom anytime, with peak bloom May to July
High light
Cool temperature
Extra humidity; best in greenhouse
p. 269

Dendrobium Blue Twinkle

Plant height: to 2 ft.
Flowers: 1½–2 in. wide
Can bloom anytime
High light
Warm temperature
Fragrant
Easy to grow into a many-flowered plant
p. 270

Dendrobium
Dawn Maree

*Plant height: to 14 in.
Flowers: 3 in. wide
Can bloom variably
twice a year, with
peak bloom in
summer
High light
Intermediate
temperature
Fragrant long-
lasting flowers
p. 270*

Dendrobium
Dok Phak Bung

*Plant height: to 3 ft.
Flowers: 3½ in.
wide
Blooms in winter
High light
Warm temperature
High humidity
while in bud
Easy
p. 270*

Dendrobium
Golden Blossom

Plant height: to 28 in.
Flowers: 3 in. wide
Blooms between February and May
High light
Intermediate temperature
Fragrant flowers last a month
p. 270

Dendrobium
Kalagas

Plant height: to 3 ft.
Flowers: 2½ in. wide on very long spike
Blooms several times a year
High light
Warm temperature
Easy to grow into a many-flowered plant
p. 270

Dendrobium
Pink Doll

Plant height: to 2 ft.
Flowers: 3 in. wide
Blooms in winter
or spring
High light
Cool to
intermediate
temperature
Many long-lasting
flowers
p. 271

Epigeneium
stella-silvae

Plant height: to 8 in.
Flowers: 3 in. long
Blooms in winter
or spring
Low light
Intermediate to
warm temperature
Extra humidity
For collectors
p. 281

Maxillaria
Tribe

Anguloa ruckeri

Plant height: to 26 in.
Flowers: 3½ in. long
Blooms between
May and July
Medium light
Intermediate to cool
temperature
Very fragrant
Easy
p. 233

Angulocaste
Olympus

Plant height: to 28 in.
Flowers: 3 in. wide
Blooms in spring
Medium light
Intermediate
temperature
Best in greenhouse
Grows well into a
many-flowered plant
p. 234

Batemania colleyi

*Plant height: to 13 in.
Flowers: 3 in. wide
Can bloom anytime
in fall or winter,
with peak bloom in
March
Medium light
Warm temperature
Unpleasant odor
p. 240*

**Bifrenaria
harrisoniae**

*Plant height: to 12 in.
Flowers: 3 in. wide
Blooms March to
May
Medium light
Intermediate
temperature
Fragrant long-
lasting flowers
Best in greenhouse
p. 241*

Bollea violacea

*Plant height: to 12 in.
Flowers: 3 in. wide
Can bloom anytime,
with peak in May
Medium light
Warm to
intermediate
temperature
High humidity; best
in greenhouse
p. 242*

**Cochleanthes
discolor**

*Plant height: to 10 in.
Flowers: 2 in. wide
Blooms between
March and June
Medium light
Intermediate to cool
temperature
High humidity and
air movement
Best in greenhouse
Difficult
p. 259*

**Gongora
armeniaca**

*Plant height: to 10 in.
Flowers: 2 in. long
on hanging spray
Blooms between
July and March
Medium to low light
Intermediate to
warm temperature
Fragrant
High humidity; best
in greenhouse*
p. 283

**Huntleya
meleagris**

*Plant height: to 12 in.
Flowers: 3 in. wide
Can bloom any
season, with peak
bloom in summer
Medium light
Cool to intermediate
temperature
Fragrant long-
lasting flowers
High humidity; best
in greenhouse*
p. 285

Lycaste macrobulbon

Plant height:
to 20 in.
Flowers: 4 in. wide
Can bloom
anytime, with peak
in July
Medium to low
light
Intermediate
temperature
Fragrant long-
lasting flowers
Best in greenhouse
p. 292

Lycaste skinneri   *Plant height: to 30 in.*
Flowers: 6 in. wide
Blooms between November and May
Medium to low light
Cool temperature
Fragrant long-lasting flowers
Best in greenhouse
p. 292

Lycaste Aquila

*Plant height:
to 30 in.
Flowers: 3½ in.
wide
Blooms in fall or
winter
Medium to low
light
Cool to
intermediate
temperature
Best in greenhouse
p. 292*

Lycaste Jackpot

*Plant height: to 30 in.
Flowers: 6 in. wide
Blooms in winter
Medium to low light
Intermediate temperature
Best in greenhouse
p. 292*

Maxillaria picta

*Plant height: to 16 in.
Flowers: 2½ in.
wide
Blooms between
October and March
High light
Intermediate to
warm temperature
Fragrant
Easy to grow into a
many-flowered plant
p. 296*

*Maxillaria
sophronitis*

*Plant height: to 2 in.
Flowers: ¼ in. wide
Blooms between
November and
January
Medium light
Cool temperature
Extra humidity
Can be difficult
p. 296*

Ornithocephalus inflexus

Plant height: to 6 in.
Flowers: ³/₁₆ in.
Blooms in summer
or fall
Low light
Intermediate to
warm temperature
Extra humidity
Can grow into a
many-flowered plant
p. 311

Pabstia jugosa

Plant height: to 12 in.
Flowers: 3 in. long
Blooms almost
anytime
Low to medium
light
Intermediate to
warm temperature
Fragrant long-
lasting flowers
Extra humidity
Relatively easy
p. 311

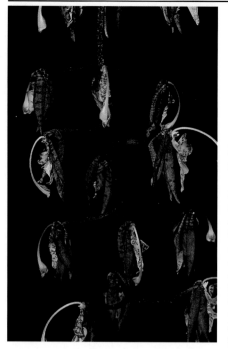

Polycycnis morganii

*Plant height:
to 14 in.
Flowers: 1½ in.
wide
Blooms in spring
Medium light
Intermediate to
warm temperature
Extra humidity;
best in greenhouse
Short-lived bloom
p. 324*

Promenaea xanthina

*Plant height: to 3 in.
Flowers: 2 in. wide
Blooms May to July
Medium to low light
Intermediate to warm temperature
Fragrant long-lasting flowers
Easy
p. 326*

Stanhopea wardii

*Plant height:
to 20 in.
Flowers: 5 in. wide
on hanging spike
Blooms between
July and October
Medium light
Intermediate to
warm temperature
Very fragrant short-
lived bloom
Easy
p. 340*

**Zygopetalum
crinitum**

*Plant height:
to 18 in.
Flowers: 3 in. wide
Blooms between
February and April
Medium light
Intermediate to
warm temperature
Very fragrant long-
lasting flowers
Easy
p. 347*

Oncidium Alliance

Baptistonia echinata

*Plant height:
to 10 in.
Flowers: ½ in. wide
Blooms between
February and May
Medium to high
light
Very warm
temperature
Grows readily into
a many-flowered
plant
p. 238*

Beallara Magic Cauldron

*Plant height:
to 20 in.
Flowers: 4 in. long
Blooms in spring or
summer
Medium light
Intermediate to
cool temperature
Flowers last 4–6
weeks
p. 240*

Brassia maculata

Plant height: 20 in.
Flowers: 8 in. long
on long sprays
Can bloom
anytime, with peak
bloom in June
Medium light
Intermediate to
warm temperature
Fragrant long-
lasting flowers
p. 244

Cochlioda
coccinea

Plant height:
to 10 in.
Flowers: 1½ in.
wide on long sprays
Blooms in spring
Medium light
Cool temperature
No heat extremes
Best in greenhouse
p. 260

**Colmanara
Wildcat**

*Plant height:
to 20 in.
Flowers: 3 in. wide
on long sprays
Peak bloom in fall;
may also bloom in
winter
Medium light
Intermediate
temperature
Free-flowering
Easy
p. 261*

**Comparettia
macroplectron**

*Plant height: to 6 in.
Flowers: 2 in. wide
Can bloom
anytime, with peak
bloom from
February to April
Low light
Intermediate
temperature
High humidity
Best in greenhouse
p. 262*

Degarmoara
Creole

Plant height: to 14 in.
Flowers: 4 in. long
Blooms in fall
Medium light
Intermediate temperature
Avoid heat
p. 266

Howeara
Mini Primi

Plant height: to 6 in.
Flowers: ½ in. wide
Blooms between
September and
February
Medium light
Intermediate
temperature
High humidity
Good in terrarium
or greenhouse
p. 285

Ionopsis hybrid

*Plant height: to 5 in.
Flowers: ¹/₂ in. wide
on 30-in. spray
Blooms winter or
spring
Low light
Intermediate
temperature
Extra humidity
Best in greenhouse
or terrarium
p. 286*

Maclellanara
Pagan Love Song

*Plant height:
to 20 in.
Flowers: 5 in. long
on 3-ft. branched
spikes
Blooms between
fall and spring
Medium light
Intermediate
temperature
Free-flowering
Easy
p. 293*

Miltonia spectabilis

Plant height: to 10 in.
Flowers: 2½ in. wide
Blooms from May to June
Medium light
Intermediate to warm temperature
Avoid high heat
Grows readily into a many-flowered plant
p. 298

Miltonia spectabilis var. **moreliana**

Plant height: to 10 in.
Flowers: 4 in. wide
Blooms between August and October
Medium light
Intermediate to warm temperature
Avoid high heat
Grows readily into a many-flowered plant
p. 298

Miltonia Seine

Plant height: to 12 in.
Flowers: 3 in. wide
Blooms in spring
Medium light
Intermediate temperature
Avoid high heat
p. 298

Miltoniopsis
roezlii

Plant height:
to 14 in.
Flowers: 2½ in.
wide
Blooms in spring
and/or fall
Medium to low
light
Cool to
intermediate
temperature
Avoid heat
Extra humidity
p. 299

Miltoniopsis
Jean Sabourin

Plant height: to 14 in.
Flowers: 3½ in. wide
Blooms in spring
Medium light
Cool to intermediate temperature
Avoid heat
Extra humidity
p. 299

Notylia barkeri

Plant height: to 7 in.
Flowers: ⅓ in. wide
Can bloom
anytime, with peak
bloom February to
March
Low light
Intermediate to
warm temperature
High humidity
For collectors
p. 302

Odontioda
Eric Young

Plant height: to 18 in.
Flowers: 4 in. wide on long sprays
Blooms in winter or spring
Medium light
Cool temperature
Extra humidity
p. 302

Odontioda
Red Riding Hood

Plant height: to 16 in.
Flowers: 3 in. wide on long sprays
Blooms in winter
Medium light
Cool temperature
Extra humidity
p. 302

Odontocidium
Artur Elle

Plant height:
to 18 in.
Flowers: 3 in. wide
on long sprays
Blooms in winter
Medium light
Intermediate
temperature
Avoid heat
Free-blooming
hybrid
p. 303

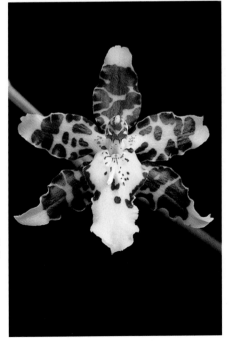

Odontocidium
Big Mac

Plant height:
to 20 in.
Flowers: 3½ in.
wide on long sprays
Blooms February to
April
Medium light
Intermediate to
cool temperature
Avoid heat
p. 303

Odontoglossum   *Plant height: to 4–13 in.*
cervantesii   *Flowers: 2½ in. wide*
Blooms in winter or spring
Medium light
Cool to intermediate temperature
Fragrant
Best in greenhouse
Can be difficult
p. 304

Odontoglossum
Stamfordiense

Plant height:
to 35 in.
Flowers: 2½ in.
wide
Blooms between
October and
February
Medium light
Cool to
intermediate
temperature
Best in greenhouse
Can be difficult
p. 304

Odontoglossum
Valeria

Plant height: to 2 ft.
Flowers: 2½ in.
wide
Can bloom spring
or fall
Medium light
Cool to
intermediate
temperature
Fragrant
Best in greenhouse
Can be difficult
p. 304

Odontonia
Debutante

Plant height:
to 18 in.
Flowers: 2½ in.
wide
Blooms between
March and July
Medium light
Intermediate
temperature
Extra humidity
p. 305

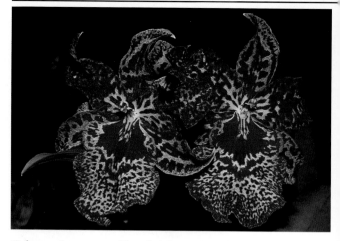

Odontonia
Susan Bogdanow

Plant height: to 14 in.
Flowers: 3½ in. wide
Blooms in winter or spring
Medium light
Intermediate to cool temperature
Extra humidity
p. 305

Odontorettia
Mandarine

Plant height:
to 16 in.
Flowers: 1½ in.
wide
Blooms in fall or
winter
Medium light
Cool to
intermediate
temperature
Extra humidity
Best in greenhouse
p. 306

Oncidium
macranthum

Plant height:
to 20 in.
Flowers: 4 in. wide on spike to 10 ft. long
Blooms from May to July; may bloom in
fall
Medium light
Cool to intermediate temperature
p. 308

Oncidium
onustum

Plant height:
to 10 in.
Flowers: 1 in. wide
on branched sprays
Blooms between
September and
November
Medium light
Intermediate
temperature
Grows well into a
many-flowered
plant
p. 308

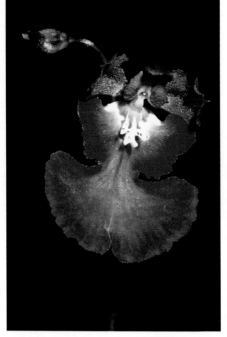

Oncidium pulchellum

Plant height: to 5 in.
Flowers: 1 in. long
Blooms between
April and June
Medium light
Warm to hot
temperature
Grows best
mounted, watered
daily
p. 309

Oncidium varicosum

Plant height:
to 14 in.
Flowers: 2 in. wide
on branched spike
to 4 ft.
Blooms primarily
in October
Medium light
Intermediate to
warm temperature
Produces
profusions of
blooms
Easy
p. 309

Oncidium
Bob Dugger

Plant height: to 6 in.
Flowers: 1½ in. long
Blooms in winter
or spring
Medium light
Intermediate to
warm temperature
Grows best
mounted, watered
daily
p. 309

Oncidium
Golden Sunset

Plant height: to 5 in.
Flowers: 1½ in. long
Can bloom three
times a year
Medium light
Warm to hot
temperature
Grows best
mounted, watered
daily
p. 309

Oncidium Good Show

*Plant height: to 7 in.
Flowers: 1½ in. wide
May bloom several times a year
Medium light
Intermediate to warm temperature
Grows best mounted, watered daily
p. 309*

Oncidium hybrid

*Plant height: to 14 in.
Flowers: 2½ in. long
Blooms in fall or winter for 4–6 weeks
Medium light
Intermediate to cool temperature
p. 309*

Psychopsis papilio

*Plant height:
to 12 in.
Flowers: 6 in. long
on 3-ft. spike
Blooms May to
September
Medium light
Intermediate to
warm temperature
Produces a
succession of long
bloom
Easy
p. 327*

**Rodricidium
Phyllis**

*Plant height: to 5 in.
Flowers: 1 in. wide
Blooms February to
March; may repeat
in fall
Medium light
Intermediate to
warm temperature
Extra humidity
p. 332*

Rodriguezia decora

*Plant height: to 4 in.
Flowers: 1½ in.
wide
Blooms between
October and
December
Medium light
Intermediate
temperature
Extra humidity
For collectors
p. 332*

Sigmatostalix sergii

*Plant height: to 7 in.
Flowers: ½ in. wide
Blooms in winter
or spring
Medium light
Intermediate to
cool temperature
Extra humidity
For collectors
p. 335*

Symphyglossum sanguineum

*Plant height: to 3½ in.
Flowers: 1 in. wide on long spray
Can bloom year-round, with peak bloom in May
Medium light
Cool to intermediate temperature
Easy
p. 342*

Trichopilia fragrans

*Plant height: to 11 in.
Flowers: 4½ in. wide
Blooms April to June
Medium to low light
Intermediate to warm temperature
Very fragrant long-lasting flowers
Easy
p. 343*

Vuylstekeara Cambria

*Plant height:
to 14 in.
Flowers: 3 in. wide
on long sprays
Variable bloom
season
Medium light
Intermediate to
cool temperature
Very free-flowering
Best in greenhouse
p. 345*

Warmingia eugenii

*Plant height: to 6 in.
Flowers: 1 in. long
Blooms between
April and July
Medium light
Intermediate to
warm temperature
For collectors
p. 346*

Wilsonara
Eurydice

Plant height: to 14 in.
Flowers: 3 in. wide on long sprays
Blooms in winter or spring
Medium light
Intermediate temperature
Avoid heat
p. 346

Wilsonara
Hambürhen Stern

Plant height:
to 14 in.
Flowers: 3½ in.
wide on long sprays
Blooms between
February and April
Medium light
Intermediate
temperature
Avoid heat
p. 347

Phalaenopsis-
Vanda Alliance

Aerides crassifolia

*Plant height: to 2 ft.
Flowers: 2½ in.
wide
Blooms between
March and July
High light
Warm to
intermediate
temperature
Very fragrant, long-
lasting, waxy
flowers
Vigorous basket
grower
p. 229*

Aeridovanda
hybrid

*Plant height: to 4 ft.
Flowers: 3 in. wide
Blooms in fall
High light
Intermediate to
warm temperature
Fragrant long-
lasting flowers
Grows best in a
basket
p. 230*

Amesiella philippinensis

Plant height: to 6 in.
Flowers: 2½ in. wide
Blooms between January and March
Medium light
Intermediate to cool temperature
Grows well into a many-flowered plant
p. 230

Ascocenda Guo Chia Long

Plant height: to 20 in.
Flowers: 2 in. wide
Blooms between spring and fall; may repeat
High light
Warm temperature
Good hanging-basket plant
Easy
p. 237

Ascocenda Mickey Nax

Plant height: to 2 ft.
Flowers: 3½ in.
wide
Blooms in spring or
summer
High light
Warm temperature
Good hanging-
basket plant
Easy
p. 237

Ascocenda Udomchai

Plant height: to 18 in.
Flowers: 2 in. wide
Blooms in spring or
summer
High light
Warm temperature
Good hanging-
basket plant
Easy
p. 237

**Ascocenda
Yip Sum Wah**

*Plant height:
to 20 in.
Flowers: 3 in. wide
Can bloom
anytime; often
repeats
Peak bloom
between March and
October
High light
Warm temperature
Easy hanging-
basket plant
p. 237*

**Ascocentrum
ampullaceum**

*Plant height:
to 16 in.
Flowers: ½ in. wide
Blooms between
March and June
High light
Warm temperature
Extra humidity
Grows readily into
a many-flowered
plant
Easy
p. 238*

Ascocentrum miniatum

*Plant height: to 16 in.
Flowers: 1 in. wide
Can bloom almost
anytime, with peak
bloom April to
June
High light
Warm temperature
Extra humidity
Easy to grow into a
many-flowered
plant
p. 238*

Doritaenopsis Asahi

*Plant height: to 14 in.
Flowers: 1½ in.
wide on long spray
Blooms in summer
Medium to low
light
Intermediate to
warm temperature
Repeats bloom
when spray is cut
back
p. 274*

**Doritaenopsis
Brazilian Legend**

*Plant height:
to 20 in.
Flowers: 4 in. wide
on arching sprays
Blooms in winter
or spring
Low light
Warm temperature
Repeats bloom
when spray is cut
back
Good cut flower
Easy
p. 274*

**Doritaenopsis
Mythic Beauty**

*Plant height: to 20 in.
Flowers: 5 in. wide on arching sprays
Blooms in winter or spring
Low light
Warm temperature
Repeats bloom when spray is cut back
Good cut flower
Easy
p. 274*

Doritis pulcherrima

*Plant height: 7 in.
Flowers: 1–1½ in.
wide on upright
spray to 3 ft.
Blooms between
July and December
Medium light
Warm to
intermediate
temperature
Long flower display
is often repeated
p. 275*

Doritis
pulcherrima var.
coerulea

*Plant height: 7 in.
Flowers: 1 in. wide
on upright spray to
3 ft.
Blooms between
July and November
Medium light
Warm to
intermediate
temperature
Long flower display
is often repeated
p. 275*

**Euanthe
sanderiana**

*Plant height: to 4 ft.
Flowers: 4½ in.
wide on 1-ft. spray
Blooms between
July and November
High light
Warm temperature
Fragrant
Good hanging-
basket plant
Easy
p. 281*

**Gastrochilus
fuscopunctatis**

*Plant height: to 2 in.
Flowers: ½ in. wide
on hanging spray
Can bloom
anytime, with peak
bloom between
April and July
Medium light
Cool temperature
Extra humidity
Difficult
p. 282*

Haraella retrocalla

*Plant height: to 2 in.
Flowers: 1 in. wide
Can bloom
anytime, with peak
bloom in fall
Low light
Intermediate to
warm temperature
High humidity
p. 284*

Mokara Redland Sunset

*Plant height: to 3 ft.
Flowers: 2½ in.
wide
Blooms between
October and March
High light
Warm temperature
Long-lasting
flowers
Easily grown in a
hanging basket
p. 300*

Neostylis
Lou Sneary

Plant height: to 6 in.
Flowers: 1½ in. long
Blooms in summer
Medium light
Intermediate
temperature
Very fragrant
Grows well into a
many-flowered
plant
Easy
p. 301

Opsistylis
Suree

Plant height: to 3 ft.
Flowers: 2 in. wide
Blooms between
February and April
Medium light
Warm temperature
Fragrant
Good plant for a
hanging basket
p. 310

Paraphalaenopsis Asean

Plant height: to 14 in
Flowers: 4 in. long
Blooms in spring or summer
Medium to low light
Warm temperature
Waxy flowers on a gangly plant
p. 316

Phalaenopsis amboinensis

Plant height: to 10 in.
Flowers: 2 in. wide
Blooms anytime
Low to medium light
Warm temperature
Very long-lasting waxy flowers
Easy
p. 318

**Phalaenopsis
aphrodite**

*Plant height: 10 in.
Flowers: 3 in. wide
on long arching
sprays
Blooms from
January to March
Low light
Intermediate to
warm temperature
Good cut flower
Easy
p. 318*

**Phalaenopsis
equestris**

*Plant height: to 6 in.
Flowers: 1½ in.
wide on 1-ft.
branching sprays
Can bloom twice a
year, in fall and
spring
Low light
Warm temperature
Showers of flowers
Good for cutting
Easy
p. 318*

Phalaenopsis
Class President

Plant height: to 14 in.
Flowers: 2½ in. wide
Blooms from March to May
Low light
Warm temperature
Long-lasting flowers, good for cutting
Easy
p. 318

Phalaenopsis
Little Hal

Plant height: to 12 in
Flowers: 1 in. wide
on branching
sprays
Blooms from
February to April
Low light
Warm temperature
Profuse bloomer
Good cut flower
Easy
p. 318

Phalaenopsis
Medford Star

Plant height:
to 20 in.
Flowers: 6 in. wide
on long arching
sprays
Blooms in winter
or spring
Low light
Warm temperature
In bloom for
months, often
repeating
Good cut flower
Easy
p. 319

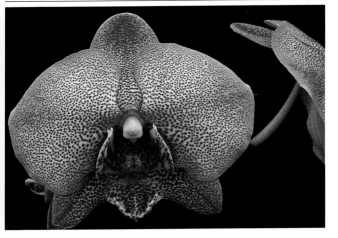

Phalaenopsis
Miva Smartissimo

Plant height: to 16 in.
Flowers: 3½ in. wide on arching sprays
Blooms in winter
Low light
Warm temperature
Can repeat bloom; good cut flower
Easy
p. 319

Phalaenopsis
Sandra Livingston

Plant height: to 16 in
Flowers: 2½ in.
wide
Blooms in winter
or spring
Low light
Warm temperature
Can repeat bloom
Good cut flower
Easy
p. 319

Phalaenopsis
Sierra Gold

Plant height: to 16 in.
Flowers: 3 in. wide
Blooms between February and May
Medium light
Warm temperature
Long-lasting waxy flowers
Can repeat bloom when spray is cut back
Good cut flower
p. 319

Phalaenopsis Zuma Aussie Delight

Plant height: to 14 in.
Flowers: 2½ in. wide
Blooms in fall or winter
Low light
Warm temperature
Can repeat bloom when spray is cut back
Good cut flower
Easy
p. 319

Phalaenopsis Zuma Urchin

Plant height:
to 20 in.
Flowers: 4 in. wide
on arching sprays
Blooms in winter
Low light
Warm temperature
Can repeat bloom
Good cut flower
Easy
p. 319

Phalaenopsis
hybrid

Plant height: to 20 in.
Flowers: 5 in. wide on arching sprays
Blooms in spring
Low light
Warm temperature
Can repeat bloom; good cut flower
Easy
p. 319

Phalaenopsis
stuartiana hybrid

Plant height: to 16 in
Flowers: 2 in. wide
on long sprays
Blooms in winter
Low light
Warm temperature
Can repeat bloom
Good cut flower
Easy
p. 319

Phalaenopsis violacea hybrid

Plant height: to 10 in.
Flowers: 2½ in. wide
Blooms in summer or fall
Low light
Warm temperature
Fragrant, waxy, long-lasting flowers
Blooms successively for a long time
p. 319

Renanthera imshootiana

Plant height: to 30 in.
Flowers: 3 in. long on 18-in. spike
Blooms from March to July
Medium light
Intermediate temperature
Profuse long-lasting flowers
An endangered species
Easy
p. 328

Renanthera monachica

Plant height: to 2 ft.
Flowers: 1½ in.
wide on 18-in.
spike
Blooms between
February and May
High light
Warm temperature
Grows well into a
many-flowered
plant
Easy
p. 328

Rhynchocentrum hybrid

Plant height: to 10 in.
Flowers: 1½ in.
wide
Blooms in spring or
summer
Medium to high
light
Warm to
intermediate
temperature
Fragrant
Good in a hanging
basket
p. 329

Plant height:
to 10 in.
Flowers: ¾ in. wide
Blooms between
June and September
Medium light
Warm temperature
Fragrant
Good plant for a
hanging basket
p. 331

Plant height: 10 in.
Flowers: 1 in. wide
Blooms May
through October,
with peak in
summer
Medium light
Warm temperature
High humidity
Fragrant long-
lasting flowers
p. 331

Sarcochilus Fitzhart

*Plant height:
to 20 in.
Flowers:* 1½ *in.
wide
Blooms February to
March
Medium light
Intermediate
temperature
High humidity
Best in greenhouse*
p. 333

Sedirea japonica

*Plant height: to 6 in.
Flowers:* 1½ *in.
wide, up to 12 on
7-in. spray
Blooms April to
June
Medium light
Intermediate
temperature
Fragrant long-
lasting flowers
Easy*
p. 334

Trichoglottis philippinensis

Plant height: to 2 ft.
Flowers: 2 in. wide
Blooms between July and October
High to medium light
Warm temperature
Fragrant
Grows well into a many-flowered plant
p. 342

Vanda coerulea

Plant height: to 4 ft.
Flowers: 4 in. wide on branched spray
Can bloom anytime, with peak bloom between July and November
High light
Intermediate to cool temperature
Extra humidity
An endangered species
p. 344

Vanda
David Gardner

*Plant height: to 3 ft.
Flowers: 3½ in.
wide on long spray
Blooms between
winter and summer
High light
Warm temperature
Long-lasting
flowers
Easy
p. 344*

Vanda
Gordon Dillon

*Plant height: to 3 ft.
Flowers: 4 in. wide
on long spray
Blooms almost
anytime
High light
Intermediate to
warm temperature
Long-lasting
flowers
p. 344*

Vanda
Motes Resplendent

*Plant height: to 3
ft. on long spray
Flowers: 4 in. wide
Blooms between
fall and spring
High light
Warm temperature
Very crystalline
flowers
Easy
p. 344*

Vanda
Patricia Low

*Plant height: to 3 ft.
Flowers: 2½ in.
wide on long spray
Blooms in spring or
summer
High light
Warm temperature
Long-lasting
flowers
Easy
p. 344*

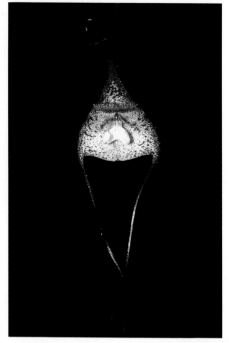

Dracula bella

*Plant height: to 7 in.
Flowers: 6 in. long
on 7-in. stem
Can bloom
anytime, with peak
bloom in May
Low light
Intermediate
temperature
Extra humidity
p. 276*

Dracula carderi

*Plant height: to 5 in.
Flowers: 2½ in.
long on 7-in. stem
Blooms between
March and
September
Low light
Cool temperature
Extra humidity
Can be difficult
p. 276*

Dracula erythrochaete

Plant height: to 12 in. Flowers: 3 in. long Blooms from March to May Low light Cool to intermediate temperature Extra humidity Easier than most Dracula p. 276

Dracula gorgona

Plant height: to 10 in. Flowers: 8 in. long on hanging stem Blooms in winter or spring Low light Cool temperature Extra humidity Can be difficult p. 277

Lepanthes delhierroi

*Plant height: to 4 in.
Flowers: ¼ in. wide
Blooms in winter
or spring
Low light
Cool to
intermediate
temperature
Extra humidity
Can be difficult
For collectors
p. 298*

Masdevallia caudata

*Plant height: to 6 in.
Flowers: 6 in. long
Can bloom
anytime, with peak
bloom March to
May
Low light
Cool to
intermediate
temperature
Extra humidity
p. 294*

Masdevallia civilis

*Plant height: to 6 in.
Flowers: 4 in. long
Can bloom
anytime, with peak
bloom March to
April
Low light
Cool to
intermediate
temperature
Extra humidity
Easy bloomer but
has unpleasant
odor
p. 294*

**Masdevallia
coccinea**

*Plant height:
to 16 in.
Flowers: 3 in. wide
on tall stem
Usually blooms
April to July, with
peak bloom in May
Low light
Cool temperature
Extra humidity
Can be difficult
p. 294*

**Masdevallia
glandulosa**

*Plant height: to 4 in.
Flowers: 3 in. wide
Blooms in winter
Low light
Intermediate to
warm temperature
Extra humidity
Sweetly fragrant
p. 294*

Masdevallia hirtzi

*Plant height: to 4 in.
Flowers: 1 in. long
Blooms in winter
or spring
Low light
Cool to
intermediate
temperature
Extra humidity
Easy bloomer
p. 295*

**Masdevallia
salatrix**

*Plant height: to 5 in.
Flowers: 1 in. long
Blooms in winter or spring
Low light
Intermediate temperature
Extra humidity
p. 295*

**Masdevallia
schroederiana**

*Plant height: to 6
in.
Flowers: 4 in. long
Blooms between
January and April
Low light
Intermediate
temperature
Extra humidity
Can grow well
into a many-
flowered plant
p. 295*

Masdevallia veitchiana

Plant height: to 14 in. Flowers: 8 in. long on tall stem Can bloom anytime, with peak bloom in May Low light Cool to intermediate temperature Extra humidity p. 295

Masdevallia Ann Jesup

Plant height: to 8 in. Flowers: 1½ in. wide Blooms in winter Medium light Cool temperature Extra humidity p. 295

***Masdevallia*
Copper Angel**

*Plant height:
to 10 in.
Flowers: 4 in. long
on sturdy upright
stem
Blooms
intermittently fall
to spring
Low light
Intermediate
temperature
Extra humidity
p. 295*

***Masdevallia*
Hincksiae**

*Plant height:
to 10 in.
Flowers: 3 in. long
Blooms in winter
or spring
Low light
Cool temperature
Extra humidity
p. 295*

Masdevallia Machu Picchu

*Plant height:
to 14 in.
Flowers: 5 in. long
on tall stem
Blooms in winter
or spring
Low light
Cool temperature
Extra humidity
p. 295*

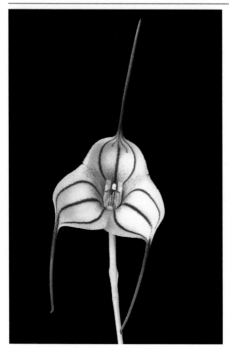

Masdevallia Tuakau Canoy

*Plant height: to 6 in.
Flowers: 3 in. long
Blooms in winter
or spring
Low light
Intermediate
temperature
Extra humidity
Can grow into a
many-flowered
plant
p. 295*

**Pleurothallis
sanderana**

*Plant height: to 3 in.
Flowers: ¼ in. long
Blooms in winter
or spring
Medium to low
light
Intermediate
temperature
Grows well into a
many-flowered
plant
Easy*
p. 323

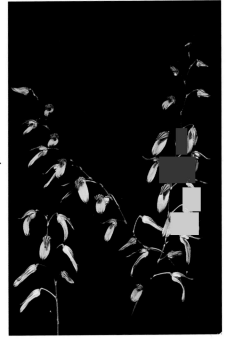

**Pleurothallis
species**

*Plant height: to 4 in.
Flowers: ¾ in. long
on tall spikes
Blooms in winter
or spring
Medium to low
light
Intermediate
temperature
Grows well into a
many-flowered
plant
Easy*
p. 323

Pleurothallis truncata

*Plant height: to 4 in.
Flowers: 1/16 in. wide
Blooms in winter
or spring
Medium to low
light
Intermediate
temperature
Charming flowers
when viewed with a
lens
Easy
p. 323*

Porroglossum olivaceum

*Plant height: to 3 in.
Flowers: 2 in. wide
Blooms in spring
Low to medium light
Intermediate to cool temperature
Flowers appear successively
p. 325*

Restrepia striata

*Plant height: to 4 in.
Flowers: 1½ in. long
Can bloom year-round, with peak bloom November to March
Low light
Intermediate to cool temperature
Extra humidity
Charming flowers, especially under a lens
p. 328*

Scaphosepalum decorum

*Plant height: to 8 in.
Flowers: 2 in. on long zigzag spike
Blooms anytime
Medium to low light
Intermediate to cool temperature
Blooms successively for a long time
For collectors
p. 334*

Other Epidendrum Subfamily

Aerangis mystacidii

*Plant height: to 4 in.
Flowers: 1 in. wide
Blooms between
August and
October; may
rebloom in March
Low light
Warm to
intermediate
temperature
Extra humidity
Fragrant and easy
p. 228*

***Aerangis
Somasticta***

*Plant height: to 3 in.
Flowers: 1½ in. wide
Peak bloom in
spring; often
reblooms in fall
Low light
Warm to
intermediate
temperature
Extra humidity
Fragrant
p. 228*

Aeranthes Grandiose

*Plant height:
to 12 in.
Flowers: 6 in. wide
Blooms on and off
all year, with peak
bloom in spring
and summer
Low light
Warm temperature
Can bloom under
extremely low light
Very easy
p. 229*

Angraecum leonis

*Plant height:
to 10 in.
Flowers: 3 in. wide
Blooms mostly in
fall
Medium to low
light
Warm temperature
Very night-fragrant
Grows well into a
many-flowered
plant
p. 232*

Angraecum longicalear

Plant height: to 4 ft.
Flowers: 16 in. long
with long spurs
Can bloom in fall
or winter, with
peak bloom in
February
Medium to high
light
Intermediate
temperature
Very fragrant
p. 232

Angraecum Orchidglade

Plant height: to 5 ft.
Flowers: 4 in. wide
with long spurs
Blooms in winter
Medium light
Warm temperature
Fragrant
Grows well into a
many-flowered
plant
p. 232

**Angranthes
Grandalena**

*Plant height:
to 14 in.
Flowers: 4 in. wide
Blooms in spring;
often reblooms in
fall
Low to medium
light
Intermediate to
warm temperature
Fragrant
Easy
p. 233*

**Oeoniella
polystachys**

*Plant height:
to 12 in.
Flowers: 1 in. wide
Blooms between
November and
April
Medium light
Warm temperature
High humidity
Very fragrant
Grows well into a
many-flowered
plant
p. 306*

Ancistrochilus rothschildianus

Plant height: to 8 in.
Flowers: 2 in. wide
Blooms January to
February; may
rebloom in summer
Low light
Warm temperature
Extra humidity
Fragrant
p. 231

Arethusa bulbosa

Plant height: to 9 in.
Flowers: 2 in. long
Blooms in spring or
summer
High light
Cool temperature
Special outdoor
conditions
Difficult
p. 235

Bletilla striata

Plant height: to 2 ft.
Flowers: 1½ in. long
Blooms in
midspring or early
summer
Medium light
Cool temperature
Hardy garden
plants
Easy
p. 242

Calanthe rubens

Plant height: to 2 ft.
Flowers: 2½ in.
wide on long spray
Blooms from
February to April
Medium light
Warm temperature
Excellent cut
flowers
p. 250

Calanthe Florence

*Plant height:
to 30 in.
Flowers: 2½ in.
wide on long spray
Blooms in winter
or spring
Medium light
Warm temperature
Excellent cut
flowers
p. 250*

**Calopogon
pulchellus**

*Plant height: to 18 in.
Flowers: 2½ in. wide
Blooms in spring or summer
High light
Cool temperature
Special outdoor conditions
Difficult
p. 251*

Chysis
Langleyensis

*Plant height:
to 20 in.
Flowers: 3 in. wide
Blooms in spring
Low to medium
light
Intermediate
temperature
Fragrant long-
lasting flowers
Easy
p. 257*

Phaius hybrid

*Plant height: to 3 ft.
Flowers: 4 in. wide
Blooms in winter
or spring
Low light
Intermediate to
warm temperature
Mild-climate
garden plant
Grows well into a
many-flowered
specimen
p. 316*

Spathoglottis vanoverberghii

*Plant height:
to 18 in.
Flowers: 1½ in.
wide
Blooms in winter
or spring
Medium to high
light
Intermediate
temperature
Mild-climate
garden plant
p. 340*

Arpophyllum spicatum

*Plant height: to 3 ft.
Flowers: ¼ in. wide
in dense spike
Can bloom
anytime, with peak
bloom in April and
May
Medium light
Intermediate to
warm temperature
Grows well into a
many-flowered
plant
p. 236*

Arundina graminifolia

Plant height: to 8 ft.
Flowers: 2½ in. long
Blooms anytime
Medium light
Warm temperature
Mild-climate
garden plant
Good in sunroom
Easy
p. 236

Calypso bulbosa

Plant height: to 5 in.
Flowers: 2 in. long
Blooms in spring or summer
Low light
Cool temperature
Fragrant
Special outdoor conditions
Difficult
p. 251

**Coelogyne
flaccida**

*Plant height:
to 12 in.
Flowers: 1½ in.
wide
Blooms between
February and
March
Medium light
Cool temperature
Unpleasant scent
Grows well into a
many-flowered
plant
p. 260*

**Coelogyne
Burfordiense**

*Plant height: to 20 in.
Flowers: 4 in. wide on long spray
Blooms in spring
Medium light
Warm temperature
Fragrant
Grows well into a many-flowered plant
p. 260*

Dendrochilum magnum

Plant height: to 18 in.
Flowers: ¼ in. wide on dense spikes to 18 in.
Blooms between August and October
Medium to low light
Intermediate to warm temperature
Grows well into a many-flowered plant
Easy
p. 271

Pleione pricei

Plant height: to 5 in.
Flowers: 3½ in. wide
Blooms between February and April
Medium light
Intermediate to cool temperature
Fragrant
p. 322

Catasetum species

*Plant height:
to 15 in.
Flowers: 2½ in.
long
Blooms in winter
or spring
Medium light
Warm to
intermediate
temperature
Extra humidity
p. 252*

Catasetum
Marge Soule

*Plant height:
to 18 in.
Flowers: 3 in. wide
on arching spray
Blooms in summer
or fall
Medium to high
light
Intermediate to
warm temperature
Very showy
fragrant display
Easy
p. 252*

**Clowesia
Grace Dunn**

*Plant height:
to 18 in.
Flowers: 1½ in.
wide
Blooms in winter
Medium light
Intermediate
temperature
Fragrant
p. 258*

*Cycnoches
chlorochilon*

*Plant height: to 2 ft.
Flowers: 5 in. wide
Blooms between
August and
November
Medium to high
light
Warm to
intermediate
temperature
Beautiful plant
habit and display
Easy
p. 263*

***Cymbidium
devonianum***

*Plant height:
to 12 in.
Flowers: 2 in. long
on hanging spray
Blooms from
March to May
High light
Cool to
intermediate
temperature
Long-lasting
flowers
Good in hanging
basket
p. 264*

***Cymbidium
goeringii***

*Plant height:
to 10 in.
Flowers: 3½ in. long
Blooms from
February to March
High light
Cool temperature
Sunroom or
greenhouse
Mild-climate
garden plant
Fragrant
p. 264*

**Cymbidium
Doris Dawson**

*Plant height:
to 30 in.
Flowers: 3 in. wide
on long many-
flowered spikes
Blooms in winter
High light
Cool temperature
Sunroom or
greenhouse
Mild-climate
garden plant
Long-lasting cut
flowers
p. 264*

**Cymbidium
Nancy Carpenter**

*Plant height: to 2 ft.
Flowers: 2½ in.
wide
Blooms in winter
High light
Intermediate
temperature
Sunroom or
greenhouse
Long-lasting cut
flowers
p. 264*

Cymbidium
Red Beauty
'Netty'

Plant height:
to 30 in.
Flowers: 3 in. wide
on long many-
flowered spikes
Blooms in winter
High light
Cool temperature
Sunroom or
greenhouse
Mild-climate
garden plant
Long-lasting cut
flowers
p. 264

Cymbidium
Red Beauty
'Wendy'

Plant height:
to 30 in.
Flowers: 3 in. wide
on long many-
flowered spikes
Blooms in winter
High light
Cool temperature
Sunroom or
greenhouse
Mild-climate
garden plant
Long-lasting cut
flowers
p. 264

Cymbidium
Showgirl

*Plant height:
to 22 in.
Flowers: 3 in. wide
Blooms in winter
High light
Cool to
intermediate
temperature
Fits on windowsill
Long-lasting cut
flowers*
p. 264

**Mormodes
histrionica**

*Plant height:
to 16 in.
Flowers: 2 in. wide
Blooms in winter
or spring
Medium light
Intermediate to
warm temperature
Fragrant
Easy*
p. 300

Ceratostylis retisquama

Plant height: to 5 in.
Flowers: 1½ in.
wide
Can bloom several
times a year
Medium light
Warm to
intermediate
temperature
Extra humidity
Short-lived flowers
p. 256

Mediocalcar
species

Plant height: to 3 in.
Flowers: ¼ in. wide
Blooms in spring
Low light
Cool to
intermediate
temperature
High humidity
Long-lasting
flowers
For collectors
p. 297

***Polystachya
paniculata***

*Plant height:
to 16 in.
Flowers: ¼ in. wide
in dense spikes
Can bloom
anytime, with peak
bloom April to
May
Medium to low
light
Intermediate
temperature
Easy
p. 324*

***Sobralia* species**

*Plant height: to 4 ft.
Flowers: 3 in. wide
Blooms in winter
Medium light
Intermediate to
warm temperature
Mild-climate
garden plant
Easy
p. 336*

Lady's Slippers
and Other
Orchids

Cypripedium acaule

*Plant height:
to 10 in.
Flowers: 2½ in.
long on tall stem
Blooms between
April and July
Low light
Cool temperature
Special outdoor
conditions
Difficult
p. 265*

**Paphiopedilum
bellatulum**

*Plant height: to 6 in.
Flowers: 3 in. wide on short stem
Can bloom anytime, with peak bloom in
May
Low light
Intermediate temperature
Extra humidity
p. 312*

Paphiopedilum delenatii

Plant height: to 10 in.
Flowers: 3 in. wide on tall stem
Blooms between March and June
Low light
Warm temperature
Mottled foliage
Can be a reluctant bloomer
p. 313

Paphiopedilum gratrixianum

Plant height: to 15 in.
Flowers: 4 in. wide on tall stem
Blooms in fall or winter
Medium light
Warm temperature
Vigorous grower
Easy
p. 313

Paphiopedilum
hirsutissimum

Plant height: to 14 in.
Flowers: 4 in. wide on hairy stem
Blooms from March to May
Medium light
Intermediate temperature
Vigorous grower
p. 313

Paphiopedilum
lowii

Plant height: 14 in.
Flowers: 5 in. wide on 2½ -ft. multifloral
spikes
Can bloom anytime, with peak bloom in
May
Medium light
Warm to intermediate temperature
Especially showy display
p. 313

Paphiopedilum micranthum

Plant height: to 6 in.
Flowers: 3 in. wide
on tall stem
Blooms in spring
Low light
Intermediate
temperature
Mottled leaves
Can be difficult
p. 313

Paphiopedilum venustum

Plant height:
to 15 in.
Flowers: 3 in. wide
on tall stem
Blooms between
December and
March
Low light
Cool to
intermediate
temperature
Mottled leaves
Grows well into a
many-flowered
plant
p. 314

Paphiopedilum
Clair de Lune

Plant height:
to 16 in.
Flowers: 3 in. wide
on tall stem
Blooms in summer
or fall
Low light
Warm temperature
Mottled leaves
Grows well into a
many-flowered
plant
Easy
p. 314

Paphiopedilum
Gilda

Plant height: to 16 in.
Flowers: 4 in. wide
Blooms in fall or winter
Medium light
Intermediate temperature
Long-lasting flowers
Easy
p. 314

Paphiopedilum
Iona

Plant height: to 9 in.
Flowers: 3 in. wide
on tall stem
Blooms between
December and
May, with peak
bloom in January
and February
Low light
Warm temperature
Mottled foliage
p. 314

Paphiopedilum
Julius

Plant height: 20 in.
Flowers: 5 in. wide on 2-ft. multifloral
spike
Blooms between March and July
Medium light
Warm temperature
Very showy display
p. 314

Paphiopedilum
Leeanum

*Plant height:
to 16 in.
Flowers: 3½ in.
wide on tall stem
Blooms in winter
Medium light
Cool to
intermediate
temperature
Grows well into a
many-flowered
plant
p. 314*

Paphiopedilum
Ma Bell

*Plant height: to 14 in.
Flowers: 4 in. wide on tall stem
Blooms in spring or summer
Low light
Intermediate temperature
Can be fragrant
p. 315*

Paphiopedilum
Raisin
Expectations

Plant height:
to 18 in.
Flowers: 3½ in.
wide on tall stem
Blooms in fall or
winter
Low light
Warm temperature
Grows well into a
many-flowered
plant
Easy
p. 315

Paphiopedilum
St. Swithin

Plant height:
to 20 in.
Flowers: 6 in. long
on 18-in.
multifloral spikes
Blooms in spring or
summer
Medium light
Warm temperature
Must be old to
bloom
Very showy display
Easy
p. 315

Phragmipedium besseae

Plant height: to 10 in.
Flowers: 2½ in. wide on tall branched stem
Blooms between February and April
Medium light
Cool temperature
Extraordinary vibrant color
Can be tricky
p. 320

Phragmipedium longifolium

Plant height:
to 20 in.
Flowers: 7 in. long
on tall stem
Blooms between
October and
December
Medium light
Intermediate
temperature
Grows well into a
many-flowered
plant
Blooms successively
for a long time
Easy
p. 320

Phragmipedium wallisi

*Plant height:
to 20 in.
Flowers: 12 in. long
on tall stem
Blooms in spring or
summer
Medium light
Intermediate
temperature
Blooms successively
for a long time
p. 321*

Phragmipedium Dominianum

*Plant height:
to 20 in.
Flowers: 8 in. long
on tall multifloral
stem
Blooms in fall
Medium light
Intermediate
temperature
Blooms successively
for a long time
p. 321*

**_Phragmipedium_
Grande**

*Plant height:
to 20 in.
Flowers: 12 in. long
on tall stem
Blooms spring or
summer
Medium light
Intermediate
temperature
Blooms successively
for a long time
p. 321*

**_Phragmipedium_
Mary Bess**

*Plant height:
to 12 in.
Flowers: 4 in. long
on several-flowered
stem
Variable bloom
season
Medium light
Intermediate to
cool temperature
Reliable bloomer
p. 321*

Phragmipedium
Schroederae

Plant height: to 2 ft.
Flowers: 4 in. wide
Blooms between
March and June
Medium light
Intermediate
temperature
Grows well into a
many-flowered
plant
p. 321

Disa tripetaloides   *Plant height: to 18 in.*
Flowers: 1 in. wide on tall spike
Can bloom twice a year
Medium light
Cool to intermediate temperature
Must be kept very damp
Special water-quality needs
p. 273

Disa Blackii

Plant height: to 2 ft.
Flowers: 3 in. wide on tall spike
Blooms in summer
Medium light
Cool to intermediate temperature
Must be kept very damp
Special water-quality needs
Good cut flower
p. 273

Disa Kirstenbosch
Pride

Plant height:
to 20 in.
Flowers: 2 in. wide
on tall stem
Blooms in summer
Medium light
Cool to
intermediate
temperature
Must be kept very
damp
Special water-
quality needs
Good cut flower
p. 273

Disa hybrid
Plant height: to 2 ft.
Flowers: 4 in. wide on tall stem
Blooms in spring or summer
Medium light
Cool to intermediate temperature
Must be kept very damp
Special water-quality needs
Good cut flower
p. 273

Goodyera
daubuzanensis
(top) and
Ludisia discolor

Plant height: to 6 in.
Flowers: ¼ in. wide
Goodyera *blooms*
in fall; Ludisia
blooms in winter
Low to medium
light
Warm temperature
Good in a
terrarium
Easy
pp. 283, 291

Sarcoglottis metallica

*Plant height: to 6 in.
Flowers: ¼ in. wide
on 3-ft. spike
Blooms between
January and March
Medium light
Intermediate to
warm temperature
Pretty mottled
rosette of leaves
p. 333*

Stenorrhynchus speciosum

*Plant height: to 7 in.
Flowers: ¼ in. long
on dense 2-ft. spike
Blooms between
December and
March
Medium light
Intermediate to
warm temperature
Often blooms at
Christmas
p. 341*

Encyclopedia
of Plants

Aerangis (Aergs.)

Ay-er-rang'giss
Dendrobium Group (Epidendrum Subfamily)
Epiphytic. Monopodial. No pseudobulbs

Description
Very popular for night fragrance and long-spurred white flowers, the small to medium-size members of the genus *Aerangis* are also handsome plants of rich green foliage. The 60 species are native to warm watery lowlands of tropical Africa and Madagascar. The name means "air vessel" in Greek.

How to Grow
Grow *Aerangis* in low light on any windowsill exposure except north, or grow them under fluorescent lights, atop humidity trays. Warm to intermediate temperatures (winter nights of 65–55°F, with narrow daytime highs never above 80°F) and humidity above 50% can help them bloom twice yearly. Grow them mounted on slabs of tree fern or cork, since they resent repotting, and water them continually throughout the year, especially when they are in bud. Allow the plants to dry slightly between waterings.

■ *mystacidii*   *p. 190*
This 10-in.-wide fragrant species from South Africa is one of the easiest *Aerangis,* a good starter for beginners. With its thicker roots, it can be grown in a pot, placed atop a humidity tray, as well as mounted on a slab. The pristine blooms appear for 4 weeks between late summer and early fall and often repeat in March.

■ **Somasticta (Somalensis** × *luteoalba*)   *p. 190*
Orange flower columns, pendent flower spikes, small plant size, and tuberose scent distinguish the pretty *luteoalba* hybrids such as this one. It always blooms in spring, although flowers can appear almost anytime.

Aeranthes (Aerth.)

Ay-er-an'theez
Dendrobium Group (Epidendrum Subfamily)
Epiphytic. Monopodial. No pseudobulbs

Description
Members of the genus *Aeranthes* have long, pendent, string-like inflorescences and translucent flowers that open succes-

sively over a long time, usually in summer. They are often fragrant. The 30 modest-size fan-shaped species are found on sides of trees in damp, shaded, Madagascar forests. The name is Greek for "air flower."

How to Grow
These easily grown, finely rooted plants need small pots of fine fir bark or moss and intermediate to warm temperatures (winter nights of 55–65°F). Grow them under low windowsill light of any exposure or under fluorescent lights. Keep *Aeranthes* moist and humid.

■ **Grandiose** *(grandiflora × ramosa) p. 191*
Hybrids involving the large-flowered *Aeranthes grandiflora* can bloom under the lowest light of any orchid, even in a north window of 600 footcandles. Don't cut old spikes since they rebloom abundantly.

Aerides (Aer.)

Ay-air′ee-deez
Dendrobium Group (Epidendrum Subfamily)
Epiphytic, lithophytic. Monopodial. No pseudobulbs

Description
Plants are large, with very fragrant and showy spring or summer blooms that open all at once on pendent spikes. A genus of 20 species from disturbed habitats of lowland Southeast Asia and Malaysia, *Aerides* generally has white and rose flowers with a spurred lip. It is involved in many intergeneric vandaceous hybrids. The name is Greek for "resembling air."

How to Grow
The thick tangle of dangling aerial roots makes basket culture a must. Give *Aerides* warm to intermediate conditions (winter nights of 65–55°F) and high light in a greenhouse or southern windowsill. Fertilize heavily throughout the year. Water them abundantly and keep them moist. When repotting is necessary, disturb the plant as little as possible, simply lifting it to another basket and adding more coarse mix. *Aerides* are generally vigorous growers. Old stems will develop a brown tone.

■ *crassifolia p. 150*
This Burmese native is not as tall and gawky as most other *Aerides*. It has pendulous or arching 2-ft.-long flower inflorescences and many fragrant waxy flowers that can last 2 months.

Aeridovanda (Aerdv.)

Ay-air-ee-doh-van'da
Dendrobium Group (Epidendrum Subfamily)
Aerides × *Vanda*
Monopodial. No pseudobulbs

Description

Large ungainly plants with colorful, often pendent flower spikes typify this hybrid vandaceous genus that was created in 1918.

How to Grow

Grow *Aeridovanda* in hanging baskets in high-light southern windowsills with warm to intermediate temperatures (65–55°F winter nights). Water and fertilize abundantly year-round. When the basket is completely overgrown, disturb the roots minimally by placing the entire thing into a larger basket.

■ **hybrid** (*Aerides lawrenceae* × *Vanda* **Fuchs Delight**) *p. 150*
Hybrids of *Aerides lawrenceae* can be even more vinelike than most other *Aeridovanda*. The flowers are fragrant.

Amesiella

Aims-ee-el'ah
Dendrobium Group (Epidendrum Subfamily)
Epiphytic. Monopodial. No pseudobulbs

Description

Found only in Philippine forests, the single species is notable for miniature plant size and very attractive habit. It is covered by large white blooms with long nectar spurs in winter. The genus is named for Oakes Ames, founder of Harvard's Orchid Herbarium.

How to Grow

Amesiella prefer small pots or baskets in medium light on eastern windowsills (keep out of direct sunlight) in intermediate to cool conditions (winter nights of 60–45°F). Water abundantly, especially while they are in active growth, so that the roots stay moist.

■ *philippinensis* *p. 151*
Until 1972, this lovely plant was considered a member of the genus *Angraecum*, and it is still registered in hybrid books as such. Unlike *Angraecum*, it is not fragrant.

Ancistrochilus

An-sis-tro'kie-lus
Epidendrum Group (Epidendrum Subfamily)
Epiphytic. Sympodial. Deciduous pseudobulbs

Description
The bare trunks of trees in tropical African forests are home to the two species of small to medium plants. The relatively large flowers appear from the base of the pseudobulbs as their leaves begin to fall off. The name means "hooked lip" in Greek.

How to Grow
Ancistrochilus need excellent drainage with humidity around the roots, so pots of chopped sphagnum mixed with tree fern or bark work best. Keep under low light on eastern windowsills or under fluorescent lights in warm conditions (60–65°F winter nights). When the leaves die, stop watering for a month or two and keep them in intermediate temperatures (50–55°F) until new growth appears, then resume watering and provide more warmth. The shriveled appearance of the onion-shaped pseudobulbs is normal.

■ *rothschildianus p. 194*
This fragrant species features 2–5 showy flowers per inflorescence on a small plant. It usually blooms in January and February.

Angraecum (Angcm.)

An-grye'kum
Dendrobium Group (Epidendrum Subfamily)
Epiphytic, lithophytic, semiterrestrial. Monopodial. No pseudobulbs

Description
The enormously popular genus *Angraecum* boasts 200 species from diverse habitats of tropical and subtropical Africa to Madagascar. Their exquisite white or green long-spurred flowers are often starry and very night-fragrant, which indicates they are pollinated by night-flying moths. The flowers last 6 weeks or more. The name is from the Malay meaning "epiphytic orchid."

How to Grow
Most *Angraecum* prefer humidity of 60% or more and medium light in any exposure except northern windowsills. The smaller ones in particular can be grown under fluores-

cent lights. Grow *Angraecum* in warm to intermediate temperatures (65–55°F winter nights). The small-growing, finely rooted plants can be mounted on bark or tree fern; the larger ones adapt to pots. Repot them infrequently, since *Angraecum* tend to resent having their roots disturbed. Keep plants well watered while they are in active growth in warm weather, fertilizing regularly; the more leaves that grow, the more flowers. *Angraecum* are very easy to grow once their roots are established. Many form keiki plantlets, which can be removed and replanted. Avoid bruising the flowers, since they easily brown.

■ *leonis* p. 191
This medium-small species from Madagascar has sickle-shaped 10-in.-long leaves. It can be grown easily under fluorescent lights and fits well in limited windowsill space. One to 6 delightfully fragrant large blooms per inflorescence appear generally for the month of October. Grow it warm (60–65°F winter nights).

■ *longicalear* p. 192
This stocky semiterrestrial comes from the 3,500-ft. highlands of Madagascar. Its 16-in. flower spur is the longest of all *Angraecum*. The plant will grow vigorously to 4 ft. tall in the high light of a southern windowsill, but protect it from direct sun. This very fragrant species often forms keiki offshoots. Flowers last 6 weeks or more.

■ Orchidglade (*sesquipedale* × *giryamae*) p. 192
This hybrid of two leggy, warm-growing (60–65°F winter nights), medium-light (eastern, western, or southern exposure) species can reach 5 ft., with abundant bloom while still young. Flowers last 6 weeks, especially if the plant is moved to a cooler spot (55–58°F) while in bloom. When the 11-in.-long nectar spur of *Angraecum sesquipedale*, or Star of Bethlehem Orchid, was first studied by Charles Darwin, he theorized, to much ridicule, that some unknown moth with an equally long proboscis must be the pollinator. Years later, exactly such an improbable moth was indeed found in the area. The nocturnal hawkmoth was named *Xanthopan morgani praedicta* to honor Darwin's prediction.

Angranthes (Angth.)
An-gran′theez
Dendrobium Group (Epidendrum Subfamily)
Aeranthes × *Angraceum*
Epiphytic. Monopodial. No pseudobulbs

Description

This beautiful hybrid genus, created in the United States in 1975, often flowers two or three times a year. The white to green spiky blooms can last for months and are often fragrant.

How to Grow

Angranthes are easy to bloom on windowsills and under fluorescent lights. They like intermediate to warm temperatures (55–65°F winter nights) and low to medium light on just about any windowsill exposure; avoid putting them in direct sun. Keep them evenly moist and humid.

■ **Grandalena** *(Aeranthes grandiflora × Angraecum magdalenae) p. 193*
This spicily fragrant hybrid is the most awarded of the genus. Let it dry slightly after bloom until new growth appears.

Anguloa (Ang.)

An-gyew-low'ah
Cymbidium Group (Epidendrum Subfamily)
Terrestrial, epiphytic. Sympodial. Deciduous pseudobulbs

Description

Often called Tulip Orchids for the round cuplike resemblance of large flowers that never open fully, the 10 species of *Anguloa* are found on steep cliffsides in the South American Andes. Most bloom in spring, producing a single flower per inflorescence from the base of new growths. The genus is closely related to *Lycaste* (with which they are often interbred) and is named for Don Francisco de Anguloa, an 18th-century Peruvian amateur naturalist.

How to Grow

Anguloa are easy to grow. Pot them in well-drained fine bark, and give them medium diffused light in an eastern or southern window, intermediate temperatures (55–60°F winter nights), and lots of water and fertilizer while they are in growth. New growths are susceptible to rot, so avoid water spotting. After the leaves fall off, stop watering for 2–4 weeks, and place the pot in a cooler (50–55°F), brighter spot during this time. Let them grow into large specimens for best show.

■ *ruckeri p. 114*
While the yellow-flowered *Anguloa clowesii* is considered showier, the *sanguinea* variety (shown in the photo) of this

very fragrant, brownish *ruckeri* species is particularly striking. Grow this one intermediate to cool (60–45°F winter nights). There is one flower per inflorescence.

Angulocaste (Angcst.)

An-gyew-low-kass'tee
Cymbidium Group (Epidendrum Subfamily)
Anguloa × *Lycaste*
Sympodial. Deciduous pseudobulbs

Description
Created in 1903, the hybrid genus *Angulocaste* has since become very popular for its beautiful large round flowers and wide range of colors — rich yellow, green, orange, rose, maroon. Many are wonderfully fragrant, even cinnamony. Most bloom in spring and summer; flowers last a month.

How to Grow
Depending on the parentage, hybrid *Angulocaste* may be deciduous, in which case they will need a reduced-water dormancy. If the leaves fall, restrict water and fertilizer and keep the plants cool (50°F) for at least a month until new growths appear. While the plants are in growth, keep the air movement and humidity high; avoid water on soft new growths; and provide intermediate temperatures (winter nights of 55°F), medium light, and regular fertilizer. They generally do best in a greenhouse. The flowers bruise easily and are better left on the plants rather than cut for a vase or corsage.

■ **Olympus** (*Angulocaste* **Apollo** × *Lycaste* **Sunrise**) *p. 114*
This gorgeous waxy hybrid from 1959 is by far the most highly awarded in the genus. There is one flower per inflorescence. The cultivar shown in the photo is 'Willow Pond.'

Arethusa (Aret.)

A-reh-thew'za
Epidendrum Group (Epidendrum Subfamily)
Terrestrial. Sympodial. Underground corm

Description
The single species of this genus is native to near-full-sun bogs and dense swamps of temperate North America and Japan. The fragrant, cheery pink flowers bloom above colonies of grasslike foliage in spring and early summer and are bum-

blebee-pollinated. The genus is named for the wood nymph Arethusa, who turned into a fountain after fleeing from the river god Alpheus.

How to Grow
The corms of this definitely tricky genus should never be transplanted from the wild unless their habitat is endangered. Create an outdoor artificial bog in full sun, lined with 4–6 mm polyethylene plastic and filled with a moist, organic, acidic mix of perlite, peat moss, and sphagnum moss in a 5:1:1 ratio, topped with live sphagnum moss dressing. The plastic lining must have a few small holes for drainage. Keep the bog constantly wet with rainwater. *Arethusa* can also be grown in large containers of the same bog mix, kept saturated. Plants need a definite winter chill (maximum 40–45°F). Give them no fertilizer or pesticides. Despite all efforts, *Arethusa* are generally short-lived.

■ *bulbosa* p. 194
These native plants have been successfully pollinated and sown artificially, and they have even been hybridized with another American native orchid, *Calopogon.*

Arpophyllum
Ar-poh-fill'um
Epidendrum Group (Epidendrum Subfamily)
Epiphytic, lithophytic, terrestrial. Sympodial. Stemlike pseudobulbs

Description
With dense clusters of many small upside-down flowers on tall spikes, the 5 species of this genus are often called Hyacinth Orchids. The medium to large tropical American plants are native from Mexico to Colombia at intermediate elevations. The generic name refers to the sickle-shaped leaves.

How to Grow
Perfect drainage is key; a potted mix of sphagnum moss and tree fern works well. Grow them in medium light but out of direct sun on windowsills of any exposure except north, with intermediate to warm temperatures (55–65°F winter nights). Keep the plants moist and weakly fertilized. Reduce water and fertilizer a bit after bloom, which generally occurs in spring.

■ *spicatum* p. 198
This epiphyte/lithophyte is found only on sierras of southern Mexico. It can bloom almost any month, with spikes to 2½ ft. tall, although peak bloom is 4 weeks in April and May.

Arundina

A-run-dee′na
Epidendrum Group (Epidendrum Subfamily)
Terrestrial. Sympodial. No pseudobulbs

Description
Nicknamed the Bamboo Orchid for its tall reedlike habit, *Arundina* has truly spectacular large flowers. The single species is native throughout tropical Southeast Asia and has many highly varietal forms. Although placed here in the Epidendrum Group, *Arundina* is a "misfit" genus that is tough to classify; its general appearance resembles *Sobralia*. The flowers can last several weeks. The name in Greek refers to the slender, reedlike stems.

How to Grow
In frost-free areas, *Arundina* grows naturally into hedges in outdoor sunny gardens in well-drained spots. The plants are as easily grown indoors, but they need large pots in a greenhouse or sunroom that can accommodate the height. Give them lots of water while in growth, warm temperatures (60–65°F winter nights), and medium light. Summer the pots outdoors. Reduce water somewhat after growth is complete.

■ *graminifolia* p. 199
This species blooms variably throughout the year, mostly in February or in July and August, though it is not an especially free-flowering plant. It can reach 8 ft. tall.

Ascocenda (Ascda.)

As-koe-sen′da
Dendrobium Group (Epidendrum Subfamily)
Ascocentrum × *Vanda*
Monopodial. No pseudobulbs

Description
Although created only in 1949, this brilliantly colored hybrid genus has recently soared in popularity. *Ascocenda* blends the best of the large *Vanda* flowers with the smaller plant size of

Ascocentrum. The easy-to-grow hybrids often bloom twice a year; flowers last a month or more.

How to Grow
Humidity above 50% is best for the warm- and sun-loving *Ascocenda*, which do best in pots or baskets of very coarse mix on high-light southern windowsills or in sunrooms or greenhouses. They are exceptionally easy in houses of humid high-light regions of the southern United States. Winter nights should not drop below 60°F. Water abundantly and fertilize heavily year-round. If aerial roots form at the top of the stem, that portion of the stem can be cut off and repotted.

■ **Guo Chia Long (Mem. Madame Pranerm × Yip Sum Wah)** *p. 151*
Spectacularly spotted hybrids are a highlight included in the genus. The cultivar pictured is 'Spotty' AM/AOS.

■ **Mickey Nax (Aribang × Duang Porn)** *p. 152*
Extremely complex parentage in this 1990 hybrid has yielded brilliant golds and yellow. The cultivar pictured is 'Robert's Gold' AM/AOS.

■ **Udomchai (*Vanda* Nam Phung × *Ascocenda* Pralor)** *p. 152*
Pictured is the less common "peloric" form of orchid flowers that occurs spontaneously when the petals attempt to form the same shape as the lip. The cultivar pictured is 'Fuch's Peloric' JC/AOS.

■ **Yip Sum Wah *(Vanda* Pukele × *Ascocentrum curvifolium)*** *p. 153*
This is the most famous *Ascocenda* cross, and the most awarded of all orchid hybrids because of beautiful flower shape and glistening colors. It has been used extensively as an excellent parent. The cultivar pictured is 'Sodsai'.

Ascocentrum (Asctm.)

Ass-koe-sen'trum
Dendrobium Group (Epidendrum Subfamily)
Epiphytic. Monopodial. No pseudobulbs

Description
Perky upright racemes of small brilliant cerise, orange, or red flowers on compact plants characterize the 5 species native to Southeast Asia and the Philippines. The successively opening flowers are showy and long-lived, each lasting a month or

more. The generic name refers to the little bagged spur at the base of the lip.

How to Grow
This popular genus is easy to grow in pots or baskets or mounted. Give it warm temperatures (60–65°F winter nights), high southern windowsill light, small pots, good humidity (add a humidity tray), and plenty of water and fertilizer, especially in summer. Let the plant dry just slightly after growth is finished for the season. *Ascocentrum* often forms a keiki plantlet at the base of the plant; remove the keiki when its roots form, and repot it separately.

■ *ampullaceum p. 153*
This tropical Himalayan-Thailand species is the most awarded in the genus. Its 6-in.-long cerise pink flower spikes appear from the base of the plant anytime between March and June. The cultivar pictured is 'Marcella' FCC/AOS.

■ *miniatum p. 154*
Neon-orange long-lasting color on upright racemes makes this species enormously popular. It usually is in bloom from April to June, although it can flower almost any time of the year.

Baptistonia (Bapt.)
Bap-tis-tone′ee-ah
Cymbidium Group (Epidendrum Subfamily)
Epiphytic. Sympodial. Pseudobulbs

Description
Although often classified as a single-genus species from southern Brazil, the increasingly popular and charming *Baptistonia* is technically considered part of *Oncidium*. The plants are compact, but they can grow into many pseudobulbs that produce hordes of tiny, cupped yellow and maroon flowers that can last 6 weeks.

How to Grow
Grow *Baptistonia* very warm (70°F winter nights) in a clay pot or on a tree-fern slab, in medium to high western or southern windowsill light or in a greenhouse. Let the plant dry just slightly between abundant waterings. After bloom, give it a short drier rest.

■ *echinata p. 126*
This species is found only in southern Brazil. It can bloom while very young. Left undivided, it grows into a breathtak-

ing specimen with hundreds of flowers on branched racemes that appear from the base of the pseudobulbs between February and May.

Barkeria (Bark.)

Bar-care'ee-ah
Epidendrum Group (Epidendrum Subfamily)
Epiphytic, lithophytic. Sympodial. Semideciduous pseudobulbs

Description
Barkeria has pretty *Cattleya*-like, successively opening flowers on canelike stems and modest-sized plants. They can bloom while very young. The 14 species were until 1970 classified as *Epidendrum* and sometimes are still listed as such. They are native primarily to intermediate-elevation Mexican forests that have distinct dry seasons. The genus is named for George Barker, a 19th-century British horticulturist who was the first to bloom it.

How to Grow
Cool to intermediate nights (45–52°F in winter) are the trick to *Barkeria*. Let it dry somewhat between waterings. When its deciduous leaves fall, give the plant a drier, cool (45°F) rest during the winter months; it goes almost dormant. Small pots or mounts work best, in medium to high light of a southern windowsill. *Barkeria* do tend to send out copious root systems, often refusing to stay within the pot and attaching instead to everything nearby.

■ *spectabilis p. 70*
The most popular and showiest of the genus has the largest flowers, borne on erect stems. Native from Mexico to Nicaragua, it usually blooms in spring or early summer, but successive flowers appear through October. Each flower lasts several weeks.

Batemania (Btmna.)

Bayt-man'ee-ah
Cymbidium Group (Epidendrum Subfamily)
Epiphytic. Sympodial. Pseudobulbs

Description
The 45 species of the genus sport somewhat bizarre, pendulous large flowers on medium to medium-small plants. *Bate-*

mania is native to hot, humid, Amazon basin areas. The genus is named for James Bateman, a 19th-century botanist.

How to Grow

Give *Batemania* warm temperatures (60–65°F winter nights), medium windowsill light of any exposure except north, 50% humidity (add humidity trays), and abundant water while they are growing. After growth is complete, move plants to a cooler (50°F), somewhat less bright spot for a few weeks to initiate flowers. Reduce watering during this time. *Batemania* resent repotting, which should be done only during the rest period. Fertilize only during the active growing phase.

■ *colleyi* *p. 115*
This plant has flowers that can last a month or more when they appear in autumn or winter; the bad news is their unpleasant odor.

Beallara (Bllra.)

Bee-al-are'ah
Cymbidium Group (Epidendrum Subfamily)
Brassia × *Cochlioda* × *Miltonia* × *Odontoglossum*
Epiphytic. Sympodial. Pseudobulbs.

Description

An intriguing blend of four natural genera in the Oncidium Alliance, *Beallara*'s intricate flower colors and markings have made this hybrid genus popular since its creation in 1970 by the American orchid company of Beall. There are usually long sprays of gorgeous flowers that last 4–6 weeks.

How to Grow

Intermediate to cool conditions (58–45°F winter nights) and medium light on an eastern or southern windowsill, or medium light in a greenhouse, generally suit *Beallara*. If the plant sulks, raise the humidity, lower the night temperatures, and avoid excessive heat above 75°F. Let it dry only slightly between waterings.

■ **Magic Cauldron (*Miltassia* Charles Marden Fitch × *Odontioda* Irene Williams)** *p. 126*
The genus *Brassia* in the genetic heritage often elongates the sepals and petals, as it has in this lovely hybrid. The cultivar pictured is 'Witch's Brew'.

Bifrenaria (Bif.)

Bye-fren-air'ee-ah
Cymbidium Group (Epidendrum Subfamily)
Epiphytic, lithophytic, terrestrial. Sympodial. Pseudobulbs

Description
The lowlands of wet tropical Amazonian forests are home to
the 24 species, where they grow on trees and atop mossy
rocks. Leathery, 5-in.-wide, foot-long leaves grow from clusters of egg-shaped pseudobulbs. The flower inflorescence
arises from the base of the pseudobulbs, and the few flowers
are similar to the beautiful *Lycaste*, although they normally
do not open as wide. The name of the genus refers to the two
appendages on the pollinia.

How to Grow
Most grow warm (60–65°F winter nights) and humid in
medium greenhouse light, with lots of water. Let the plants
rest after growth, in a cooler, less bright spot with reduced
watering, to stimulate buds. Divide only when necessary, during the rest period. Bloom is usually not generous.

■ *harrisoniae* *p. 115*
The sweet scent of this Brazilian epiphytic species comes
from March to May blooms that sit atop 4-angled pseudobulbs. The waxy flowers last up to 6 weeks, borne 1 per
inflorescence. It grows well if given constant watering and
intermediate temperatures (55–60°F winter nights). This
species needs no rest period. The cultivar pictured is 'Ruth'
AM/AOS.

Bletilla (Ble.)

Ble-till'ah
Epidendrum Group (Epidendrum Subfamily)
Terrestrial. Sympodial. Deciduous underground tubers

Description
Known both as the Hardy Chinese Orchid and the Hyacinth
Orchid (for its slight sweet scent), *Bletilla* is a popular and
very easy outdoor garden plant even in cold areas, one of the
best hardy orchids. Its 9 species are native to margins of
woods in temperate areas of eastern Asia. The name is the
diminutive form of *Bletia,* a genus *Bletilla* somewhat resembles, although they are only vaguely related.

How to Grow
Plant the tubers 2 in. deep in loamy well-drained garden soil in light shade or full sun protected from noon heat. Do not dig them up in winter; mulch with 2–3 in. of compost where winter temperatures drop below 5°F. *Bletilla* can also be grown indoors in an 8-in. pot filled with a woodland mix of loam, leaf mold, sphagnum moss, and sharp sand (2:2:1:1 ratio). Put it outdoors for the summer (protected from midday sun), watering carefully to prevent rot when the new growths appear. After the leaves fall, keep the plant in a cool (40–45°F) shaded spot, and water it only enough to prevent shriveling.

■ *striata* p. 195
Often sold in garden catalogs as *hyacinthina*, this Chinese/Japanese/Tibetan species blooms for 2 weeks in midspring to early summer with up to 12 successive, half-open, pink flowers per 16-in. inflorescence. There are also *alba* forms. The pretty pleated leaves remain on the plant all summer.

Bollea (Bol.)

Boh'lee-ah
Cymbidium Group (Epidendrum Subfamily)
Epiphytic. Sympodial. No pseudobulbs (or minuscule)

Description
The thick, waxy, large *Bollea* flowers seem carved from velvety stone, spectacularly surreal, yet they are not long-lasting; they are in bloom perhaps 2 weeks. There is only one bloom per floppy flower scape. Very wet mid-elevation cloud forests of South America are home to *Bollea*'s 10 large, fan-shaped species. The genus is named for Dr. Karl Boll, a German patron of horticulture.

How to Grow
Cool nights (45°F), intermediate day temperatures (not above 75°F), high humidity, and good air movement to ward off fungal attack are essential. *Bollea* is best grown in a greenhouse, in a very well drained pot or basket. Its heavy roots often push the plant up out of the pot, which is nothing to worry about; when repotting, simply position the plant lower in the pot. Give medium greenhouse light (slightly less than for *Cattleya*), and don't let the plant dry out. Fertilize regularly.

■ *violacea* *p. 116*
This fragrant blue-violet species grows warmer than most other *Bollea,* needing warm to intermediate temperatures (65–55°F). It generally blooms in May, with several solitary-flowered inflorescences; flowers may also appear in early winter. The cultivar pictured is 'Walter'.

Brassavola (B.)

Bra-sah'vol-lah
Epidendrum Group (Epidendrum Subfamily)
Epiphytic, lithophytic. Sympodial. Small pseudobulbs

Description

Some of the easiest orchids to grow are found among the 17 compact species of *Brassavola.* This Cattleya Alliance genus is native to moist lowland forests of tropical Central and South America and the Caribbean. Many species are night fragrant, such as the well-known Lady of the Night (*Brassavola nodosa*), and most bloom between summer and fall, although *B. nodosa* in particular can be almost everblooming. The plants have thin cylindrical pseudobulbs with long terete leaves. *Brassavola* was named to honor a 16th-century Venetian botanist, Sr. Antonio Musa Brassavola. See also *Rhyncholaelia,* since two very popular species originally classified as *Brassavola* (*B. digbyana* and *B. glauca*) have been reclassified into that genus.

How to Grow

Easy *Brassavola* need intermediate to warm temperatures (55–65°F winter nights; summer day maximum of 86°F) and the medium- to high-light conditions of a southern windowsill. Baskets of coarse mix or mounted slabs work best for the somewhat pendulous growths. Extra humidity from misting and humidity trays during growth periods will give better bloom. Fertilize regularly while they are growing, and let the plants dry between waterings. After bloom, reduce water for several weeks, but don't allow the pseudobulbs to shrivel. Rather than dividing them, grow the plants into large specimens of many growths and flowers.

■ *perrinii* *p. 70*
This Brazilian species is one of the largest-flowered *Brassavola.* Each inflorescence can carry 3–6 flowers that are each 3 in. across. Peak bloom is in July, although flowers can appear unexpectedly anytime.

Brassia (Brs.)

Brass'ee-ah
Cymbidium Group (Epidendrum Subfamily)
Epiphytic. Sympodial. Large pseudobulbs

Description

The 35 spectacular, free-blooming species of Spider Orchids mimic the look of spiders to attract their spider-hunting wasp pollinators. They are found in wet forests from sea level to 5,000 ft. in the tropical Americas. The yellowy green flowers are often fragrant. They appear from the base of the large pseudobulb and are usually beautifully spaced on long inflorescences that last 6 weeks or more. Most bloom generously on gracefully held, well-spaced flowering sprays in late spring or summer, but twice-a-year bloom is common. They are often interbred within the Oncidium Alliance, their presence in a pedigree signaled by the spidery or pointy look of the blooms. The genus was named for 18th-century botanical artist William Brass.

How to Grow

All *Brassia* are easy to grow and flower in medium light on any windowsill except northern ones (give them slightly less light than *Cattleya*), and in greenhouses under medium light, in intermediate to warm temperatures (55–65°F winter nights). Grow them in baskets or pots; the roots will often climb out of the mix, which is normal. Add humidity with misting and humidity trays. Fertilize regularly while they are growing, which helps encourage twice-a-year bloom. Give plants a decided 2–4-week rest with higher light after growth is complete. *Brassia* don't like to be repotted often.

■ *maculata* p. 127
Large in habit, this West Indian–Honduras species has many long, fragrant, waxy blooms that last at least 6 weeks. June is its peak flowering time, often repeating in fall. The cultivar pictured is 'Majus'.

Brassocattleya (Bc.)

Brass-oh-kat'lee-yah
Epidendrum Group (Epidendrum Subfamily)
Brassavola (and/or *Rhyncholaelia*) × *Cattleya*
Sympodial. Pseudobulbs

Description

Although it is a hybrid genus in the Cattleya Alliance, *Brassocattleya* can cross naturally in the wild. The first artificial hybrid in this genus was created in 1889. *Brassocattleya* are very popular for the ruffled lips of the large-flowered hybrids that originated most often from the species once called *Brassavola digbyana;* technically, many hybrids come from the genus *Rhyncholaelia* rather than *Brassavola,* since *digbyana* has been reclassified as *Rhyncholaelia digbyana,* but hybrid registration still considers that species, and thus its hybrids, as *Brassavola* to avoid chaos. Today's hybrids are often compact plants. Many are wonderfully fragrant, and the flowers last 4–6 weeks.

How to Grow
Brassocattleya are easy to grow on medium- to high-light windowsills of southern or eastern exposure, with intermediate temperatures (55–60°F winter nights). Pot them in coarse mix (bark and perlite works well in most situations). Let the plants dry somewhat between waterings. Fertilize only when they are actively growing. If the bloom seems reluctant, increase the light.

■ **Angel Lace** *(Cattleya* Little Angel × *Rhyncholaelia digbyana) p. 71*
This heady 1988 hybrid has won fragrance judgings. It usually produces 1–2 lovely pink flowers per inflorescence, on medium-size plants. The cultivar photographed is 'Breckinridge' AM/AOS.

■ *Binosa (Cattleya bicolor × Brassavola nodosa) p. 71*
The tall *Cattleya bicolor* from Brazil often lends cerise lips to its offspring, as it has in this much-awarded hybrid. The compact *Brassavola nodosa* parent reduces size and encourages free-flowering. Both parents impart great fragrance. The hybrid bears up to 7 flowers per inflorescence. The cultivar photographed is 'Kirk' AM/AOS.

■ **Green Dragoon** (*Brassocattleya* Harriet Moseley × *Cattleya bicolor*) *p. 72*
Sturdy flower shape and beautiful pale green color both come from the *alba* variety of the *Cattleya bicolor* parent. This hybrid cross is vigorous. The cultivar photographed is 'Mendenhall'.

Brassoepidendrum (Bepi.)

Brass-oh-ep-ee-den'drum
Epidendrum Group (Epidendrum Subfamily)
Brassavola (and/or *Rhyncholaelia*) × *Epidendrum*
Sympodial. Pseudobulbs

Description

Most of the crosses in this 1906 hybrid genus of the Cattleya Alliance are made using the free-blooming *Brassavola nodosa* with a variety of *Epidendrum,* yielding perky, interestingly shaped and colored flowers that can bloom in succession for a long time.

How to Grow

If the hybrid has produced a plant with small pseudobulbs, keep it more moist than plants with more-prominent pseudobulbs, which need to dry out between waterings. Grow *Brassoepidendrum* in pots of medium-coarse mix on windowsills of any exposure except north in medium light in intermediate temperatures (55–60°F winter nights).

■ **Peggy Ann** *(Epidendrum pseudepidendrum × Rhyncholaelia glauca)* *p. 72*
The *Rhyncholaelia* parent produces hybrids that need a bit brighter light than most other *Brassoepidendrum.* The brilliant waxy color and tolerance for warmer temperatures comes from the reed-stem *Epidendrum* parent. Grow this hybrid intermediate to warm (55–65°F winter nights) on southern windowsills in medium to high light. Allow to dry slightly between waterings. There are usually several flowers per inflorescence.

Brassolaelia (Bl.)

Brass-oh-lay′lee-ah
Epidendrum Group (Epidendrum Subfamily)
Brassavola (and/or *Rhyncholaelia*) × *Laelia*
Sympodial. Pseudobulbs

Description

This hybrid genus in the Cattleya Alliance was created in 1898. The plant size and flower color usually depend on which *Laelia* parent is used. Flowers are often a lovely starry shape. *Brassolaelia* hybrids may actually be the result of using *Rhyncholaelia* species instead of *Brassavola,* since two major species of the latter have been reclassified as *Rhyncholaelia.* Their offspring continue to be registered as *Brassavola* origin for hybrid purposes.

How to Grow

Many *Brassolaelia* do well on mounts or in pots of coarse mix, in the medium to high light of a southern windowsill, in intermediate temperatures (55–60°F winter nights). Let them dry somewhat between waterings, and fertilize regularly except for a short 2-week rest after growth, when both water and fertilizer should be reduced. If a hybrid does not bloom, increase the light.

■ **Richard Mueller** *(Brassavola nodosa × Laelia milleri)* *p. 73*
This compact grower is one of the better-known *Brassolaelia* hybrids. It blooms anytime from fall to spring, with peak bloom in summer. It is content with medium light of any windowsill exposure except north. Flowers last 6 weeks.

Brassolaeliocattleya (Blc.)

Brass-oh-lay-lee-oh-kat'lee-yah
Epidendrum Group (Epidendrum Subfamily)
Brassavola (and/or *Rhyncholaelia*) × *Laelia* × *Cattleya*
Sympodial. Pseudobulbs

Description
The big, beautiful, richly colored, frilly-lipped flowers of this trigeneric hybrid genus classically signal "orchid" to most people. This enormously popular Cattleya Alliance genus was created in 1897; there are now more than 5,000 complex hybrids. The showy, often fragrant flowers have traditionally been the prom corsage of choice and can measure up to 8 in. across. Flowers last a week or more in water and 4–6 weeks in bloom.

How to Grow
These are generally medium to tall plants. They do well on medium-light southern or eastern windowsills, in intermediate temperatures (55–60°F winter nights). Pot in coarse mix (bark and perlite usually works well). Let them dry out between waterings, and fertilize regularly. The flower sheaths sometimes are too dry and stiff, and they may need to be carefully sliced open so the buds can emerge.

■ **Mem. Dorothy Bertsch** *(Iliad × Midas Charm)* *p. 73*
Suffusions of glistening colors are common among *Brassolaeliocattleya* hybrids. The abbreviation "Mem." in an orchid name means it is named "in memoriam" of someone. The cultivar pictured is 'Copper Glow' AM/AOS.

■ **Port Royal Sound** *(Laeliocattleya* Amber Glow × *Brassocattleya* Oconee) *p. 74*
The overlapping sepals and petals achieved in this cross are a desired goal of hybridizers. The cultivar pictured is '# 1'

HCC/AOS. The *Laeliocattleya* Amber Glow parent of this cross is also pictured in the color plates (see p. 89).

Bulbophyllum (Bulb.)

Bulb-oh-fill'um
Dendrobium Group (Epidendrum Subfamily)
Epiphytic. Sympodial. Pseudobulbs

Description

Bulbophyllum boasts some of the most bizarre orchids, in a dizzying array of color, shapes, and odors. Tropical African and Asian rain forests and cloud forests are home to the 1,000 species, many of which are worth growing for curiosity's sake. *Bulbophyllum* was for many years the genus with the largest number of species; it has recently been dislodged by *Pleurothallis*. The genus's name refers to the prominent "bulbous" pseudobulbs with fleshy leaves. See also *Cirrhopetalum;* many popular *Bulbophyllum* are often classified as such, although most taxonomists agree that *Cirrhopetalum* is merely a subsection of *Bulbophyllum*.

How to Grow

Bulbophyllum creeps along a rhizome with its pseudobulbs spaced widely apart, and resents repotting, so it is best grown on a mount or in a shallow hanging basket. The trick to *Bulbophyllum* is humidity above 60%; good air movement is then also essential to prevent rot. Many grow well under fluorescent lights, in warm environments (60–65°F winter nights) such as a plastic-draped light cart or in a basement, or in a warm greenhouse in shaded light. Water well while in active growth.

■ *phalaenopsis* p. 100
As with most *Bulbophyllum,* this species, rarely seen until the 1980s, is pollinated by flies that are drawn to the rotting meat scent. This is one of the largest species in the genus. The cultivar pictured is humorously named 'Pleasant Dreams'. Grow it warm to intermediate (65–55°F winter nights).

Cadetia

Ka-det'ee-ah
Dendrobium Group (Epidendrum Subfamily)
Epiphytic, lithophytic. Sympodial. No pseudobulbs

Description

Charming diminutive tufts covered with a succession of tiny blooms make this primarily New Guinea genus of 67 species jewels in any collection. The genus, once part of *Dendrobium,* is named in honor of French chemist Charles Cadet.

How to Grow

High humidity (above 60%) and constant moisture in cool to intermediate temperatures (45–58°F winter nights) can help *Cadetia* bloom more than once yearly. Medium light in a greenhouse is best. Grow them on mounts or in small pots of osmunda. Don't let the plants dry out at all.

■ *chionantha* p. 100
Found at mid-elevations on trees, this precious species combines robust growth with bouquets of fragrant white blooms that appear continuously between November and March.

Calanthe (Cal.)

Ka-lan'thee
Epidendrum Group (Epidendrum Subfamily)
Terrestrial, semiterrestrial, epiphytic. Sympodial. Pseudobulbs

Description

Calanthe is Greek for "beautiful flower." The 150 species of this genus from tropical Southeast and East Asia are increasing rapidly in popularity, as are the intensely colored newer hybrids. There are two types of *Calanthe:* evergreen with virtually no pseudobulbs, and deciduous with prominent ones, which flower from bare, angular pseudobulbs. The profuse blooms last 6 weeks or more. Like many orchid flowers, *Calanthe* last very well cut; because their sprays of 6–12 flowers can reach 30 in., they have become a commercial cutflower industry.

How to Grow

The evergreen *Calanthe* like warm (60–65°F winter nights), low-light conditions on windowsills of any exposure except north, or they can be grown under fluorescent lights. Give them constant water and heavy fertilizer while in active growth; let them dry only very slightly after growth is complete. The deciduous pseudobulb types need brighter light (medium southern light), intermediate to warm temperatures (55–65°F winter nights), and lots of water and fertilizer while growing. Plant them in a peaty, stony mix. After the deciduous *Calanthe* leaves fall, turn the pot on its side in a dry, cool spot (45°F) and keep the plant absolutely dry until the new growth is several inches high, when water and fertilizer can be resumed.

■ *rubens*   p. 195
A deciduous species that grows on limestone in Thailand, this spring bloomer needs warm temperatures (60–65°F winter nights) while in growth. The multiflowered inflorescence is 18 in. long. Add limestone to the potting mix for best results.

■ Florence (*sedenii* × Veitchii)   p. 196
Brilliant color on long inflorescences makes this deciduous hybrid — and most *Calanthe* — excellent for cut flowers. This is a warm-loving *Calanthe,* needing 60–65°F winter nights.

Calopogon (Cpg.)
Kal-oh-poe′gon
Epidendrum Group (Epidendrum Subfamily)
Terrestrial. Sympodial. Underground corms

Description
Native mostly to the United States and known as Grass Pinks, the 4 species inhabit acid bogs as well as highly alkaline sandy fens. The showy pink flowers bloom upside down with the lip uppermost; the plant is a single grasslike leaf. The generic name is Greek for "beautiful beard," referring to the yellow beard on the lip.

How to Grow
Unless their habitat is endangered, leave *Calopogon* in site. Laboratory seedlings can grow in an outdoor artificial bog as for *Arethusa* (see p. 234) or in an artificial sunny calcareous meadow. To make the meadow, line a 20-in.-deep bed with plastic, fill it with equal parts sand and loam, and add lime chunks. Seed the bed thickly with grass. Keep the grass mowed short. In spring or fall, plant the *Calopogon* corms 2 in. deep after the grass has grown enough to have been mowed twice. Keep the bed constantly wet, watering with collected rainwater. Use no tap water or fertilizer. Corms can be divided in spring (make sure there is an eye on each piece) or transplanted in fall. *Calopogon* can also be grown indoors in sunrooms in large containers of sphagnum moss, kept saturated, with a definite winter chill (maximum 40–45°F). Give them no fertilizer or pesticides.

■ *pulchellus* *p. 196*
This species is widespread in central and eastern North America. The name means "little beauty" in Latin, for the spike of 2–10 sequentially opening pink flowers. Depending on location, it blooms for 2 weeks between March and August.

Calypso
Kal-lip′so
Cymbidium Group (Epidendrum Subfamily)
Terrestrial. Sympodial. Underground tuber

Description
The 1 species, known as the Native Calypso Orchid, is widespread in both hemispheres of the north temperate zone in low-nutrient areas such as deep coniferous forests, shoreline sand dunes, and damp marshes. The plant is a solitary 4-in. leaf that produces a single pendent flower. The genus is named for the enchanting Greek sea nymph of Homer's *Odyssey* who charmed Ulysses to stay 7 years on her island.

How to Grow
Unless their habitat is threatened, do not try to transplant these native orchids. *Calypso* cannot tolerate high summer heat, which bleaches their leaves. Grow them in low light, either outdoors in a similar habitat from which they came, or indoors in any windowsill exposure where they do not receive direct sunlight, where they can be grown in pots filled with live sphagnum moss and leaf mold. Keep them moist, using rainwater rather than tap water, and apply no fertilizer or pesticides. After bloom, the solitary leaf will wither. Let the pots dry out a bit in summer. Growth begins in autumn, when an overwintering leaf is produced. Give the plant a cool (45°F) spot for the necessary winter chill.

■ *bulbosa* *p. 199*
Fragrant and perky, this species can often be found at bases of trees in rotting leaf mold. It blooms for 2 weeks between May and July.

Catasetum (Ctsm.)
Kat-a-see′tum
Cymbidium Group (Epidendrum Subfamily)
Epiphytic, lithophytic, semiterrestrial.
Sympodial. Deciduous pseudobulbs

Description

While the vast majority of orchids have hermaphroditic flowers (wherein the male and female portions are fused together), the bristly-fringed *Catasetum* can have separate, complicated, male or female unisex flowers, sometimes together on the same plant at the same time. Female flowers are usually less numerous, fleshier, more hooded, often nonresupinate (upside down), and yellow-green. The more common male flowers have trigger-sensitive antennae that forcibly shoot pollen when the column is touched; this is fun to demonstrate, but note that the flowers will wilt afterward. The 100 medium to large species are native mostly to the Amazon basin. The hybrids are spectacular. Most bloom from the base of the large pseudobulb with an arching inflorescence. Flowers are often fragrant, but they do not last long, fading within 2 weeks, although twice-a-year bloom is not uncommon. The plants are not very attractive out of bloom. The generic name is a mixture of Greek and Latin, meaning "downward bristle."

How to Grow

Easily grown in warm to intermediate temperatures (65–55°F) on medium to high light of eastern, western, or southern windowsills, *Catasetum* need lots of water and fertilizer during growth. Grow them in small hanging pots or baskets of tree fern or osmunda. Provide extra humidity via humidity trays and grouping plants together during growth. Summer the plants outdoors. When their deciduous leaves fall, reduce water for several weeks until the new roots appear, which is when they can be repotted if necessary. Water new growth carefully, since it can rot easily if left damp. Higher light produces the less numerous female flowers; both sexes of flowers are interesting and can be very different.

■ **species** *p. 202*
The bristles on the male flowers of this unidentified Peruvian species are typical of the genus.

■ **Marge Soule** (*fimbriatum* × *expansum*) *p. 202*
A large plant with 15 or so flowers on an 18-in. inflorescence, this 1985 hybrid has a spicy scent. It blooms for several weeks in summer or fall.

Cattleya (C.)

Kat'lee-ya
Epidendrum Group (Epidendrum Subfamily)
Epiphytic, lithophytic. Sympodial. Pseudobulbs

Description

Cattleya defines "orchid" for most people, and its popularity is well deserved for its long-lasting gorgeous flowers and easy culture. The 45 Central and South American species usually grow near treetops in moist forests. One-leaved (unifoliate) types have larger and fewer flowers than the taller, two-leaved (bifoliate) species. Both types have prominent pseudobulbs; the bifoliate ones are more elongated. Classic for prom corsages, *Cattleya* flowers last at least a week in water and bloom for about 4 weeks on the plant, with buds arising from a sheath. The genus is named for William Cattley, a wealthy English horticulturist who successfully bloomed some of the first known. The words *"Cattleya"* or "Cattleya Alliance" are often loosely used to refer to the numerous genera that interbreed readily, including *Cattleya, Brassavola, Epidendrum, Laelia, Rhyncholaelia,* and *Sophronitis,* along with the many artificially made intergeneric hybrid genera such as *Brassolaeliocattleya.*

How to Grow

Cattleya are among the easiest and showiest of all orchids to grow, in intermediate to warm temperatures (55–65°F winter nights) in medium bright light of southern, eastern, or western windowsills. Blooms are most abundant in the higher light range; leaf margins will often develop a reddish tinge that lets you know they are at the upper limit of light. Pot them in coarse mix; fir bark and perlite often works well. Let them dry out a bit between waterings, and fertilize regularly while they are actively growing. Reduce both somewhat for a short rest when the pseudobulbs mature; during this time they will appreciate misting more than they will water. Unifoliate species prefer cooler nights (50–55°F).

■ *amethystoglossa* p. 74
This tall Brazilian species, often with heads of 30 fragrant flowers, is highly awarded and coveted. A bifoliate, it blooms for 6 weeks between February and April. The cultivar pictured is 'El Camino'.

■ *aurantiaca* p. 75
The brilliant glowing flowers on this Mexican bifoliate don't open fully. Unlike most orchids, its many flowers often self-pollinate, in which case the blooms wilt within a week of opening. It blooms easily even while young, in late winter or spring. There are also yellow varieties.

■ *forbesii* p. 75
One or two fragrant and waxy flowers per inflorescence ap-

pear for 4–6 weeks between May and October on this mid-size Brazilian bifoliate. Usually tannish, this is an *alba* green form. The cultivar pictured is 'Ilgenfritz'.

■ *harrisoniana* *p. 76*
Sometimes considered a variety of *Cattleya loddigesii*, this pink Brazilian bifoliate blooms between July and October. It is nicely fragrant, with flowers held well on strong stalks for up to 6 weeks.

■ *intermedia* *p. 76*
This is a fragrant bifoliate from Brazilian regions. Although the flowers are usually solid pink, there is a white, pink-tipped variety (*aquinii*) responsible for much of the so-called splashed petal coloration in Cattleya Alliance hybrids. The 2–5 blooms last 4–6 weeks.

■ *skinneri* *p. 77*
By far the most awarded *Cattleya*, this gorgeous bifoliate species is considered one of the most endangered orchids, its trade severely restricted. Fortunately, it is available via seed and tissue propagation. The plant produces many huge clusters of up to 12 intensely crystalline flowers per inflorescence, which appear between February and June; the blooms don't last long, folding after several weeks. The plant must be mature before it blooms well. The rarer lilac-blue *coerulea* variety is pictured.

■ *walkeriana* *p. 77*
The combination of waxy big flowers on short plants has won popularity and many awards for this winter or spring Brazilian bloomer. The bifoliate species usually has 1–3 rose-purple flowers with a darker lip, but the *alba* varieties are quite popular. The cultivar pictured is var. *alba* 'Pendentive' AM/AOS. Flowers last 4 weeks and are very fragrant.

■ Carla Avila (**Luxury** × **Louise Georgianna**) *p. 78*
Classic white *Cattleya* such as these often have *alba* forms of *Cattleya intermedia* in their heritage. They are sometimes still referred to as "Henrietta Japhet"–type orchids, excellent for corsages. Blooms last a month or more. Grow it intermediate (55–60°F winter nights).

■ Chocolate Drop (*guttata* × *aurantiaca*) *p. 78*
This is a famous and much awarded 1965 primary cross between two bifoliate species. Chocolate Drop is tall with unbelievably waxy flower heads. The cultivar pictured is 'Kodoma' AM/AOS. The many blooms last about a month.

■ **Pumpernickel (***loddigesii*** × Gloriette)** *p. 79*
Different-colored lips such as seen in this hybrid often trace back to a unifoliate *Cattleya dowiana* influence, a yellow species with large red lips that often imparts fragrance. The cultivar pictured is 'Stardust'. The multiple blooms last a month.

■ **Sophia Martin (***guttata*** × Summer Stars)** *p. 79*
Intensely fragrant *Cattleya guttata* may impart its scent to its offspring, as well as speckled flowers. The cultivar pictured is 'Sprite'. The blooms last 4–6 weeks.

Cattleytonia (Ctna.)

Kat-lee-tone′ee-ah
Epidendrum Group (Epidendrum Subfamily)
Broughtonia × *Cattleya*
Sympodial. Pseudobulbs

Description
Created in 1956, *Cattleytonia* has become very popular for the rich crystalline colors and round full shape of its flowers and compact plant habits. Virtually all crosses in this hybrid genus have been made using Jamaican-native *Broughtonia sanguinea*, with many types of *Cattleya* used.

How to Grow
Cattleytonia prefer higher light than *Cattleya*. Place them in bright southern windowsills of medium to high light in intermediate to warm temperatures (55–65°F winter nights). Pot in a medium coarse mix; fir bark and perlite often works well, or grow them on mounts where humidity is very good. Water them abundantly, but let them dry out somewhat between waterings.

■ **Why Not (***Cattleya aurantiaca*** × *Broughtonia sanguinea***)** *p. 80*
This 1979 primary cross is one of the most awarded and sought-after *Cattleytonia* hybrids because of its intense colors. Blooms last a month or more.

Ceratostylis

Se-rat-oh-sty′lis
Dendrobium Group (Epidendrum Subfamily)
Epiphytic. Sympodial. Pseudobulbs

Description

Small yet brightly colored numerous flowers produced several times a year atop grassy tufts make this genus of 70 species worth collecting. Each pseudobulb carries a single leaf. Most of the species are native to New Guinea. The name is Greek for "horned stylis," referring to the hornlike flower column.

How to Grow

Since many have pendent growth and wandering rhizomes, mounts or baskets often work best. *Ceratostylis* must be kept constantly moist while in growth, in intermediate to warm temperatures (55–62°F) with medium filtered light, never in direct sun. Since they prefer humidity above 60%, they are usually easiest in a greenhouse, although they will grow in humid basements under fluorescent lights, or wherever *Bulbophyllum* are flourishing. Let plants dry only slightly between waterings after growth is complete.

■ *retisquama* *p. 208*

The showiest, most awarded species, found only in the Philippines, always has a brownish papery sheath surrounding the rhizome and pseudobulbs. It sometimes is found under the synonym *rubra*. Fall is usually its peak bloom. The flowers last but a week, although a plant often can flower in succession several times a year from the base of the new growths.

Chysis (Chy.)

Kye'siss
Epidendrum Group (Epidendrum Subfamily)
Epiphytic, lithophytic. Sympodial. Deciduous pseudobulbs

Description

The large, long-lasting waxy flowers arise from the sides of the old club-shaped deciduous pseudobulbs to make interesting and distinctive plants. The 7 Mexican to Andean species inhabit tree trunks in damp shaded forests at mid-elevations. *Chysis* means "fusion" in Greek, which probably refers to the fused look of the pollen clumps, although it may have alluded to the way flowers sometimes self-pollinate without ever opening.

How to Grow

To accommodate its pendent pseudobulbs and rampantly wandering root system that resents repotting, the easily grown *Chysis* grows best in a basket or on a mount. Give it intermediate temperatures (55–60°F winter nights) in low to medium light on humid windowsills of any exposure except north; keep it away from direct sun. Water and fertilize well while it is making its fast growth in spring and summer. After the deciduous leaves drop, place the plant in a cooler spot (50°F) and reduce the water and fertilizer during the winter. When new growths appear, bring it back to the warmer spot.

■ **Langleyensis (***bractescens*** × Chelsonii)** *p. 197*
The striking fragrant flowers bloom between March and May on a somewhat coarse plant. There can be 6 or more blooms per inflorescence, with flowers lasting 6 weeks. The cultivar pictured is 'Diane' AM/AOS.

Cirrhopetalum (Cirr.)

Seer'oh-pet-al-um
Dendrobium Group (Epidendrum Subfamily)
Epiphytic. Sympodial. Pseudobulbs

Description
Cirrhopetalum are nicknamed the Daisy-Chain Orchids because the circular, umbellate flower head often resembles a yellow daisy. Each "petal" of the "daisy" is, however, actually a separate and complete flower. The name comes from either the Greek for "tawny yellow petals" or the Latin for "fringed petals." Successive blooming can keep *Cirrhopetalum* in flower almost year-round. The small to medium creeping plants are native mostly to tropical India and other Asiatic regions. Widely known as a separate genus of 30–100 species, and registered as such for hybridizing, the popular *Cirrhopetalum* is technically considered part of *Bulbophyllum* by most taxonomists. *Cirrhopetalum* has the same egg-shaped pseudobulbs widely spaced along the rhizome. Also see *Bulbophyllum* (p. 248).

How to Grow
Warm (60–65°F winter nights), humid environments under fluorescent lights suit *Cirrhopetalum* well. Pot them in shallow baskets or on mounts to accommodate the wandering rhizomes. Give them plenty of water and regular fertilizer while in active growth; they should never really dry out at any time of the year.

■ *gracillimum* *p. 101*
Long-tailed and brilliant red, this fragrant Thailand to New Guinea native has an arching 10-in.-long inflorescence. It blooms successively from October to January on a miniature plant.

■ *makoyanum* p. 101
The very popular, fragrant Singapore species can bloom successively almost any time of the year. It is the species most well known as the Daisy-Chain Orchid.

■ *medusae* p. 102
The Medusa Orchid is aptly named for the snake-headed Gorgon of Greek myth. The 6-in.-long, musty-scented, dense flower clusters bloom in fall or early winter. It is native from Thailand to the Philippines.

Clowesia (Clow.)
Klow′eez-ee-ah
Cymbidium Group (Epidendrum Subfamily)
Epiphytic. Sympodial. Deciduous pseudobulbs

Description
Until 1975, *Clowesia* was considered part of *Catasetum,* and the spectacular hybrids are still registered as such. Plants of the genus *Clowesia* do not have *Catasetum*'s separate male and female flowers (*Clowesia* are, like most orchids, hermaphroditic), although they do possess the same fascinating trigger-shot pollen mechanism and similarly frilly or fringed lips. The 6 fragrant species are found in forests from Mexico to northern South America. The genus is named for 19th-century English orchidist Rev. John Clowes.

How to Grow
Medium windowsill light of any exposure except north, and intermediate temperatures (55–60°F winter nights) make *Clowesia* relatively easy. The pendent inflorescence is best accommodated in a small hanging pot or basket. Water and fertilize well when the plant is growing, but when its deciduous leaves fall, reduce the water for several weeks and let it rest.

■ Grace Dunn *(warscewiczii × rosea)* p. 203
The frilly lip of both parents yields a beautiful hybrid that blooms for a month between January and April.

Cochleanthes (Cnths.)
Kok-lee-an′theez
Cymbidium Group (Epidendrum Subfamily)
Epiphytic. Sympodial. No pseudobulbs

Description

The 15 species of medium-size fanlike plants from low to mid-elevation Costa Rican to Peruvian cloud forests have large, white and blue-toned fragrant flowers that bloom successively. The name is Greek for "spiral-shelled flower."

How to Grow

The need for high humidity and good air movement to prevent common fungal leaf spotting makes *Cochleanthes* somewhat tricky. Give it frequent water (its elaborate root system should never dry out), intermediate greenhouse temperatures (55–60°F winter nights), and low shady light. Add sphagnum to the potting mix to retain water; it can also be grown mounted on tree fern or cork. If all conditions are met, *Cochleanthes* grow easily into large specimens; they resent repotting and division.

■ *discolor* *p. 116*

The most familiar and most awarded species is native from Costa Rica to Venezuela. Its showy 2-in-wide flowers bloom 1 per inflorescence anytime from March to June, and sometimes again in summer. Grow it a bit cooler (low 50–55°F winter nights) with a bit higher light (slightly less than for *Cattleya*).

Cochlioda (Cda.)

Kok-lee-oh′dah
Cymbidium Group (Epidendrum Subfamily)
Epiphytic, lithophytic. Sympodial. Pseudobulbs

Description

These 5 small to medium-size species are native to high-elevation Andean cloud forests. The brilliant, often scarlet flowers have been used extensively in intergeneric hybridizing within the Oncidium Alliance. The generic name refers to the lip calluses that resemble shells. See also *Symphyglossum*, since a prominent species, *sanguineum,* was once considered part of *Cochlioda,* and *Cochlioda sanguinea* is still its official name for hybrid registration purposes.

How to Grow

Cochlioda are narrow-temperature cool growers, needing 45°F winter nights and resenting any daytime temperature over 78°F. Medium light in a humid greenhouse is generally best; they grow well alongside *Odontoglossum*. Give them lots of water year-round, but don't let water sit on the growths, since they rot easily.

■ *coccinea* *p. 127*
This small plant blooms for 4–6 weeks in spring on a long inflorescence of up to 20 flowers.

Coelogyne (Coel.)

See-loj'in-ee
Epidendrum Group (Epidendrum Subfamily)
Epiphytic. Sympodial. Sometimes deciduous pseudobulbs

Description

With 100 very varied species, this desirable and usually fragrant tropical Asian genus has racemes of showy blooms with bristly colorful lips. There are two basic types of growth, either deciduous or evergreen, with leaves on large angular pseudobulbs. The flower stems arise either from the center of new growths or from the base of the pseudobulbs. The name is Greek for "hollow female," referring to the very deep stigma in the flower column.

How to Grow

The deciduous, high-elevation Indian, Burmese, and Malaysian species are grown cool (45–50°F winter nights; summer daytime highs never above 80°F). Give them medium light on any windowsill exposure except north; protect them from direct sun. These types need a strict rest after growth, when the leaves may fall. If the resting pseudobulbs overshrivel, mist them. Species from the warm low altitudes of New Guinea, Borneo, and the Far East grow continuously and must never dry out. They need warm to intermediate temperatures (65–55°F winter nights). All like lots of fertilizer during growth, and good air movement. All particularly resent repotting, preferring to be grown into large specimens. Types with wandering pseudobulbs do best mounted; those with tight clusters of pseudobulbs can be potted.

■ *flaccida* *p. 200*
Native to high elevations of the Himalaya Mountains, this species has a slightly unpleasant odor. Up to 8 flowers are borne on pendent spikes for a month between February and March and are best displayed in hanging baskets. Grow it cool (45–55°F winter nights, with daytime highs below 80°F), and give it a dry rest after its leaves fall.

■ Burfordiense (*asperata* × *pandurata*) *p. 200*
An old hybrid from 1911 between two warm-growing species, Burfordiense can boast 10 flowers per inflorescence.

The wonderful black lip markings come from the *Coelogyne pandurata* parent. Grow it warm (60–65°F winter nights), potted in sphagnum moss; never let it dry out.

Colmanara (Colm.)

Kole-man-ah'rah
Cymbidium Group (Epidendrum Subfamily)
Miltonia × *Odontoglossum* × *Oncidium*
Sympodial. Pseudobulbs

Description
This is a hybrid genus in the Oncidium Alliance. These 3 genera were first interbred in 1963, creating racemes of many flowers in a diverse variety of colors and markings, even within the same cross, although brilliant yellow tones are often encountered. The generic name suitably honors hybridizing pioneer Sir Jeremiah Coleman, a 19th–20th-century Englishman who specialized in breeding yellow orchids.

How to Grow
Most *Colmanara* hybrids grow on medium-light windowsills of any exposure except north, in intermediate temperatures (55–60°F winter nights). Water them throughout the year; let them dry only slightly in between waterings. Maintain humidity at 50% or above with humidity trays and by grouping plants together. If a plant seems unhappy with this regimen, drop the night temperature 5°F, avoid heat above 78°F, and don't allow it to dry out.

■ Wildcat (*Odontonia* Rustic Bridge × *Odontocidium* Crowborough) *p. 128*
A 1992 hybrid from cool *Miltoniopsis* and *Odontoglossum* grandparents and an intermediate to warm *Oncidium* one yields brilliantly patterned, temperature-tolerant offspring bearing up to 50 flowers on branched spikes. Grow it intermediate (52–60°F), but avoid daytime temperatures above 80°F.

Comparettia (Comp.)

Kom-pa-ret'ee-ah
Cymbidium Group (Epidendrum Subfamily)
Epiphytic. Sympodial. Pseudobulbs

Description
A desirable genus of 10 mostly mid-elevation Colombian

Andes species, *Comparettia* offers miniature plants that bear racemes of uniquely shaped pink, rose, or red-orange flowers that arise from the base of the unifoliate pseudobulbs. *Comparettia* are often used in intergeneric hybridizing to impart brilliant color. The generic name honors 19th-century Italian botanist Sr. Andreo Comparetti.

How to Grow
Comparettia live on twigs on guava trees and do best mounted on wood. They thrive in a greenhouse, in high humidity, or can be grown under fluorescent lights in a humid spot. Water them daily year-round, and give them low to medium shaded light and intermediate to cool temperatures, with no extremes of heat (58–45°F winter nights; daytime highs below 78°F). The root system must be extensive to sustain blooming; otherwise pinch off flowers. Despite all best efforts, *Comparettia* are often short-lived.

■ *macroplectron   p. 128*
One of the most popular species, and certainly the most awarded, comes from Colombia. The 4–8 light violet flowers bloom mostly in January and February, but they can appear almost any time of the year. Grow it in intermediate temperatures (55°F winter nights) and low light.

Cycnoches (Cyc.)
Sik'no-keez
Cymbidium Group (Epidendrum Subfamily)
Epiphytic. Sympodial. Deciduous pseudobulbs

Description
The stunning and fragrant Swan Orchids (named for a swan-like neck on the column) have separate male and female flowers rather than the standard hermaphroditic orchid flowers. Although the two sexes usually look fairly similar, the males have the swan necks and brighter colors. *Cycnoches* bloom with the flower lip uppermost, in late summer through fall, with a swinging-lip, trigger-shot pollen mechanism activated by euglossine bee pollinators. The 23 medium-size species, found on decomposing wood in warm, moist Amazonian forests, are handsome out of bloom as well.

How to Grow
The easily grown *Cycnoches* do best in warm to intermediate temperatures (65–55°F) and medium windowsill light of

any exposure except north (more light will yield less-colorful female flowers), protected from direct noon sun. Give them small well-drained pots or hanging baskets with a fine mix. When their leaves fall in winter, provide a cool (45–50°F), drier rest with brighter southern light. *Cycnoches* respond well to repotting, which is best done when their pseudobulbs are bare.

■ *chlorochilon* *p. 203*
By far the most awarded and recognized *Cycnoches,* this large plant boasts flowers up to 6 in. across that are spicily fragrant in the morning. Blooms last 4–6 weeks. The male flowers are pictured.

Cymbidium (Cym.)

Sim-bid′ee-um
Cymbidium Group (Epidendrum Subfamily)
Epiphytic, lithophytic, terrestrial. Sympodial. Pseudobulbs

Description
The beloved *Cymbidium* yields bountiful tall spikes of many exquisite flowers amid elegant grassy-leaved foliage and short, fat, egg-shaped pseudobulbs. Plants can stay in bloom for 3 months; the waxy long-lasting flowers make classic corsages and are a commercial cut-flower industry. Flowers come in just about every shade except blue and purple. The 45 species range from low to high elevations of India to Japan down to Australia, often in exposed habitats in full sun. Some, such as *Cymbidium ensifolium, Cym. sinense,* and *Cym. kanran,* are intensely fragrant. While traditional hybrids are large cool-growing plants, newer breeding has introduced smaller, warmer-growing hybrids. The generic name is from the Greek for "hull of a boat," referring to the boat-shaped lip.

How to Grow
Most *Cymbidium* are very easy to grow if they have cool nights and high light. All *Cymbidium* need high light, whether in a greenhouse or sunroom, although the smaller types can be grown on southern windowsills. All need a decided drop in nighttime temperatures for at least 6 weeks, generally in late summer and fall, in order to induce buds, and it's best if this drop can be maintained throughout winter as well. High-altitude species and most large hybrids will need cool night temperatures of 40–45°F; the warmer types

will need to drop to a more intermediate 52–55°F. The big types have copious root systems and do best in large deep pots of semiterrestrial mix. The warmer-growing species do better in baskets, since many are pendent-flowered. In mild climates, *Cymbidium* can also be grown outdoors as landscape plants, in well-drained humusy garden soil. Give all types even moisture and heavy regular fertilizer. Most will bloom from February to April. For best floral display, stake the erect inflorescence when it is 4 in. tall, then again at 8 in., but first put the plant in a warm spot for several hours to make the inflorescence less brittle.

■ *devonianum* *p. 204*
This cool to intermediate (45–52°F fall and winter nights) epiphytic species grows only a foot tall, and it blooms with a 14-in.-long, pendent, many-flowered spike in spring. It can fit as a hanging plant in a windowsill.

■ *goeringii* *p. 204*
This cool-growing (45°F fall and winter nights) small plant is often classically drawn in Oriental art. The solitary fragrant flower is borne on a short scape. The variety *tortispalum* shown in the photo has twisted sepals.

■ **Doris Dawson (Dag × Greenstone)** *p. 205*
Complex breeding of many generations turns small-flowered green species into big round standards. The cultivar pictured is 'Copenhagen' HCC/AOS. Grow it cool (45–50°F fall and winter nights).

■ **Nancy Carpenter (Korintji × *chloranthum*)** *p. 205*
The Malayan *chloranthum* species provides green color and open shape as well as warmth tolerance. Grow it intermediate (52–58°F fall and winter nights).

■ **Red Beauty (Vanguard × Tapestry)** *p. 206*
Two different cultivars of this cross demonstrate complex hybrid variation. Pictured are 'Netty' and 'Wendy'. Grow plants cool (45–50°F fall and winter nights).

■ **Showgirl (Sweetheart × Alexanderi)** *p. 207*
This hybrid is considered a "miniature" *Cymbidium*, growing under 2 ft. tall, and can be suitable for a southern windowsill. Grow cool to intermediate (45–55°F fall and winter nights).

Cypripedium (Cyp.)

Sip-ree-pee'dee-um
Cypripedium Subfamily
Terrestrial. Sympodial. No pseudobulbs

Description

The well-known and beloved Native Lady's Slipper Orchids inhabit arctic to subtropical North America, Europe, and Asia. The 40 species can be found in deciduous forests, swamps, and bogs, in acidic to alkaline spots. Some have been seed-grown successfully (although they take notoriously long to flower, typically 8–10 years, with 19 years the record for some *Cypripedium reginae*). Others still resist artificial propagation of any type, including meristem tissue culture. *Cypripedium* is from the Greek and Latin for "Aphrodite's shoe," referring to the very prominent pouched, slipper-toed lip.

How to Grow

Do not take lady's slippers from their native habitats unless those habitats are threatened, and do not buy wild-collected plants. In most areas of the country, wild collecting is prohibited. If transplanting is absolutely necessary, disturb the roots as little as possible during the process, taking as much of the root ball as you can and wrapping it tightly during the move. Still, you will have more transplant failures than successes. Grow *Cypripedium* outdoors in acid bogs as for *Arethusa* or in calcareous meadows as for *Calopogon*; take care to place the bog or meadow under deciduous trees so that it receives full sun in early spring, but is shaded later in the season. If the site is successful, *Cypripedium* will increase in colony size. It is not uncommon, however, for even thriving colonies to fade away in 5–7 years. To grow *Cypripedium* in pots, use a mix of loam, sharp sand, milled oak leaf, medium pine bark, and limestone chips (3:3:2:1:1), and provide a cold rest treatment in winter of 35–40°F after its leaves fall, withholding water. Use rainwater and no fertilizer. The potted plants are best divided every 2 years in spring.

■ *acaule p. 212*

The Pink Lady's Slipper, or Moccasin Flower, is the most common American orchid, growing in very acidic deciduous pine or hemlock forests. It blooms in spring, with a solitary flower. Grow it in a very acidic spot or acid mix, incorporating pine needles. There are *alba* forms.

Degarmoara (Dgmra.)

De-gar-moe-are'ah
Cymbidium Group (Epidendrum Subfamily)
Brassia × *Miltonia* × *Odontoglossum*
Sympodial. Pseudobulbs

Description

This trigeneric hybrid genus in the Oncidium Alliance was created in 1967. The offspring vary widely in color and patterns, but they generally display sprays of many flowers with elongated sepals and petals on medium-size plants. *Degarmoara* usually are plants with hybrid vigor, more tolerant than their *Miltonia* and *Odontoglossum* parentage. The genus was named for its Californian creator, Lloyd De Garmo.

How to Grow

Place in medium windowsill light of any exposure except north and intermediate temperatures (55–60°F winter nights) that do not go above 78°F during summer days. Let the plants dry only slightly between waterings, and fertilize regularly. If plants seem unhappy with this regimen, raise the humidity and drop the night temperatures 5°F.

■ **Creole (*Miltassia* Aztec × *Odontonia* Glass Creek)** *p. 129*
With *Miltonia* heritage from both parents, this 1986 hybrid shows classic *Miltonia* coloring, while the elongated spidery sepals are from the *Brassia* genes. This hybrid does best with higher humidity; add a humidity tray and mist often. The flowers last a month or more.

Dendrobium (Den.)

Den-droh'bee-um
Dendrobium Group (Epidendrum Subfamily)
Epiphytic, lithophytic, or terrestrial. Sympodial. Pseudobulbs or canes

Description

While two genera boast more species, the enormously popular and beautiful *Dendrobium* has by far the most horticulturally worthwhile diversity. Its 900 Asian and Pacific tropical and subtropical species range from hot lowlands to Himalayan snowtops. A third of them are found in Papua New Guinea. Most have pseudobulbs, although elongated canes are also a common growth type; flowers range from tiny to exceptionally showy and are often very long-lasting. More than 6,000 *Dendrobium* hybrids have been made. The casual hobbyist is most likely to encounter the brilliant "Ya-mamoto" *Dendrobium nobile* hybrids or the *Den. pha-laenopsis* types; both are cane-growers, with the first type de-ciduous and the second evergreen. *Dendrobium* is Greek for "life in a tree," testament to the plants' mostly epiphytic na-ture.

How to Grow
Most *Dendrobium* want high light on southern windowsills and intermediate temperatures (55–60°F nights). Give them small pots of well-drained mix (rock works well, as does medium bark with coarse perlite). Pendent types will do bet-ter in small baskets or mounts. The taller cane-type *Dendro-bium* tend to be top-heavy in small pots, so place the pots in-side larger clay pots to help steady them. Let *Dendrobium* dry out somewhat between waterings. Good air movement is a boon, as is humidity of 50–70%; grow over pebble trays and group plants together. They are heavy feeders; fertilize regularly only while in growth. *Dendrobium* are either ever-green or deciduous. Both types may need a dormant rest, gen-erally 2 months in winter after the canes or pseudobulbs ma-ture; others grow continuously year-round with no rest needed. It is therefore important to find out what type your plant is. Dormancy falls into three basic categories: some plants want cooler temperatures and restricted water, others need cooler temperatures and the same watering, and still others get the same temperatures year-round but less water after growth. If your *Dendrobium* doesn't bloom, the most likely cause is insufficient light; the strongest clue will be weak, thin stems. If the light doesn't seem to be the problem, you probably are not providing the proper dormant rest.

■ *atroviolaceum* *p. 102*
Evergreen and fragrant, this New Guinea species is exten-sively used in hybridizing because of how continuously its crosses stay in bloom. Grow it warm (60–65°F nights), but avoid daytime temperatures above 75°F. Give it a cool rest in winter (45–50°F), and water it the same throughout the year. Each plant produces many flowers that last 3 months or more.

■ *chrysotoxum* *p. 103*
The evergreen, yellow pendent-flowered species such as *Den-drobium chrysotoxum* need intermediate temperatures (55–60°F nights), except in winter, when temperatures during the short dormancy period should be cool (45–50°F); reduce wa-tering to just enough to prevent shriveling. Since the 12–20 blooms are pendent, grow the plants in hanging baskets to

show the very fragrant, fringed, spring flowers to best advantage. Blooms last 6 weeks or more.

■ *cuthbertsonii* *p. 103*
This dwarf, evergreen species from high cloud forests of New Guinea is one of the most exquisite *Dendrobium*. It has special needs, however, requiring high humidity (65%+) and narrow cool conditions (45–50°F nights; below 80°F days). It grows well under fluorescent lights in an enclosed area such as a basement or a plastic-draped light cart or in low greenhouse light, although a bit higher light results in less space between the leaves, creating a neater, denser plant. The diminutive rhizome wanders, so it is best on a mount or in a shallow pot, watered daily, but not soggy. It grows year-round and needs no rest. The brilliant nonresupinate flowers are much larger than the exquisitely marked foliage, and each can last up to an astonishing 11 months. Some clones are reluctant to bloom. A variety of color forms are pictured.

■ *kingianum* *p. 104*
This easy-to-grow, compact evergreen Australian lithophyte with pseudobulbs needs intermediate temperatures (55–60°F winter nights) and no rest period. It resents wet feet, but if it is allowed to dry out at all, many keikis form instead of flowers; try using clay pots and coarse mix, and water it daily. Some clones are reluctant to flower; discard these and purchase proven bloomers. The fragrant flowers appear between February and March, with up to 15 blooms per branching inflorescence.

■ *loddigesii* *p. 104*
This small, easy-to-grow Chinese beauty needs cool to intermediate temperatures (45–60°F nights) with a cool (45–50°F), dry rest in winter after its deciduous leaves fall off the canes. It can be grown either in a pot, where aerial roots will be common, or on a mount. The fragrant flowers are borne 1 per inflorescence all along the bare cane and last 6 weeks or more.

■ *nobile* *p. 105*
This very popular, high-altitude Indian species is deciduous. Grow it in cool to intermediate temperatures (45–58°F nights). It needs a dormant rest in late autumn, when leaves drop off the year-old canes; give it cool temperatures (45–50°F) and reduce water dramatically, only enough to prevent the plant from shriveling. Flowering begins at the end of the rest, so resume watering when the buds are well formed. This regimen also applies to the popular "Ya-

mamoto" *Dendrobium nobile* hybrids. The 2–4 fragrant blooms per inflorescence last a month or more.

▪ *pendulum* p. 105
Long-lasting fragrant flowers bloom off deciduous knobby canes in this Indian-Chinese species. Grow it intermediate (55–60°F nights). After its leaves fall, give the plant a cool (45–50°F) dry rest. Flowering begins at the end of the rest, when you should resume watering. The 1–3 blooms per inflorescence last 6 weeks or more, with peak flowering in February and March.

▪ *primulinum* p. 106
This pendent, fragrant, Himalayan to Malay species, which flowers on new growth, needs a distinct cool (45–50°F), dry spell in winter after its deciduous leaves fall. The rest of the year it is grown intermediate (55–60°F nights). The *giganteum* form, shown in the photo, is exceptionally large-flowered. There is usually only 1 flower per inflorescence, with many borne along the bare cane. They last 6 weeks or more.

▪ *speciosum* p. 106
This Australian native has quite a number of white to yellow varietal forms. Give it cool to intermediate temperatures (45–58°F nights) and a cool (45°F), dry winter rest with bright light, such as in a sunroom or a garage with a southern window. The *pedunculatum* form (not pictured) is yellow. The fragrant flowers appear profusely for weeks.

▪ *subacaule* p. 107
This diminutive evergreen species from New Guinea needs cool temperatures (45–50°F nights) and continual dampness year-round. It is best grown in a greenhouse. In most sympodial orchids, each pseudobulb flowers only once, with new flowers produced by new pseudobulbs; this species is unusual in that its dwarf pseudobulbs flower 2 years in a row in spring or summer. It is also known as *oreocharis*.

▪ *toressae* p. 107
This Australian evergreen has unusual alternating leaves that form a tiny mat. Grow it cool (45–50°F nights), constantly damp, and shady year-round. It does well under fluorescent lights in a cool basement, or in a greenhouse spot protected from direct light.

▪ *victoria-reginae* p. 108
This high-altitude Philippine native is named to commemorate Queen Victoria's Golden Jubilee, since it was discovered

in the late 1890s. Its canes can be erect or pendent, and the plant is notable for the wonderful violet to sky blue half-open blooms that appear 3–12 per inflorescence on old stems from May to July. It needs very cool (40–45°F nights) and humid conditions, with a dry rest after the growths mature. It is best grown in a cool greenhouse.

■ **Blue Twinkle (Betty Goto × *canaliculatum*)** *p. 108*
This easy-to-grow hybrid has evergreen warm parentage. Grow it on a southern windowsill in warm conditions (60–65°F winter nights), and keep it fairly wet from spring to fall. Let it dry out and rest in winter. Blue Twinkle is a profuse, fragrant bloomer. The cultivar pictured is 'Carmela'.

■ **Dawn Maree *(formosum × cruentum)* *p. 109*
This hybrid is an example of the hirsute *Dendrobium*, which has black fuzzy stems. The *Dendrobium formosum* types (including the very similar and commonly grown *Den. bellatulum*), are small evergreens that resent heat and grow best on slabs. The other parent of this hybrid, *Den. cruentum,* is deciduous and needs warmth (60–65°F winter nights). Offspring such as this one can be grown narrow intermediate (55–60°F winter nights; not above 80°F days). Reduce watering somewhat in winter. The 3–5 flowers last 3 months. The cultivar pictured is 'G.J.W.' AM/AOS.

■ **Dok Phak Bung (Bandung White × Theodore Takiguchi)** *p. 109*
This is an example of the popular, easy-to-grow hybrids that have *Dendrobium phalaenopsis* heritage. They are evergreen warm (60–65°F winter nights) growers well suited to a southern windowsill. While they need no dormancy, they bloom best if water is reduced slightly after the canes mature but before the multi-flowering inflorescences appear. Keep the humidity high while plants are in bud to help the flowers open; use humidity trays and group plants together. The lower leaves may eventually fall off. The cultivar pictured is 'Lile'. Blooms last a month or so.

■ **Golden Blossom (Golden Eagle × Dream)** *p. 110*
This fragrant hybrid has deciduous *Dendrobium nobile* ancestry as well as other types. Grow it in intermediate temperatures (55–60°F nights), and give the plant a cool (45–50°F), dry rest in winter after its leaves fall. The cultivar pictured is 'Venus' HCC/AOS. Blooms last a month or more.

■ **Kalagas (Lili Marlene × *stratiotes*)** *p. 110*
These easy-to-grow Antelope Orchids are large evergreens

and need no rest. Give them warm (60–65°F winter nights) conditions on a southern windowsill atop humidity trays. Avoid excessive daytime temperatures above 80°F. Antelope *Dendrobium* can bloom more than once a year; it's also likely to have as many as 15 flowers per inflorescence, which last 6 weeks.

■ **Pink Doll (Isochidori × Utopia)** *p. 111*
The colorful "Yamamoto" hybrids such as this beauty are bred from deciduous *Dendrobium nobile*. Give them cool to intermediate temperatures (45–58°F nights) and a cool (45–50°F winter nights) dormancy with reduced water after leaves fall. They often do well in unheated sunrooms. The cultivar pictured is 'Elegance'. The multiple blooms last a month or more.

Dendrochilum
Den-droh-kye'lum
Epidendrum Group (Epidendrum Subfamily)
Epiphytic, lithophytic. Sympodial. Usually pseudobulbs

Description
The 100 species of Asiatic Golden Chain, or Necklace, Orchids send out arching racemes of numerous tiny, fragrant blooms atop gracefully arching grassy foliage on crowded pseudobulbs. Each species is often found in just a single limited habitat. Many come only from the Philippines and Borneo, and of these, *Dendrochilum filiforme* and *cobbianum* are the showiest and the most awarded. The generic name is from the Greek for "tree lip"; it's anyone's guess as to the origin.

How to Grow
Let the easy-to-grow *Dendrochilum* grow pot-bound into large specimen clumps in small pots of sphagnum moss and tree fern, or grow them on mounts; they resent repotting. They need intermediate to warm temperatures (55–65°F winter nights) with medium to low windowsill light of any exposure except north, or grow them under fluorescent lights. Provide good air movement and 50% humidity with humidity trays, and keep them evenly moist and heavily fertilized year-round.

■ *magnum* *p. 201*
As with most *Dendrochilum*, the showy inflorescences of this species remain after bloom to interesting effect.

Dialaelia (Dial.)

Dye-ah-lay′lee-ah
Epidendrum Group (Epidendrum Subfamily)
Diacrium × *Laelia*
Sympodial. Pseudobulbs

Description

The Central American species known as the Virgin Orchid *Diacrium bicornutum* is the one most often used in this 1905 hybrid genus, with a variety of *Laelia* parents. The result usually yields sprays of lovely white flowers on long spikes. The hybrid genus is still called *Dialaelia* for *Diacrium* and *Laelia*, even though *Diacrium bicornutum* is now technically known as *Caularthron bicornutum*. The pseudobulbs sometimes hollow with age; in the wild, the *Diacrium* species is often home to fire ants, which make their nests inside the empty growths.

How to Grow

Give *Dialaelia* medium to high light on any windowsill exposure except north, with intermediate temperatures (55–60°F winter nights). Let the plants dry only slightly between waterings, but reduce watering while they are not in active growth. Bloom is sometimes better in some hybrids if they are given higher light (southern windowsill).

■ **Snowflake** *(Diacrium bicornutum* × *Laelia albida)* *p. 80*
This is the most famous and most awarded hybrid, from two white parents. The 10 or more flowers can last 6 weeks. The cultivar pictured is 'Northland'.

Disa

Dee′zah; dye′zah
Orchid Subfamily
Terrestrial. Sympodial. Underground tubers

Description

Growing by the thousands in often flooded wet grasslands of tropical Africa, this spectacularly beautiful genus of 99 species has recently surged in popularity and hybridizing. The flower shape is unusual, with large sepals and intricate dorsal sepal; colors are usually brilliant. Most bloom in summer; the long-lasting tall spikes make excellent cut flowers. The name honors Queen Disa of Swedish mythology, who, when ordered to appear at a state banquet unclothed but not nude, showed up dressed in a fishnet.

How to Grow

Grow *Disa* in cool to intermediate temperatures (45–60°F winter nights; daytime highs should stay under 80°F) and medium light on any windowsill exposure except north, or grow them under fluorescent lights or in a greenhouse. Water quality is critical with *Disa*, which do not tolerate salts well and must be kept almost constantly wet. Grow them in well-drained pots filled with a mixture of peat, builder's sand, and sphagnum moss. Stand the pots in rainwater that has a pH of 4.5–6.0 to keep the plants constantly wet. Use extremely dilute fertilizer; organic fish emulsion works well. The old stem will die after bloom, when a brief drier rest is helpful; allow the standing water below the pots to dry up between waterings during this time. Unlike most orchids, *Disa* are very easy to grow from seed without laboratory conditions; seed sown at the base of the plant often germinates, and the new plant can bloom in 2 years.

■ *tripetaloides* *p. 223*
This South African streamside native has an inflorescence up to 2 ft. long. It blooms from May through August and often again in November to December. The cultivar pictured is 'Cream Kew', an exceptionally fine spotted white form from Kew Gardens; other colors include pink or yellow.

■ Blackii (*uniflora* × Luna) *p. 224*
The exquisite hooded flowers of this hybrid reach nearly 4 in. wide. The several blooms can last 2 months.

■ Kirstenbosch Pride (*uniflora* × *cardinalis*) *p. 224*
The vibrant red of *Disa uniflora* has long been the most important parent used in hybridizing this genus. The inflorescence, 2 ft. tall or more, can last 2 months, usually bearing 1–2 flowers.

■ hybrid (Kirstenbosch Pride × Kirstendior) *p. 225*
Brilliant orange is another trademark color in *Disa* hybrids. *Disa* last for weeks as cut flowers, for which there is a commercial industry.

Doritaenopsis (Dtps.)

Doe-rye-tye-nop'siss
Dendrobium Group (Epidendrum Subfamily)
Doritis × *Phalaenopsis*
Monopodial. No pseudobulbs

Description

This very popular hybrid genus is virtually synonymous with *Phalaenopsis;* both are known as Moth Orchids, bearing long sprays of exquisite flowers that last for months and months. The two genera often look and act identical, since sometimes the only difference between them is that the *Doritaenopsis* hybrid may have had a single instance of the closely related multi-flowered cerise species, *Doritis pulcherrima,* used somewhere in its ancestry. Such heritage often imparts pink or striped coloration, summer blooming, and repeat flowering to its *Doritaenopsis* hybrids. If you are looking for summer-blooming *Phalaenopsis* types, you will often find them in *Doritaenopsis.* Although the genus was created in 1923, only 6 crosses were registered in the first 30 years; there are now almost 1,500. See also *Phalaenopsis* (p. 317).

How to Grow

Easy *Doritaenopsis* prefer warm to intermediate temperatures (65–55°F winter nights) of the average home and low to medium light on any windowsill exposure except north, or they can be grown under fluorescent lights. Pot them in plastic pots filled with a well-drained mix such as medium bark and chopped sphagnum moss. Those with *Doritis* very recently in the parentage bloom better with higher light (put the plants closer to the windowpane) and a slightly finer medium; add seedling-grade bark to the mix. Keep them moist year-round. Avoid moving the pot while the inflorescence is developing, since that results in blooms twisting oddly in order to reorient to the light; water in place during this time. After bloom, cut the inflorescence just above the second node from the bottom to encourage a repeat flowering.

■ Asahi (*Phalaenopsis lindenii* × *Doritis pulcherrima*) *p. 154*
This is the first *Doritaenopsis* hybrid, from 1923, bred from two pink parents. It does best over a humidity tray.

■ Brazilian Legend (Brazilian Connection × Hawaiian Glow) *p. 155*
Pink stripes occur often in *Doritaenopsis* hybrids. The cultivar pictured is 'Maria Teresa' HCC/AOS.

■ Mythic Beauty (Chamopix × Orglade's Puff) *p. 155*
Big white *Doritaenopsis* are virtually indistinguishable from complex white *Phalaenopsis* hybrids. The cultivar pictured is 'Prince Mulligan' HCC/AOS.

Doritis (Dor.)

Doe-rye'tis
Dendrobium Group (Epidendrum Subfamily)
Terrestrial. Monopodial. No pseudobulbs

Description

The 2 species from Sri Lanka to Sumatra have small but showy, chiefly deep pink blooms on stiffly upright, 3-ft.-long inflorescences. Other colors include bluish lavender, white, and white with a colored lip. The plants are short and compact. Summer-blooming *Doritis* has been used extensively in hybridizing with *Phalaenopsis* to make the very popular *Doritaenopsis,* which has pink coloration, long spikes, and summer bloom. *Doritis* is the Greek name for the goddess Aphrodite.

How to Grow

Doritis prefers slightly higher windowsill light (any exposure except north) than *Phalaenopsis* but the same warm to intermediate temperatures (65–55°F winter nights). Pot it in fine bark and keep moist, fertilizing frequently. The roots often push the plant up out of the pot, which is normal; when repotting, simply set the roots deeper into the new pot so that the plant sits atop the mix, although it will regrow in a similar way. Evenly high humidity helps avoid bud blast. After bloom, the inflorescence can be cut just above the second jointed node from the bottom, which may encourage a repeat inflorescence.

■ *pulcherrima* p. 156
The typical color of this species most used in *Doritis* hybridizing is deep cerise, and the upright inflorescence can reach 3 ft. long, bearing many flowers. This is the species that has been used to create virtually every *Doritaenopsis* hybrid.

■ *pulcherrima* var. *coerulea* p. 156
The unusual *coerulea* variety of *Doritis pulcherrima* shown in the photo is lavender-blue. It flowers with the same upright inflorescence but has an even smaller plant habit. It grows very quickly.

Dracula (Drac.)

Drack'yule-ah
Epidendrum Group (Epidendrum Subfamily)
Epiphytic, lithophytic. Sympodial. No pseudobulbs

Description
Bizarre and furry *Dracula* have inspired many monster-evoking names (*Dracula vampira* is quintessential); the name of the genus itself is Latin for "little dragon." The small to medium-size plants are native to trees in very humid mid- to high-elevation forests, with half of them found in Colombia. Until 1978, this fascinating genus of 90 species was considered part of the genus *Masdevallia*. Plants differ from *Masdevallia* in having a prominent midrib down the center of the leaves. The flower shape is unusual, generally triangular with long-tailed sepals, and the inflorescence is often pendent, producing a succession of solitary blooms that typically peak in May.

How to Grow
Although *Dracula* have special needs, their year-round spectacular and unusual blooms make them well worth the trouble. Most species are pendent-flowered and bloom from the bottom of the container, so use hanging mesh baskets with a fine mix (seedling bark and tree fern often works well). They need high humidity, above 60% (flowers frequently wilt when brought out of humid areas for display); good air movement; narrow cool to intermediate temperatures (45–58°F winter nights; avoid daytime highs above 80°F); constant rainwater; and very little fertilizer. If the leaf tips turn black or die back, you are either fertilizing too heavily or not giving the plant enough water. *Dracula* grow well under fluorescent lights, particularly in a humid light cart or basement, or in low greenhouse light. They cannot be propagated via meristem tissue culture, only by division or from seed.

■ *bella p. 176*
One of the prettiest of these bizarre species is this one from Colombia, which can withstand lower humidity and warmer temperatures than most in the genus, making it relatively easy to grow. Grow it intermediate (52–58°F winter nights).

■ *carderi p. 176*
This cup-shaped species is found only in a limited area in Colombia. A cool grower (45–50°F nights), it can be difficult, resenting heat and low humidity.

■ *erythrochaete p. 177*
The cultivar pictured, 'Longwood Gardens' CCM/AOS, is more easily grown than most *Dracula*, tolerating lower humidity. Native to Central America and Colombia, it can be grown into a large specimen and is a good starter in the genus.

■ *gorgona* *p. 177*
The spectacular, hairy Colombian species is a showstopper, but it folds quickly if brought into low humidity.

Encyclia (Encycl.)
En-sik'klee-ah
Epidendrum Group (Epidendrum Subfamily)
Epiphytic. Sympodial. Pseudobulbs

Description
Often very fragrant, *Encyclia* generally have interesting, long-lasting flowers, some of which bloom so successively that they appear virtually year-round. Seasonally dry tropical forests of the Americas (particularly of Mexico and the West Indies) are home to most of the 235 species. Until 1974 they were classified as *Epidendrum,* and they are still registered under that genus for hybridization purposes. *Epidendrum* tend to have no pseudobulbs, whereas *Encyclia* do; they also have leathery leaves. The derivation of the generic name is Greek for "surround," referring to the flower lip that encircles the column.

How to Grow
Encyclia are easy to grow. Medium to high windowsill light of southern exposure and intermediate temperatures (55–60°F winter nights) suit most of them. They can be grown mounted or in pots of medium-coarse mix. Let them dry somewhat between waterings. Fertilize only while they are actively growing and flowering. When pseudobulb and leaf growth are finished, give the plants an even drier rest until new growth begins, but make sure the light stays bright.

■ *atropurpurea* *p. 81*
The Spice Orchid is spicily fragrant and long-lasting. It blooms from March to June. The green and white *alba* variety is pictured. Flowers can last for months. Grow it intermediate to warm (55–65°F winter nights).

■ *cochleata* *p. 81*
The modest-size Cockleshell Orchid is found from Florida to Venezuela and is one of the easiest orchids for beginners. It blooms in long succession, at least 6 months of the year, often longer, usually with 4 blooms per inflorescence open at once. Grow it intermediate to warm (55–65°F winter nights) in medium light on an eastern exposure; it will flower even under artificial light.

■ *prismatocarpa*   p. 82
This fragrant waxy-flowered species is native to Costa Rica and Panama. It blooms anytime from July to October. Give it intermediate to warm temperatures (55–62°F winter nights).

Epicattleya (Epc.)

Eh-pi-kat′lee-yah
Epidendrum Group (Epidendrum Subfamily)
Cattleya × Epidendrum
Sympodial. Pseudobulbs

Description
This 19th-century hybrid genus of the Cattleya Alliance, familiarly called "epicatts," generally has starry, open-shaped flowers and bright combinations of contrasting colors. Some epicatts really have *Encyclia* in their parentage rather than *Epidendrum,* since both genera are treated as the same for hybrid registrations. Those with reed-stem *Epidendrum* heritage can be leggy. Regardless of parentage, most are very easy to grow.

How to Grow
Grow *Epicattleya* on medium-light windowsills of any exposure except north, and give them intermediate temperatures (55–60°F winter nights). Pot them in a well-drained medium mix (fir bark and perlite works well). Let the plants dry between waterings. Fertilize them while they are actively growing.

■ Fireball *(Cattleya* Lutata × *Epidendrum cinnabarinum)*
p. 82
A tall hybrid, Fireball can grow a bit warmer and drier than most *Epicattleya,* with winter nights to 65°F. The cultivar pictured is 'Enewetok' AM/AOS.

Epidendrum (Epi.)

Eh-pi-den′drum
Epidendrum Group (Epidendrum Subfamily)
Epiphytic, lithophytic. Sympodial. Thickened canes (reed-stem) or pseudobulbs

Description
There is enormous diversity among the 800 species of *Epidendrum,* which tend to grow easily into large specimens with

hoards of often fragrant blooms. They are found from the southeastern United States to Argentina in a wide range of habitats and temperatures, typically growing on moss or rocks. Most of the types with pseudobulbs have been transferred to the genus *Encyclia*, although hybrid and award registrations still record them as *Epidendrum.* The vast majority of *Epidendrum,* therefore, have tall canelike reed-stems rather than pseudobulbs. Aerial roots commonly surround the stems, and flower inflorescences are usually branched. *Epidendrum* have been extensively interbred within the Cattleya Alliance, often imparting freedom of bloom. The generic name is from the Greek for "upon a tree."

How to Grow
There are two basic growth habits: pseudobulbous and reed-stem. Those with pseudobulbs need a drier rest after maturation of growth, while the reed-stem types, which make up the majority of *Epidendrum,* do not. Most grow in intermediate temperatures (55–60°F winter nights) in medium to high windowsill light (eastern, western, or southern exposure). All need good drainage; small pots filled with medium bark often work well, especially for those with pseudobulbs. They are normally top-heavy; place the pots inside larger clay pots to help steady them. Fertilize the plants regularly while they are in growth. The reed-stem *Epidendrum* can be divided and/or kept to manageable size by stem cuttings.

■ *cinnabarinum* *p. 83*
From coastal Brazil, this warm-growing (60–65°F winter nights), nonresupinate, successive summer bloomer likes full sun in a southern windowsill. Let it dry between waterings, and give it a dry rest after growth is finished.

■ *conopseum* *p. 83*
This is the northernmost epiphytic orchid, found from North Carolina to Mexico. Grow it cool (45–50°F winter nights) in low light on any windowsill exposure or under fluorescent lights. It likes its roots to dry out, and it often grows well on a mount.

■ *ilense* *p. 84*
This famous Ecuadorian species was eliminated from the wild by destruction of its habitat and was successfully saved from extinction by laboratory propagation at Selby Gardens in Florida. Grow it warm (60–65°F winter nights) in a hanging pot or basket in medium light of an eastern windowsill. Its pendent multiflowered bloom can appear almost anytime between June and January.

■ *porpax* *p. 84*
This dwarf, waxy-flowered species from Mexico to Peru grows into thick mats. It is sometimes placed by taxonomists into its own genus, *Neolehmannia*. The photo shows the greenish *alba* variety rather than the more common purple-green. Give it medium light (any windowsill exposure except north) and intermediate temperatures (55–60°F winter nights).

■ *stamfordianum* *p. 85*
This is the most awarded *Epidendrum*. It is a warm, seasonally dry Colombian species that easily grows into a magnificent specimen with long spikes of hundreds, sometimes thousands, of fragrant flowers on 2-ft.-long inflorescences that last a month. Grow it on a warm (60–65°F winter nights) windowsill of any medium light exposure except north. Give it a definite dry rest after it blooms.

■ Costa Rica *(schumannianum × pseudowallisii)* *p. 85*
The cross of two Costa Rican reed-stem species has produced a popular, winter- or spring-blooming clustered beauty. Grow it in any medium-light windowsill exposure except north, with intermediate temperatures (55–60°F winter nights). The cultivar pictured is 'J&L' AM/AOS.

Epigeneium

Eh-pi-gee-nee'um
Dendrobium Group (Epidendrum Subfamily)
Epiphytic. Sympodial. Angular pseudobulbs

Description
Epigeneium has a creeping habit, similar to *Bulbophyllum* growth, wherein egg-shaped pseudobulbs appear at widely spaced intervals along a wandering rhizome; some species were originally classified as *Bulbophyllum*. Unlike *Bulbophyllum*, however, this genus has very beautiful, large, showy flowers. The 12 species are native to the Asiatic tropics. The generic name is Greek for "upon the chin," describing how the petals and lateral sepals sit on the foot of the column.

How to Grow
These creeping plants do best on mounts or in shallow pots or baskets. Excellent drainage is critical. Water the plants carefully year-round, making sure water doesn't sit on the growths, since they rot very easily. Give *Epigeneium* intermediate to warm temperatures (55–65°F winter nights) and

low windowsill light of any exposure (high light can burn the leaves), or grow them under fluorescent lights. They appreciate extra humidity; add humidity trays.

■ *stella-silvae* *p. 281*
This beautiful species, which blooms for several weeks in winter or spring, is rare in cultivation. Give it extra humidity, or grow it in a greenhouse.

Euanthe (Enth.)
Yew-an'thee
Dendrobium Group (Epidendrum Subfamily)
Epiphytic. Monopodial. No pseudobulbs

Description
The single species in this vandaceous genus is native to the Philippines. Its very large three-toned flowers make it decidedly one of the showiest of the Asian orchid species. The generic name is derived from the Greek for "blooming," testament to the 6–10 flat, full blooms that are borne on each foot-long inflorescence. Plants are large and rather vinelike. Many taxonomists technically classify *Euanthe* as *Vanda* rather than as a separate genus; the difference is its balloon-like base on a 2-part lip. *Euanthe* will continue to be registered as *Vanda;* it has been used so extensively in hybridizing *Vanda* hybrids that any change would cause chaos. See also *Vanda* (p. 343).

How to Grow
Growing on trees near the sea in high sun, *Euanthe* likes warm temperatures (60–65°F winter nights; daytime highs can reach into the 90s) and the high light of a greenhouse, sunroom, or large southern windowsill. It is a superb Florida plant, loving the heat, humidity, and sun, and is easy to grow in almost any warm sunny spot. Its tangle of roots does best in a coarse open mix in a basket. When repotting is necessary, simply lift the entire basket and put it into a larger one. *Euanthe* grows best when given abundant, consistent water, never neglected. The bottom leaves will normally fall off with age.

■ *sanderiana* *p. 157*
Plants of this species with very full, overlapping petal and sepals have often been crossed and recrossed together ("line-bred"). The result are offspring with very fine floral forms that would never have appeared in the wild. The fragrant

flowers bloom for at least a month in late summer or fall, with several blooms per inflorescence.

Gastrochilus (Gchls.)

Gas-tro-kye'lus
Dendrobium Group (Epidendrum Subfamily)
Epiphytic. Monopodial. No pseudobulbs

Description
A dwarf, fan-shaped Asiatic genus of 50 species, *Gastrochilus* is notable for colorful, sometimes fringed little blooms. The generic name is Greek for "stomach lip," describing the bellylike shape of the floral lip.

How to Grow
Keep *Gastrochilus* evenly moist year-round, with high humidity and medium greenhouse light. Most will prefer intermediate temperatures (55–60°F winter nights). Put the smallest plants on mounts.

■ *fuscopunctatis* p. 157
This pendent-blooming, multibranched Taiwan native can be difficult. Mount it on cork with a base of moss and let it hang; the flowers face downward. Keep the plant moist in cool temperatures (50–55°F). It does well with *Dendrobium cuthbertsonii*. Bloom is anytime from April to July, although flowers can appear intermittently throughout the year. The cultivar pictured is 'Lil' CBR/AOS.

Gongora (Gga.)

Gon-gor'ah
Cymbidium Group (Epidendrum Subfamily)
Epiphytic. Sympodial. Small pseudobulbs

Description
The 50 species of *Gongora* inhabit ant nests in wet forests from Mexico to Bolivia. The long pendulous chains of fascinatingly complex, upside-down flowers arise from the base of the bifoliate wrinkled pseudobulbs. They are often spicily fragrant, a lure for the euglossine bee pollinators, but generally have dull colors. The name of the genus honors Don Gongora, an 18th-century Spanish bishop.

How to Grow
A hanging basket is essential, with the plant positioned so

that its pseudobulbs hang over the edge. Grow *Gongora* in intermediate to warm temperatures (55–65°F winter nights) but not above 70°F days. Give it high humidity in medium to low greenhouse light, or grow it under fluorescent lights. Keep it evenly moist, since *Gongora* does not like dry roots. Heavy fertilizer can encourage twice-a-year bloom. Move the basket to a slightly cooler spot with lower light when the flowers bloom, which will help them last longer. After bloom, let the plant have a short rest period, reducing water and fertilizer.

■ *armeniaca* p. 117
This apricot-scented, Punch and Judy Orchid is native to Nicaragua, Costa Rica, and Panama. The dangling inflorescence reaches 3 ft. long, with up to 15 flowers. It blooms primarily in summer, although flowers can appear again anytime through March.

Goodyera

Good-yer'ah
Spiranthes Subfamily
Terrestrial. Sympodial. Pseudobulbs

Description
Striking, marbled leaves are the highlight in this 55-species genus that spans the temperate and tropical world. The plants grow from a basal rosette with creeping stolons, and the small flowers borne on upright inflorescences are usually not noteworthy. The genus honors John Goodyer, an 18th-century English botanist. *Goodyera* are often called Jewel Orchids. See also *Ludisia,* another of the Jewel Orchids grown mostly for its foliage.

How to Grow
Its preference for a fine mix in a shallow pot, kept evenly moist, makes *Goodyera* more like a houseplant than many orchids. Give it low light on any windowsill exposure, or grow it under fluorescent lights. Temperate or tropical origin of a particular species will determine the growing temperature it needs; the tropicals are easiest, and most of these will be fine grown intermediate to warm (55–65°F winter nights).

■ *daubuzanensis* p. 225
From tropical Taiwan, this species with green-and-white marbled foliage blooms with white flowers from September to November. Grow it in intermediate to warm temperatures

(55–65°F winter nights). (Also pictured are two varieties of *Ludisia discolor*, another Jewel Orchid.)

Haraella

Ha-rah-el′ah
Dendrobium Group (Epidendrum Subfamily)
Epiphytic. Monopodial. No pseudobulbs

Description
Tiny plants boast relatively large fringed blooms that resemble insects, particularly bees, presumably evolved to lure them as pollinators by mimicking a possible mate. The 1 species is found only on Taiwan. The genus is named after Yoshie Hara, its 20th-century Tawainese discoverer.

How to Grow
Give *Haraella* high humidity and constant water in intermediate to warm temperatures (55–65°F winter nights). Grow them in small pots or on mounts. *Haraella* do well under fluorescent lights or in low, shaded light in a greenhouse.

■ *retrocalla p. 158*
Also known as *Haraella odorata,* this diminutive plant has beelike flowers that can appear throughout the year, with peak bloom in the fall. The several flowers last a few weeks.

Howeara (Hwra.)

How-ee-are′ah
Cymbidium Group (Epidendrum Subfamily)
Leochilus × Oncidium × Rodriguezia
Sympodial. Pseudobulbs

Description
This trigeneric hybrid genus of the Oncidium Alliance was created in 1976. *Howeara* offers charming little flowers on small plants. The genus was named for the American hybridizer of its first cross, Stephen Howe.

How to Grow
Howeara do best with humidity above 50%, abundant water, intermediate temperatures (55–60°F winter nights), and medium light. They do well in greenhouses or in humid terrariums. Both the *Leochilus* and *Rodriguezia* parents grow on guava tree twigs, so mounting the hybrids on wood is usually beneficial.

■ **Mini Primi** *(Rodricidium* Primi × *Leochilus oncidiodes)* *p. 129*
This first *Howeara* hybrid has won many awards and is still the most popular of the genus. If given high humidity, it grows very easily.

Huntleya (Hya.)

Hunt′lee-ah
Cymbidium Group (Epidendrum Subfamily)
Epiphytic. Sympodial. No pseudobulbs

Description
The fanlike *Huntleya* range from Costa Rica to Bolivia, found attached to tree trunks in wet cloud forests. The 10 species are notable for large, striking, very glossy, often bumpy flowers borne 1 to an inflorescence. Flowers can be nicely fragrant. The genus is named for an early-19th-century English orchidist, Rev. J. T. Huntley.

How to Grow
Huntleya is best grown in a greenhouse, since high humidity is preferred. Give it medium light. Most will do fine in intermediate to warm temperatures (55–65°F winter nights). Good drainage is absolutely essential. Put the creeping rhizome on a mount or use a large basket. Let the plant dry only slightly between waterings; it should never go completely dry.

■ *meleagris p. 117*
A medium-size plant from wet high-elevation forests of Brazil, Venezuela, and Guyana, this summer bloomer is fragrant. The flowers are very waxy and last at least 6 weeks. Grow it in cool temperatures (45–50°F winter nights). It is sometimes found under the name *Zygopetalum meleagris.*

Ionopsis (Inps.)

Eye-o-nop′siss
Cymbidium Group (Epidendrum Subfamily)
Epiphytic, terrestrial. Sympodial. Pseudobulbs

Description
The 3 species of *Ionopsis* bear long sprays of fragile-looking, violetlike blooms with large flat lips on diminutive plants. They are native to humid lowland tropics from Florida to

Brazil. The pseudobulbs bear 1 leaf each. The generic name is Greek for "violet appearance."

How to Grow
Ionopsis need constant year-round water, humid conditions, intermediate temperatures (55–60°F winter nights), and low greenhouse light, or they can be grown under fluorescent lights in humid terrariums. They do best mounted on twigs or in small pots, and they resent repotting. The roots prefer not to be forced down into the mix; a topping of damp moss helps keep them from drying. Mist them often. Despite all best efforts, it is not unusual for a plant to be short-lived, dying after 5 years.

■ **hybrid** *(utricularioides × paniculata)* *p. 130*
This cross may actually be a species rather than a hybrid. Some taxonomists consider these two parents to be simply varieties of the same species, but hybrid registrations have long considered them as separate. The many-flowered inflorescence can reach 30 in. long, and flowers last several weeks.

Isabelia
Iz-a-bell′ee-ah
Epidendrum Group (Epidendrum Subfamily)
Epiphytic. Sympodial. Small pseudobulbs

Description
The dwarf, tufted, needle-leaved *Isabelia* can be covered with relatively large, lovely blooms, 1–2 per inflorescence. The 2 species are found only in humid Brazilian forests. *Isabelia* is named for Isabel d'Eu, a Brazilian countess and 19th-century patron of flowers.

How to Grow
Grow *Isabelia* either on mounts or in well-drained small pots on medium-light windowsills of any exposure except north, with intermediate to warm temperatures (55–62°F winter nights). Let the plants dry out somewhat between waterings. They flower best in extra humidity; add humidity trays under the pots.

■ *violacea* *p. 86*
Although the February flowers last but a week, this easy species is a treasure in or out of bloom. Until recently it was known as *Sophronitella violacea*. The cultivar pictured is 'Christopher Bailes'.

Iwanagaara (Iwan.)

Ee-wan-ah-gah'rah
Epidendrum Group (Epidendrum Subfamily)
Brassavola × *Cattleya* × *Diacrium* × *Laelia*
Sympodial. Pseudobulbs

Description
Created in 1960, this easy hybrid genus involves four genera in the Cattleya Alliance, interbreeding that has yielded some beautiful new shapes and color blends. It deserves wider attention. The genus is named for the Hawaiian family who hybridized it, Iwanaga.

How to Grow
Place *Iwanagaara* in medium to high light on eastern, western or southern windowsills with intermediate temperatures (55–60°F winter nights). Pot them in a medium-coarse mix (bark and perlite is often fine), and allow plants to dry out somewhat between waterings. Fertilize while in active growth.

■ **Apple Blossom (*Dialaelia* Snowflake × *Brassolaeliocattleya* Orange Nuggett)** *p. 86*
This exquisite 1992 cross has been given an Award of Quality for producing offspring of exceptionally high quality. The multiple flowers last a month.

Laelia (L.)

Lay'lee-ah
Epidendrum Group (Epidendrum Subfamily)
Lithophytic, epiphytic. Sympodial. Pseudobulbs

Description
The truly gracefully beautiful *Laelia*, named for one of the Vestal Virgins, offers a long succession of multiple blooms on inflorescences that can extend to 6 ft. The 69 tiny to tall species are native to tropical America, particularly Brazil, often at high elevations. They are so closely related to the genus *Cattleya* that some taxonomists consider them "doubtfully distinct."

How to Grow
Many *Laelia* bloom best in brighter light than most in the Cattleya Alliance, preferring the high light of a southern windowsill; the Brazilian species need almost full sun. Intermediate temperatures (55–60°F winter nights) are a good start;

if plants stagnate, move them to a cooler (50°F nights) or warmer (65°F nights) spot. Mounts or well-drained pots of coarse bark and stone work best. Let the plants dry out between waterings. Give them humidity of 40–60%; humidity trays are helpful. Fertilize only during active growth. After seasonal growth is complete, let them have a dormant rest in high light, providing little water; reduce the humidity as well. Some cultivars of the dwarf "rupicolous" (*Laelia briegeri, milleri, lucasiana*) that grow on stone can be reluctant to flower. For success with these, buy proven bloomers, pot them in gravel, fertilize minimally, regularly strip dry sheaths off the pseudobulbs, and give them cool nights (45–50°F); they need a decided dormant rest after growth.

■ *anceps* p. 87
Many color forms of this famous Mexican winter bloomer exist. The short pseudobulbs of this species do best mounted or in a hanging basket of open mix. Place it in the high-light "burn" zone at the top of an intermediate-temperature (55–60°F winter nights) greenhouse. It does not like to be watered near night. Give it a decided dry dormancy period after growth is complete, keeping it in a cooler (45–50°F nights) spot. It often produces 2–5 flowers per 3-ft. inflorescence, which last about a month.

■ *harpophylla* p. 87
This Brazilian epiphyte grows intermediate to warm (55–65°F winter nights) on high-light southern windowsills. It needs no dormancy. The inflorescence bears 5–10 flowers between February and May; if given less light and cooler temperatures during this time, the blooms will last 8 weeks.

■ *jongheana* p. 88
This very beautiful, compact Brazilian species boasts 1–2 large blooms per inflorescence. It blooms for 4–6 weeks between February and May. Although it flowers best in high light, it can also be flowered under fluorescent lights.

■ *pumila* p. 88
A coveted Brazilian miniature with many color forms, this fragrant fall-blooming species needs high humidity and a decided dry rest season after growth. It often does best in a greenhouse, in medium light and cool to intermediate temperatures (48–58°F winter nights). It carries a single flower per inflorescence that lasts a month or more. The cultivar pictured is 'Black Diamond' HCC/AOS.

■ *purpurata* *p. 89*
Named the National Flower of Brazil, *Laelia purpurata* is the largest-flowered "queen" of all *Laelia*. This very fragrant species from southern Brazil often has 2–5 blooms per inflorescence and many variable color forms. The plant must be large in order to first bloom. Flowers last 4 weeks or more. Grow it intermediate to warm (55–62°F winter nights).

Laeliocattleya (Lc.)

Lay-lee-oh-kat′lee-yah
Epidendrum Group (Epidendrum Subfamily)
Cattleya × *Laelia*
Sympodial. Pseudobulbs

Description
This naturally occurring hybrid genus has become the most popular of all *Cattleya* types, with more hybrids than any other in the alliance. In 1863 it was the first intergeneric orchid genus ever created. Modern breeding has reduced the size of many of the plants, yet has left them with spectacular, large, beautiful blooms on sturdy, pronounced inflorescences that usually are in flower for about a month.

How to Grow
Medium bright light of eastern, southern, or western windowsills and intermediate temperatures (55–60°F winter nights) are fine for most *Laeliocattleya*. Pot them in medium-coarse mix (bark and perlite often works well). Let the plants dry out somewhat between waterings, and fertilize them regularly while they are in growth. Smaller types may need higher light (southern exposures) and cooler nights (50°F).

■ **Amber Glow (Derna** × **Anne Walker)** *p. 89*
A spectacular yellow Cattleya Alliance flower with a red lip such as this famous cross immediately signals the cooler-growing unifoliate *Cattleya dowiana* in the genetic background. Grow the vigorous hybrid in medium light of any exposure except north and somewhat cooler intermediate temperatures (52–58°F winter nights).

■ **Mary Ellen Carter (S. J. Bracey** × **Amber Glow)** *p. 90*
Proudly held multiple flowers well above the pseudobulbs are often a hallmark of *Laeliocattleya* breeding. The vigorous, twice-yearly blooming cultivar pictured is 'Dixie Hummingbird'.

■ **Mini Purple** *(Laelia pumila* × *Cattleya walkeriana)* *p. 90*
This diminutive plant is the product of two small species
highly prized for their large beautiful flowers. It prefers higher
humidity than most *Laeliocattleya;* grow it atop humidity
trays in medium light of an eastern or southern windowsill.
It blooms in a 3-in. pot; it also does well mounted. The cultivar pictured is 'Tamani' BM/JOGA.

■ **Platinum Sun** *(Cattleya* Francis T.C. Au × *Laeliocattleya*
Colorama) *p. 91*
"Splash-petal" *Cattleya* types such as this tricolor hybrid
harken back to *Cattleya intermedia* var. *aquinii* heritage. The
cultivar pictured is '0-1' AM/AOS.

Lepanthes (Lths.)
Le-pan'theez
Epidendrum Group (Epidendrum Subfamily)
Epiphytic, lithophytic. Sympodial. No pseudobulbs

Description
You'll need a hand lens to see the glory of the minuscule *Lepanthes* flowers to full glory, grown by connoisseurs. Most of
the 460 species, which inhabit moist high-elevation forests
from Mexico to Bolivia, are difficult to identify. The fragile
little blooms arise from the base of the leaf and often fade in
a week or so. The dwarf plants have aerial stems surrounded
by sheaths. One Ecuadorian/Colombian species in particular,
Lepanthes calodictyon, is collected primarily because of its
exquisite, scallop-edged, mottled foliage.

How to Grow
Lepanthes can be difficult. Pot them in small pots or on
mounts in airy, humid conditions with abundant water so
they never dry out. They do well under fluorescent lights, in
cool to intermediate temperatures (45–58°F winter nights),
and resent summer heat above 78°F.

■ *delhierroi* *p. 178*
Like many *Lepanthes,* this species blooms in late winter or
early spring from a delicate inflorescence.

Ludisia (Lds.)
Loo-dis'ee-ah
Spiranthes Subfamily
Terrestrial. Sympodial. No pseudobulbs

Description

Grown primarily for its remarkable, gemlike rosettes of leaves along fleshy stems, the 1 species of *Ludisia* (formerly known as *Haemaria*) has several varieties. It is native to humusy soils of tropical China and Southeast Asia. The small, fragrant, white flowers are borne on a foot-high inflorescence. *Ludisia* is often grouped with *Anoectochilus*, *Macradenia*, and *Goodyera* as the Jewel Orchids. See also *Goodyera* (p. 283).

How to Grow

Often sold as a standard houseplant in potting mix, *Ludisia* likes constant moisture, humid conditions, and very warm temperatures (65–75°F winter nights). Shallow pots are helpful, as is an equal mix of peat, chopped sphagnum moss, and sharp sand, with some ⅜-in. gravel. Let the mix dry out completely between waterings. Regular fertilizer can stimulate lavish white blooms in winter. Grow on medium- to low-light (avoid direct sun) windowsills of any exposure or under fluorescent lights. High light causes the leaf color to fade; light too low will make the stems leggy. *Ludisia* also make good terrarium candidates; line the terrarium with moist peat moss, provide an air vent through the cover, and keep at a constant temperature of 75°F for the most superb growth. To propagate new plants, cut the stem into pieces, each with two dormant buds, and place on moist sphagnum moss in a terrarium-like box with bottom heat of 80°F.

■ *discolor* *p. 225*
The velvety black, heavily veined leaves make this the most popular Jewel Orchid. The *nigra* variety (also pictured) has a single vein through the center. It blooms anytime from December through March. (Also pictured is *Goodyera daubuzanensis,* another Jewel Orchid.)

Lycaste (Lyc.)

Lye-kass′tee
Cymbidium Group (Epidendrum Subfamily)
Epiphytic, lithophytic, semiterrestrial. Sympodial. Deciduous pseudobulbs

Description

Some of the most beautiful and enchantingly fragrant orchids have been named for the lovely sister of Helen of Troy. Native from Mexico to Bolivia, the 49 medium to large species grow in shaded mid- to high elevations; some are even subjected to nighttime frosts. Their long, broad, thin leaves atop plump, tightly grown oval pseudobulbs make them distinguished-looking plants. The inflorescence arises from the base of the pseudobulb, bearing 1–2 flowers that last at least 4 weeks; it is not uncommon to have 10 inflorescences in bloom at one time on a well-grown plant.

How to Grow
Filtered light in airy greenhouses is best for *Lycaste*, which prefer to be pot-bound in loose, acidic fine mixes in small plastic pots or open baskets. Water generously but carefully to avoid easy rot of soft new growths. Let the mix dry out slightly between waterings. Provide cool to intermediate nights (45–60°F winter nights), with summer day maximum below 80°F. The yellow types often go dormant and deciduous for several months in winter; reduce watering dramatically during this time but mist them to keep the pseudobulbs from shriveling, and increase the light until new roots appear. If left undisturbed in the same pot, and fed regularly in growth, *Lycaste* grow to handsome specimen sizes with many blooms. Take care not to touch the flowers, since they bruise easily.

■ *macrobulbon*   *p. 118*
This exquisite, fragrant, deciduous yellow Colombian species blooms almost anytime, but especially in July. Grow it intermediate (55–60°F nights) and give it a cool (45–50°F), dry, higher-light rest after its leaves fall. Flowers last at least 6 weeks.

■ *skinneri*   *p. 118*
This most popular and awarded species of *Lycaste* is the National Flower of its native Guatemala. The *alba* form, known as "White Nun," is also enormously popular. Once considered one of the most endangered of all orchids, it happily has recently been taken off that list. One fragrant flower is borne per 6–12-in. spike and lasts at least 6 weeks. Grow this high-elevation species cool (48–53°F). It needs no dormancy. The cultivar pictured is 'Par-O-Bek's Sugarplum' JC/AOS.

■ Aquila (Brugensis × Jason)   *p. 119*
Peach tones can result of a blend of yellow and red parentage. The cultivar pictured is 'Detente' AM/AOS. Allow to dry somewhat after growth is complete; if its leaves fall, reduce the water even further and increase the light.

■ Jackpot (Auburn × Wyld Court)   *p. 119*
The most spectacular of *Lycaste* hybrids reveal the influence of the most popular species in hybridizing, *Lycaste skinneri*, also pictured in the color plates (p. 118). Grow it intermedi-

ate, and allow to dry somewhat after growth is complete. The hybrid cultivar pictured is 'Willow Pond' HCC/AOS.

Maclellanara (Mclna.)

Mac-lell-an-are′ah
Cymbidium Group (Epidendrum Subfamily)
Brassia × *Odontoglossum* × *Oncidium*
Sympodial. Pseudobulbs

Description
Created in 1978, this trigeneric hybrid genus boasts some of the best of the Oncidium Alliance, usually bearing long sprays of astonishingly marked red, brown, green, and yellow multicolored flowers. This freely blooming genus of good hybrid vigor is named for the Californian orchid firm of Rod MacLellan Co., which originated it.

How to Grow
Grow *Maclellanara* in pots on windowsills of any exposure except north, in medium light and intermediate temperatures (55–60°F winter nights). Let the plants dry slightly between waterings, and avoid daytime temperatures above 80°F. If a plant sulks, try a cooler spot.

■ **Pagan Love Song** (*Odontocidium* Tiger Butter × *Brassia verrucosa*) *p. 130*
This first *Maclellanara* hybrid is still the most popular by far, an extraordinary bloomer with great vigor and ease of growth. The long flower spikes last for more than a month.

Masdevallia (Masd.)

Maz-de-val′ee-ah
Epidendrum Group (Epidendrum Subfamily)
Epiphytic, lithophytic, terrestrial. Sympodial. No pseudobulbs

Description
For spectacular neon colors, amazing shapes, and "fragrances" that range from candy to carrion, few orchids rival the diminutive *Masdevallia*. The flowers are deceptively un-orchidlike in structure, since the sepals overwhelm the entire flower, often elongating into long tails, with the petals and lip so minuscule that they almost disappear. The inflorescences arise from the base of the leaves, and the majority bear a single flower each; most blooms last about a month. The 380 species are native mostly to high-elevation South American

Andean cloud forests, with more than half in Colombia. Recent discoveries of new species have brought an explosion of hybridizing, producing plants more temperature-tolerant and freer to bloom. The easiest, warmest species include *Masdevallia floribunda, bicolor, infracta, angulata, attenuata,* and *tovarensis,* although these are admittedly not especially showy. The genus is named for an 18th-century Spanish botanist, Dr. Jose Masdevall.

How to Grow
Humidity above 60% and good air movement are the true keys to success with *Masdevallia.* Keep them in small pots constantly moist with rainwater, in a shaded greenhouse or under fluorescent lights of a plastic-draped light cart or humid basement. Fertilize sparingly. Most need cool to intermediate temperatures (45–58°F winter nights). The trick to blooming even the "warmer" species is not so much keeping them cold as it is protecting them from temperatures above 80°F for any prolonged length of time. Reduce stress during hot spells on all *Masdevallia* by keeping the roots drier while increasing the humidity in the air with misting. To divide, simply pull the plants apart. *Masdevallia* cannot be cultivated via meristem tissue culture, only from division or from seed.

■ *caudata   p. 178*
This fragrant high-altitude South American species holds perky flowers, 1 per inflorescence, well above its 6-in. foliage for about a month. It needs cool to intermediate conditions (45–55°F winter nights).

■ *civilis   p. 179*
The easy flowering of this high-altitude Peruvian species is offset by the foul scent. Grow it cool to intermediate (45–58°F winter nights). Peak bloom is in March and April, although the singly borne flowers can appear all year.

■ *coccinea   p. 179*
Highly coveted for the foot-long spike with 3-in.-wide exquisite solitary bloom, this terrestrial Colombian species needs constant cool temperatures (45–50°F winter nights; not above 75°F during summer days). The solitary bloom can last a month or more. The two cultivars pictured together are 'Deep Purple' and 'Dwarf Pink' HCC/AOS.

■ *glandulosa   p. 180*
This mid-elevation Peruvian-Ecuadorian species grows intermediate to warm (55–62°F winter nights). Its pretty little flowers have a delightful fragrance of sweet-tart candy.

■ *hirtzi*   *p. 180*
This neon-flowered species was discovered in Ecuador in 1988. It grows easily and blooms freely if given a cool to intermediate spot (45–60°F winter nights).

■ *salatrix*   *p. 181*
With glossy, strikingly shaped, tubed flowers, this mid-elevation Colombian species often holds its blooms out to the sides of the medium-size leaves. Grow it in intermediate temperatures (55–60°F winter nights).

■ *schroederiana*   *p. 181*
A medium-size plant from medium elevation, this solitary-flowered, month-long winter bloomer is satisfied with intermediate temperatures (55–60°F winter nights).

■ *veitchiana*   *p. 182*
The amazing, free-blooming 8-in.-long flowers, borne 1 per inflorescence, make this high-altitude Machu Picchu lithophyte the easiest of the large showy types to grow and bloom. Grow it cool to intermediate (45–58°F winter nights). It is enormously popular in hybridizing. The cultivar pictured is 'Prince de Gaulle' AM/AOS.

■ Ann Jesup *(uniflora × veitchiana)*   *p. 182*
A decided cool-grower (45–50°F winter nights), this new hybrid is named for one of the finest *Masdevallia* growers in the country. There is 1 month-long flower per inflorescence.

■ Copper Angel *(veitchiana × strobelii)*   *p. 183*
This hybrid is one of the finest *Masdevallia* crosses ever made. It combines a tolerance for somewhat warmer temperatures with excellent shape and color; it also withstands lower humidity. Grow it intermediate (55°F winter nights). The plant grows quickly into a showy specimen of many well-held flowers that put on a month-long display. The cultivar pictured is 'Highland' AM/AOS.

■ Hincksiae *(caudata × Gairiana)*   *p. 183*
Pink coloration from *caudata* makes this 1902 hybrid still worthy of growing. Grow it cool (45–50°F winter nights)

■ Machu Picchu *(ayabacana × coccinea)*   *p. 184*
A large plant, this hybrid has beautiful long-tailed flowers that last a month. Grow it cool (45–50°F winter nights).

■ Taukau Candy *(yunganensis ssp. calogodon × triangularis)*
p. 184
The striped markings of cool-growing *Masdevallia yunga-*

nensis dominated in this recent hybrid. Grow it on the low side of intermediate temperatures (55°F winter nights). The cultivar pictured is 'Patricia' HCC/AOS.

Maxillaria (Max.)

Mak-sil-lair′ee-ah
Cymbidium Group (Epidendrum Subfamily)
Epiphytic, lithophytic. Sympodial. Pseudobulbs or no pseudobulbs

Description

A widely variable genus of 420 species from humid forests of the American tropics, *Maxillaria* is increasing in popularity because of its easy growth, intriguing flowers, and scents from chocolate to watermelon. The inflorescence often bears a single flower that arises from the base of the pseudobulb. There are two types, those with pseudobulbs and those without. The generic name is derived from the Latin for "jawbone," because the flower columns resemble insect jaws.

How to Grow

Most are easy if kept moist and given good air movement. Place them in either pots or baskets in the medium filtered light of any windowsill exposure except north, but not in direct light, and give intermediate to warm temperatures (55–65°F winter nights). Add humidity trays. Reduce water and fertilizer after flowering. Let them grow into specimens; *Maxillaria* resent repotting.

■ *picta   p. 120*
Easy and usually fragrant, this mid-elevation Brazilian species likes high southern light and tolerates lower humidity well. It blooms abundantly with many inflorescences anytime between October and March, flowering from the base of the pseudobulb on well-held stems. Grow either in a well-drained pot or on a slab. Let it dry somewhat between waterings.

■ *sophronitis   p. 120*
The dwarf creeping habit of this mid-elevation Venezuelan/Colombian species, with its pseudobulbs spaced at intervals along the brown-sheathed rhizome, makes mounting a must (tree fern works well). The relatively large flowers bloom for several weeks from the base of the pseudobulb. Keep the plant moist year-round, and give it coolish 50–55°F winter nights. It can be difficult, resenting stale conditions; keep it near a fan in good humidity.

Mediocalcar

Meed-ee-oh-kal′kar
Dendrobium Group (Epidendrum Subfamily)
Epiphytic. Sympodial. Pseudobulbs

Description
The 20 species from high-elevation New Guinea cloud forests
are notable for their un-orchidlike puffed little flowers, which
last in brilliant colors for a long time. This is a collector's item.

How to Grow
Keep moist year-round, in cool to intermediate temperatures
(45–53°F winter nights) with high humidity. Low greenhouse
or artificial light is best.

■ **species** *p. 208*
This unidentified species comes from the highlands of Papua
New Guinea, blooming in spring for at least 6 weeks.

Miltonia (Milt.)

Mil-tone′ee-ah
Cymbidium Group (Epidendrum Subfamily)
Epiphytic. Sympodial. Pseudobulbs

Description
Miltonia often look familiar, since their exquisite flowers,
known as Pansy Orchids, indeed resemble those favorite garden blooms. The 9 chiefly Brazilian species have graceful,
grassy foliage and are native from sea level to mid-elevations.
Plant growth is small to medium size. Flowers arise from the
base of new pseudobulbs. The genus is a bit confusing to
many people, because the cooler-growing *Miltoniopsis* species
were until 1976 lumped into this genus, and all hybrids and
awards, regardless of genus, continue to be registered simply
as *Miltonia*. The 1,000 hybrids are often a mix of *Miltonia*
and *Miltoniopsis* species. Both genera belong to the Oncidium Alliance and are named for the Earl Fitzwilliam, Viscount
Milton, an 18th–19th-century patron of horticulture.

How to Grow
Easier than the closely related *Miltoniopsis, Miltonia* prefer
intermediate temperatures without excessive heat (55–60°F
winter nights; summer highs below 80°F) and medium windowsill light of any exposure except north. They also bloom
under fluorescent lights. Keep them moist, but reduce watering just slightly after growth is complete. If the grassy leaves

"accordion" into crinkled pleats, the watering is insufficient or the humidity is too low; raise humidity to 40–60% by keeping the plants in groups atop humidity trays. Once the leaves accordion, they will not revert to normal shape, but the new leaves will come in fine. Pot in small well-drained pots of fine mix such as tree fern and charcoal. If hybrids seem to sulk, they may have more *Miltoniopsis* in them; give them cooler nights (45–52°F) and increase the humidity even further.

■ *spectabilis* *p. 131*
This compact Brazilian blooms massively, with 1 long-lived flower per erect inflorescence. It flowers for 6 weeks from May to June. The creeping rhizomes are often best in a basket. Grow it intermediate to warm (55–65°F winter nights).

■ *spectabilis* var. *moreliana* *p. 131*
The flowers of the variety *moreliana* are consistently much darker and larger than the typical *spectabilis,* making it the most awarded and popular *Miltonia* species. It also blooms later in the season, between August and October. The cultivar pictured is 'Linda Dayan' HCC/AOS. Grow it intermediate to warm (55–65°F winter nights).

■ Seine (Diademe × Edwidge Sabourin) *p. 132*
White *Miltonia* hybrids often glisten pristinely. But leave them on the plant; *Miltonia* flowers wilt promptly upon cutting. The cultivar pictured is 'Diamant'.

Miltoniopsis (Milt.)

Mill-tone-ee-op′siss
Cymbidium Group (Epidendrum Subfamily)
Epiphytic, lithophytic. Sympodial. Flat pseudobulbs

Description
The 5 cool-growing Costa Rican–Peruvian species were removed from the genus *Miltonia* in 1976, although they continue to be registered as such for hybridization. Often called the Pansy Orchids, these pretty, grayish green, grassy-leaved plants with flat pseudobulbs are native to mid- and high-elevation, wet cloud forests. *Miltoniopsis* is derived from the Greek for "appearance like a *Miltonia.*" See also *Miltonia* (p. 297).

How to Grow
Intermediate to cool temperatures (58–50°F winter nights)

that do not exceed the upper 70s during the day are essential; *Miltoniopsis* do best at temperatures that are never at either extreme. They also prefer humidity above 50%; add humidity trays and mist often. If the leaves "accordion," the humidity is too low. (New growth will not show the crinkling, although leaves already affected will not revert to normal.) Provide medium light on any windowsill exposure except north, or grow them in a greenhouse. They will also bloom under artificial light. Keep them moist, watering evenly year-round. *Miltoniopsis* respond well to repotting and division.

■ *roezlii*   *p. 132*
This species from lower elevations of Panama and Colombia can bloom twice a year, with 2–5 flowers per inflorescence in spring and fall. It cannot tolerate temperatures above 70°F and prefers less light than most other *Miltoniopsis;* it may even bloom in a northerly exposure.

■ Jean Sabourin (Aurora × Piccadilly) *p. 133*
The dramatic waterfall patterns in *Miltonia* hybrids such as that seen in this one usually come from cool-growing *Miltoniopsis phalaenopsis* heritage, a species found only in Colombia. There are often 3–5 blooms per inflorescence. Grow this cool to intermediate (45–58°F winter nights). The cultivar pictured is 'Vulcain' AM/AOS.

Mokara (Mkra.)
Moe-kare′ah
Dendrobium Group (Epidendrum Subfamily)
Arachnis × *Ascocentrum* × *Vanda*
Monopodial. No pseudobulbs

Description
This trigeneric hybrid vandaceous genus, created in Singapore in 1969, incorporates the scorpion-shaped barred flowers of *Arachnis* but not its ungainly height. The brilliant colors are imparted from the other genera. *Mokara* often resemble *Ascocenda* hybrids, and the blooms can last a similar 4–6 weeks. The generic name honors the hybridizer, C. Y. Mok.

How to Grow
Mokara are best suited to a bright southern windowsill, sunroom, or greenhouse, with warm temperatures (60–65°F winter nights). Give them heavy fertilizer for best bloom, and copious consistent watering. The often lanky habit is well

adapted for a hanging basket, with the roots infrequently disturbed. To repot, simply lift the entire plant and basket and place in a larger basket.

■ **Redland Sunset** (*Aranda* **Singapura** × *Ascocenda* **Yip Sum Wah**) *p. 158*
This 1983 hybrid is the most awarded of all *Mokara* crosses and exhibits brilliant coloration and lovely floral form. The cultivar pictured is 'Robert' AM/AOS. One of its parents, the famous *Ascocenda* Yip Sum Wah, is pictured on p. 153.

Mormodes (Morm.)

More-moe'deez
Cymbidium Group (Epidendrum Subfamily)
Epiphytic, lithophytic, semiterrestrial. Sympodial. Deciduous pseudobulbs

Description
The generic name means "frightful phantom" in Greek, testament to the strangely contorted and hairy flowers that arise on racemes from the base of leafless pseudobulbs. The 60 species of these Goblin Orchids are often confusing and can have separate male and female flowers, with a trigger-shot male pollen mechanism triggered by euglossine bee pollinators, similar to the closely related *Catasetum*. They range from Mexico to Brazil on decaying matter in moist forests. The fascinatingly bizarre flowers are often pendulous.

How to Grow
Although bizarre, *Mormodes* are relatively easy to grow on intermediate to warm (55–62°F winter nights) windowsills in medium light of any exposure except north. Give them plenty of water and fertilizer while they are in growth. Avoid getting water on the leaves and growths, and don't mist them, since they tend to rot. Reduce water after growth just enough so the pseudobulbs don't shrivel (the leaves will fall), then resume normal watering when the flower spikes begin to show. *Mormodes* tend to be short-lived even under excellent conditions.

■ *histrionica* *p. 207*
This small species blooms from the base of the pseudobulb for a month or so in winter or spring. The name probably refers to the torment its taxonomist had in trying to figure out which species it was; there are many confused names within this genus.

Neostylis (Neost.)

Nee-oh-sty′liss
Dendrobium Group (Epidendrum Subfamily)
Neofinetia × *Rhynchostylis*
Monopodial. No pseudobulbs

Description

This is a hybrid genus recently gaining in popularity. The diminutive single species of the long-spurred *Neofinetia* (Samurai Orchid) was first crossed with *Rhynchostylis* in 1965. The result is a sweetly fragrant and very charming genus of excellent little pot plants that grow easily and flower for at least a month.

How to Grow

Windowsill culture with medium light from any exposure except north, intermediate temperatures (55–60°F winter nights), a well-drained epiphytic mix, and even watering are best. Let plants dry slightly after flowering, until you see new leaf growth. New plantlets often form at the base and can be potted separately.

■ **Lou Sneary** *(Neofinetia falcata × Rhynchostylis coelestis)* *p. 159*
Usually a summer bloomer, Lou Sneary can flower twice a year. The fragrance is more pronounced at night.

Notylia (Ntl.)

No-till′ee-ah
Cymbidium Group (Epidendrum Subfamily)
Epiphytic, lithophytic. Sympodial. Pseudobulbs

Description

Flowers hang like dense little tails from the 50 species of compact plants of *Notylia,* found in wet lowland forests from Mexico to Brazil. The bee-pollinated inflorescence begins from the base of the unifoliate pseudobulb. The generic name is Greek for "humpback," referring to the pronounced anther callus on the column.

How to Grow

Because of the pendent blooms, pot *Notylia* in small hanging pots or on tree-fern mounts. Grow them under fluorescent lights or in low greenhouse light in intermediate to warm temperatures (55–65°F winter nights) with high humidity of

70%. Keep them constantly wet, and fertilize moderately throughout the year. *Notylia* resent repotting.

■ *barkeri*　*p. 133*
This species with prickly leaves and 12-in.-long flower chains is often found on the sides of the trees on coffee plantations of Mexico to Panama. It blooms from February to March and has a light fragrance.

Odontioda (Oda.)
Oh-don-tee-oh′dah
Cymbidium Group (Epidendrum Subfamily)
Cochlioda × *Odontoglossum*
Sympodial. Pseudobulbs

Description
This very popular intergeneric hybrid genus in the Oncidium Alliance was created in 1906, blending red *Cochlioda* color to the big beautiful *Odontoglossum* sprays. Some of the *Cochlioda* parents used are actually now classified as *Symphyglossum*, but the offspring continue to be registered as *Odontioda* to avoid hybrid list chaos. The gorgeous sprays of flowers last a month or longer.

How to Grow
Cool to intermediate temperatures of 45–55°F winter nights and summer highs that never exceed 75°F during the day are key. Grow them in medium light of eastern or southern windowsills atop humidity trays, or in a greenhouse, where the even greater humidity will be appreciated, resulting in more blooms. Provide abundant water and fertilizer year-round. Let plants dry only slightly between waterings.

■ **Eric Young (Golden Rialto** × **Niamatto)**　*p. 134*
Exquisite white flowers marked with yellow exemplify the very cool and coveted *Odontoglossum crispum* hybrids. Grow this hybrid cool (45–52°F winter nights). The cultivar pictured is 'Exotic Sunglow'.

■ **Red Riding Hood (*Odontioda* Bradsawiae × *Odontoglossum rossii*)**　*p. 134*
This 1913 hybrid is still popular today for its vivid coloring. The red coloring comes from *Cochlioda noezliana*, the species most commonly used in *Odontioda* hybridizing. This hybrid prefers cooler temperatures (45–52°F).

Odontocidium (Odcdm.)

Oh-don-toh-sid'ee-um
Cymbidium Group (Epidendrum Subfamily)
Odontoglossum × *Oncidium*
Sympodial. Pseudobulbs

Description
Two enormously popular, very closely related genera were crossed in 1911 to create an Oncidium Alliance genus of exquisitely marked, often yellow-toned sprays of big blooms. Plants are typically bountiful bloomers, with flowers that last at least a month, frequently longer.

How to Grow
Grow *Odontocidium* in the medium light of eastern or southern windowsills, with narrow intermediate temperatures (53–60°F winter nights) that don't exceed the 70s during hottest summer days. Water and fertilize well; after growth is complete, the plant may appreciate a slight drying between waterings.

■ **Artur Elle (*Oncidium tigrinum* × *Odontoglossum* Hambürhen Gold)** *p. 135*
The free-blooming, warm (60–65°F winter nights) Mexican *Oncidium* parent lends temperature tolerance and long inflorescence to this hybrid. Blooms last 6 weeks or more. Grow it 55–62°F. The cultivar pictured is 'Colombien'.

■ **Big Mac (*Oncidium maculatum* × *Odontoglossum hallii*)** *p. 135*
Lots of glossy flowers highlight this pretty hybrid that flowers winter to spring. Blooms last 6 weeks or more.

Odontoglossum (Odm.)

Oh-don-toh-gloss'um
Cymbidium Group (Epidendrum Subfamily)
Epiphytic, lithophytic, terrestrial. Sympodial. Pseudobulbs

Description
Very showy sprays of flowers with exquisite markings have made this tropical American genus of 140 medium to large species popular, despite sometimes recalcitrant growth. *Odontoglossum* are found in mountains at altitudes from 5,000 to 11,500 ft., which makes them intolerant of warm temperatures. Most of the beautifully patterned standard hy-

brids are descended from the high-altitude, wet cloud-forest Andean species, *Odontoglossum crispum*. Colors range from pure white to yellow, green, pink, brown, purple, and red, often mottled with spots, stripes, or bars. Flowers generally last at least a month. *Odontoglossum* has been extensively interbred with others in the Oncidium Alliance; in fact, taxonomists consider it very closely related to the genus *Oncidium*. The name of the genus is Greek for "tooth tongue," a reference to the toothlike crest found on most flower lips.

How to Grow
Odontoglossum can be difficult and fickle, although hobbyists on the cool, humid Pacific coast often find them very easy on windowsills. Most are cool to intermediate growers (low to mid 50s winter nights). Those with high-altitude *Odontoglossum crispum* in the heritage — ordinarily typified by predominantly white blooms — are cool-temperature growers (48°F winter nights). All *Odontoglossum* decidedly dislike heat over 75°F during the day. Although many are large plants, the roots are fine. Grow the plants in medium greenhouse light in small pots with rockwool added to the mix. Give them copious water and fertilizer year-round. Provide 60% humidity and good air movement to prevent stale conditions, which they resent. New growth is generally between fall and spring.

■ *cervantesii* p. 136
One of the smaller-growing species from high elevations of Mexico-Guatamala, this fragrant epiphyte has 3–6 flowers that appear anytime between January and May. Grow it cool to intermediate (45–58°F winter nights). The cultivar pictured is 'Celestial' AM/AOS.

■ **Stamfordiense** *(bictoniense × uro-skinneri)* p. 136
A large, robust plant with glorious, intensely colored floriferous sprays, this 1909 hybrid needs a semiterrestrial mix that incorporates finer bits than for most *Odontoglossum*. It blooms for 6 weeks in fall or winter. The cultivar pictured is 'Willow Pond' AM/AOS.

■ **Valeria** *(edwardii × Vuylstekei)* p. 137
This 1911 hybrid is fragrant. The inflorescence can reach 30 in. long, and flowers last 6 weeks.

Odontonia (Odtna.)
Oh-don-tone'ee-ah
Cymbidium Group (Epidendrum Subfamily)

Miltonia (and/or *Miltoniopsis*) × *Odontoglossum*
Sympodial. Pseudobulbs

Description
The first *Odontonia* hybrids, from 1905, were made using what is now known as *Miltoniopsis*. This Oncidium Alliance genus is popular for beautifully marked sprays on relatively compact plants. Flowers often last 4–6 weeks.

How to Grow
Odontonia are usually cool to intermediate growers, needing 45–55°F winter nights and no daytime highs above 75°F. Humidity above 50% is best. They generally grow best in a greenhouse, in medium light, although the more temperature-tolerant hybrids are often fine atop humidity trays on an eastern windowsill. Grow them in small well-drained pots of medium-fine mix, and keep them watered year-round.

■ **Debutante** *(Miltoniopsis warscewiczii* × *Odontoglossum cariniferum) p. 137*
This is the most famous and awarded *Odontonia* hybrid, registered in 1960. Its intermediate- to warm-growing *Odontoglossum* parent lends a bit more temperature tolerance. Grow the hybrid on a humid eastern windowsill in intermediate temperatures (55°F winter nights), but still avoid daytime temperatures above 75°F. The cultivar pictured is 'Oxbow' AM/AOS.

■ **Susan Bogdanow** (*Odontonia* Avril Gay × *Miltonia* Franz Wichmann) *p. 138*
Generations of complex hybridization produced this 1977 cross. The result is a vigorous hybrid that can be grown on a humid eastern windowsill in intermediate temperatures (55–60°F winter nights). The cultivar pictured is 'Aalsmeer'.

Odontorettia (Odrta.)
Oh-don-toh-ret′tee-ah
Cymbidium Group (Epidendrum Subfamily)
Comparettia × *Odontoglossum*
Sympodial. Pseudobulbs

Description
An exciting Oncidium Alliance hybrid genus created in Germany in 1975 has produced medium-small plants with floral sprays of brilliant color and striking shapes that last about a month.

How to Grow
Odontorettia do best in cool to intermediate temperatures (45–58°F winter nights), with daytime temperatures below 75°F. Grow them in medium greenhouse light with humidity of at least 50%. Water them abundantly year–round. Mount smaller types on wood; larger plants can be potted in fine bark and perlite.

■ **Mandarine** *(Odontoglossum bictoniense* × *Comparettia speciosa) p. 138*
This is an outstanding medium-size plant with excellent hybrid vigor. It can be grown on a mount.

Oeoniella (Oenla.)

Ee-oh-nee-el'ah
Dendrobium Group (Epidendrum Subfamily)
Epiphytic. Monopodial. No pseudobulbs

Description
Hot seashore lowlands of Madagascar are home to 5 small species with racemes of many small, wonderfully fragrant flowers. The generic name is from the Greek for "little bird of prey," since the flowers have the appearance of birds in flight; the vandaceous genus is named after *Oeonia,* a rarely cultivated Madagascar genus to which *Oeoniella* is closely allied.

How to Grow
High humidity is essential, so *Oeoniella* do best in a warm (60–70°F winter nights) greenhouse with medium shaded light, or under fluorescent lights in a humid environment. It's best to grow them mounted to accommodate the many aerial roots. Be sure to water and mist daily. Since these plants tend to get leggy, cut them back when they exceed 12 in.

■ *polystachys p. 193*
The tiny fringed flowers have an incredible evening scent. The inflorescence carries 7–12 blooms in winter or spring and lasts a month. If provided its high humidity, this adorable species is easy to grow into a specimen of many growths and flowers that wins many cultural awards.

Oerstedella

Oar-ste-del'ah
Epidendrum Group (Epidendrum Subfamily)
Epiphytic. Sympodial. Reed-stems

Description
This genus of 32 reed-stemmed species is found from Mexico to Bolivia, often at lower elevations. Several species are popular for their hordes of pretty little blooms. The plants have reed-stems covered with purple warts. Once part of *Epidendrum, Oerstedella* is still listed as such for hybrid registration. The genus is named for 19th-century Danish ecologist Anders Oersted.

How to Grow
Mount the plant on twiggy wood or grow it in a small well-drained pot in medium light in a greenhouse or in any windowsill exposure except north. Give it warm temperatures (60–65°F winter nights). Most *Oerstedella* do not like to dry out.

■ *centradenia* *p. 91*
A low-elevation, Pacific coast species from Costa Rica and Panama, this most familiar and easy-to-grow *Oerstedella* blooms for 6 weeks between January and March, with upside-down flowers. Since it experiences distinct wet and dry seasons in its natural habitat, it needs a drier rest after growth. It does best on a mount, as the roots must be well aired. It is sometimes found under the erroneous name *Epidendrum oerstedii*. The cultivar pictured is 'Maria Teresa' HCC/AOS.

Oncidium (Onc.)

On-sid'ee-um
Cymbidium Group (Epidendrum Subfamily)
Epiphytic, lithophytic, terrestrial. Sympodial. Pseudobulbs

Description
Long dancing sprays of little yellow flowers with big lips typify the immensely popular *Oncidium*, although its 420 species are actually very diverse. They are native to a wide range of tropical and subtropical American habitats, with most in the Andes and Brazil. "Mule-ear" *Oncidium* have large pseudobulbs and mule-ear-shaped leaves, with larger flowers. The

diminutive "equitant" (or "variegata") *Oncidium* from the warm Caribbean, with their fans of virtually pseudobulbless leaves in one plane, boast some of the most brilliant flower colors of all orchids. Many taxonomists now believe the 22 or so species of equitants should be moved to a separate genus, *Tolumnia*. Even when this becomes a firm reality, the equitants will continue to be listed for hybrid registration purposes as *Oncidium*. *Oncidium* has been extensively interbred, occurring in more than 50 new genera. The term "Oncidium Alliance" refers to the entire related group that includes *Odontoglossum*, *Miltonia*, *Cochlioda*, *Brassia*, and *Comparettia*. See also *Psychopsis* and *Baptistonia* (p. 326 and p. 238), since those genera are technically considered part of the genus *Oncidium*. *Oncidium* is from the Greek *onkos*, which means "swelling," in reference to the warty lip callus.

How to Grow
With habitats from sea level to 13,000 ft., *Oncidium* runs the gamut of cultural needs. Most are easy and tolerant and do fine in intermediate temperatures (55–60°F winter nights), in medium windowsill light of any exposure except north, with good breezes. Mount them on slabs or in small well-drained pots of medium bark and perlite. Water them well year-round, but allow them to dry out somewhat between waterings. Fertilizer will help give the most abundant bloom. More difficult are the equitant types; most people fail with the equitants when they do not provide the necessary warm to hot temperatures during the day (equitants can tolerate up 100°F if the air movement is high), with nights never below 64°F. Root health is also especially critical, requiring high air movement via fans and sharp drainage. If their special needs can be met, however, the equitants grow easily. Pot them in clay pots filled with equal parts of open mix (medium bark, or tree fern and charcoal; they can even grow in empty clay pots), or grow them mounted on cork slabs. Water and mist them daily, and keep humidity high. Give them high-nitrogen fertilizer, but only while they are actively growing. They resent repotting; let them grow into specimens.

■ *macranthum* *p. 139*
This is a high-elevation Andean epiphyte. It blooms for 4–6 weeks from May to July with large multiple flowers on a branched inflorescence that can reach 10 ft. long. Grow it cool to intermediate (45–53°F winter nights). Flowers can last 4–6 weeks.

■ *onustum* *p. 139*
Found in very dry regions of Ecuador and Peru, this very

highly awarded medium-small fall bloomer must dry completely after growth so that the pseudobulbs shrivel a bit; resume watering when new growth begins. Grow it on a mount, in intermediate temperatures (55–60°F winter nights). The inflorescence can reach 20 in., with many flowers that last at least a month. The cultivar pictured is 'Everglades' AM/AOS.

■ *pulchellum* *p. 140*
This is an equitant *Oncidium* found only in humid forests of Jamaica. Many of the equitant hybrids stem from this brilliant species. Blooms last 6 weeks. Grow it warm to hot (at least 64°F winter nights). The cultivar pictured is the outstanding form 'Skippy' FCC/AOS.

■ *varicosum* *p. 140*
Intensely yellow, many-flowered branching sprays make this easy fall bloomer widely grown and much awarded. This rewarding species from Bolivia, Brazil, and Paraguay will even bloom under fluorescent lights. Floral inflorescence extends 3–5 ft. long and lasts for 6–8 weeks. Grow it intermediate to warm (55–65°F winter nights). The preferred *rogersii* variety shown in the photo has a much larger lip and is even more branching.

■ **Bob Dugger (Gypsy Beauty × Susan Perreira)** *p. 141*
Distinct red and yellow combine in a compact equitant *Oncidium* that does well mounted. It tolerates cooler temperatures than most equitants. Grow it intermediate to warm (58–65°F winter nights).

■ **Golden Sunset (Stanley Smith × Tiny Tim)** *p. 141*
This equitant is the most heavily awarded *Oncidium* hybrid. The cultivar pictured is 'Glenn Nitta'. Grow it warm to hot (at least 64°F winter nights).

■ **Good Show (Phyllis Hetfield × Springfield)** *p. 142*
Complex breeding has produced distinctly marked equitant hybrids. This one tolerates cooler temperatures than most equitants. Grow it intermediate to warm (a minimum of 58°F winter nights). The cultivar pictured is 'Eichenfels' AM/AOS.

■ **hybrid (Nondmyre × Enderianum)** *p. 142*
There is much cool heritage in this hybrid's background, including Enderianum, a naturally occurring Brazilian hybrid, which allows it to tolerate intermediate to cool temperatures (58–45°F winter nights). It flowers for 4–6 weeks in fall or winter.

Opsistylis (Opst.)

Ahp-si-sty'liss
Dendrobium Group (Epidendrum Subfamily)
Rhynchostylis × Vandopsis
Monopodial. No pseudobulbs

Description
Opsistylis is a hybrid vandaceous genus created in 1970. It is the showiest of all the genera that have been created using the genus *Rhynchostylis*. The other parent genus, *Vandopsis*, produces massive plants with large rounded, often golden-toned flowers. The hybrid results are plants of manageable size with large, round, richly colored flowers borne in summer. The flowers last 6 weeks or more.

How to Grow
Warmth (60–65°F winter nights) and medium to high windowsill light of southern or western exposures, or greenhouse light, are best for these easy-to-grow plants. Place them in hanging baskets of open mix and disturb the roots as little as possible. When repotting, simply place the entire basket into a larger one. Water and fertilize the plants well year-round.

■ Suree *(Opsistylis* Lanna Thai × *Rhynchostylis gigantea) p. 159*
This hybrid from the first *Opsistylis* has *Rhynchostylis gigantea* (pictured on p. 169) from both parents. The flowers are among the most deeply pigmented of all vandaceous orchids and last at least 6 weeks. It needs somewhat less light; an eastern exposure works well, and prefers even more warmth (at least 64°F nights). The cultivar pictured is 'See's' AM/AOS.

Ornithocephalus

Or-nith-o-seff'ah-lus
Cymbidium Group (Epidendrum Subfamily)
Epiphytic. Sympodial. No pseudobulbs

Description
The 28 species known as Bird's-Head Orchids are diminutive fan-shaped plants with showy racemes of numerous tiny whitish blooms. They are found at low elevations in misty forests from Mexico to Brazil, often growing on small twigs with their roots moss-covered.

How to Grow
Ornithocephalus grow easily if they are kept moist in a humid, low-light spot (fluorescent lights in a basement or a plastic-draped light cart works well). Give them intermediate to warm temperatures (55–65°F winter nights). Mossy twigs are their natural homes, so mounts work best, or else use small pots of moss and tree fern. The plants should dry slightly between waterings. They flower best if given regular weak fertilizer. Plantlets that arise at the base of the plants can be removed and potted separately.

■ *inflexus* p. 121
Native from Mexico to Panama, this species blooms for 3–4 weeks in summer or fall. The several-flowered inflorescence is usually 3–4 in. long.

Pabstia (Pab.)
Pab'stee-ah
Cymbidium Group (Epidendrum Subfamily)
Epiphytic, lithophytic. Sympodial. Pseudobulbs

Description
The five species are found only in Brazil. The pretty, long-lasting, waxy flowers are borne 2–4 per inflorescence on medium-size plants with small clusters of unifoliate pseudobulbs. Leaves are glossy green. The genus was called *Colax* until 1975, when it was realized that another genus named *Colax* already existed. *Pabstia* honors Brazilian orchid scientist Guido Pabst.

How to Grow
Easy *Pabstia* like humid, intermediate to warm conditions (55–65°F winter nights). They can be grown in low to medium light of any windowsill exposure except north, or under fluorescent lights. Add humidity trays under the pots. Water and fertilize them well during growth, reducing water slightly after growth is complete. Pot them in a coarse mix such as bark, repotting infrequently. They grow well alongside *Zygopetalum*.

■ *jugosa* p. 121
This is the most familiar species. It can bloom almost anytime, with as many as 4 very waxy, fragrant flowers per inflorescence that last 6 weeks. It is often found under the name *Colax jugosus*.

Paphiopedilum (Paph.)

Paff-ee-oh-ped'i-lum
Cypripedium Subfamily
Terrestrial, (rarely) epiphytic. Sympodial. No pseudobulbs

Description

These enormously popular tropical lady's slippers are the single most hybridized and awarded orchid genus. The flowers of the 60 species and thousands of hybrids run the gamut of oddly pouched shapes and colors, often with stripes, spots, and "warts," inspiring great passion in collectors. Many types also have beautifully mottled foliage, pretty even out of bloom. Flowers can last for months. *Paphiopedilum* are found from southern India through New Guinea and the Philippines, mostly in montane forests with high seasonal rains and frequently long dry seasons. Paphos is a Mediterranean island with a temple devoted to Venus; *pedilum* is Greek for "slipper," referring to the pouched slipper shape of the lip.

How to Grow

Many *Paphiopedilum* make good houseplants on low- to medium-light windowsills of almost any exposure except north, or under fluorescent lights. Multifloral types, often with long unmarked green leaves, do better in the higher light of southeastern exposures. Most *Paphiopedilum* are intermediate to warm (55–65°F winter nights) growers, although the green-leaved types that do not produce long multifloral sprays tend to like cooler temperatures (45–55°F winter nights). *Paphiopedilum* prefer small deep pots to accommodate the large furry root system, with semiterrestrial mix (such as fine bark and chopped sphagnum moss). Water so that the mix never quite dries out. These plants respond well to repotting; repot often, as soon as the mix seems the least bit stale. If bloom appears reluctant, provide the plant with cooler nights (50–55°F) and more humidity, although patience and age may be more the factors. *Paphiopedilum* cannot be propagated via meristem tissue culture, only by division or from seed.

■ *bellatulum* *p. 212*

From Burma-Thailand, this mottled-leaved, highly awarded species from the Brachypetalum (broad-petaled) section of *Paphiopedilum* grows on mossy limestone. One or two flowers bloom on a short stem usually for the month of May. The leaves have spotted purple undersides. Grow it in low light and intermediate temperatures (55–60°F winter nights). Provide extra humidity from a humidity tray under the pot. Add limestone to the mix. Allow it to dry out between waterings and also after growth. Similar species are *Paphio-pedilum concolor* and *Paph. niveum,* which are grown the same.

■ *delenatii p. 213*
Everyone seems to like this species, even people who usually don't like *Paphiopedilum.* Found only in northern Vietnam, the prized pink beauty flowers from March to June, with 1–2 fragrant flowers per inflorescence. The mottled leaves have spotted purple undersides. All the plants known today stem from a single specimen saved in 1922 and successfully grown in France. Grow it in sheet moss, low light of any exposure except north, and warm temperatures (60–65°F); a somewhat cooler period (55°F) in winter can help in flowering this sometimes reluctant bloomer.

■ *gratrixianum p. 213*
Glossy-flowered and green-leaved with spotted purple leaf undersides, this easy-to-grow solitary-bloomed terrestrial from Laos grows readily into specimen size. Two color forms are shown. Grow it warm (60–65°F winter nights), in medium light of any exposure except north. Similar species are *Paphiopedilum insigne* and *Paph. exul,* which are grown the same.

■ *hirsutissimum p. 214*
The hairs on the back and stem of the solitary flower give this robust Indian-Chinese green-leaved species its name. The vigorous plants bloom from March to May. Grow them in intermediate temperatures (55–60°F winter nights), medium light, and provide a distinct dry period after growth.

■ *lowii p. 214*
An epiphytic green-leaved species from the Malay area, this generally blooms from March to May, although it can surprise you with flowers almost anytime. Its floral inflorescence can reach 30 in. and, when well grown, can have up to 10 flowers. Grow it warm to intermediate (65–55°F winter nights) in medium light.

■ *micranthum p. 215*
Found only in Yunnan, China, this recently introduced little species has beautifully mottled purple and dark green foliage. The name is misleading, since the solitary flower is huge, with an incredible balloonlike pouch. It has won many awards. Grow this terrestrial intermediate (55–60°F winter nights), with low light. Add limestone to the mix. It can be a very slow and reluctant grower.

■ *venustum* *p. 215*

The Snakeskin Orchid from lowland Nepalese regions is so named for its gorgeous foliage, which is marbled green above, with purple undersides. It is also notable for the heavily veined pouch of its solitary winter flower. Grow it in low light in a warm and humid spot in summer (to 90°F), and keep it very moist; let the night temperatures drop to cool to intermediate (45–55°F nights) in winter and spring, and let it dry somewhat between waterings.

■ Clair de Lune (Emerald × Alma Gavaert) *p. 216*

This 1927 hybrid is a classic example of the very popular, easy-to-grow "Maudiae"- or *callosum*-type *Paphiopedilum*. Maudiae types are so named because the first of this type was bred from the lowland Southeast Asian species *Paphiopedilum callosum*, (with *Paph. lawrenceanum*) to create *Paph.* Maudiae. They are highly coveted for the exquisite, usually solitary bloom per inflorescence and mottled foliage. Grow them warm (60–65°F winter nights) in low light. The cultivar pictured, 'Edgar Van Bell' AM/AOS, is considered an *alba* form, even though it is green and white rather than pure white.

■ Gilda (Dena × Dramatic) *p. 216*

Big, complex hybrids have astonishingly round and waxy flowers. The plants are easy to grow in the medium light of almost any windowsill except north and in intermediate temperatures (55–60°F winter nights).

■ Iona (*bellatulum* × *fairrieanum*) *p. 217*

An exquisite 1986 primary hybrid between two species, Iona grows warm (60–65°F winter nights) in low light. It has mottled foliage and bears a solitary bloom per inflorescence. The cultivar pictured is 'A&P'.

■ Julius (*lowii* × *rothschildianum*) *p. 217*

An old (1914) but magnificent multifloral with a 2-ft. flower stem, Julius still wins awards when the cross is remade. Five to 8 flowers per inflorescence is not uncommon. Grow it in medium light in warm temperatures (60–65°F winter nights). The cultivar pictured is 'Maria Teresa' FCC/AOS.

■ Leeanum (*insigne* × *spicerianum*) *p. 218*

Created more than 100 years ago, this vigorous hybrid blooms in winter. It usually has a solitary flower per inflorescence, sometimes double-bloomed. Grow it cool to intermediate (45–60°F winter nights) in medium light.

■ **Ma Bell** *(bellatulum × malipoense) p. 218*
This is an unusual newer primary hybrid using the green-flowered *Paphiopedilum malipoense,* a Chinese species often strongly scented of raspberries, although the fragrance can be nonexistent in other cultivars. Grow this hybrid in intermediate temperatures (55–60°F winter nights) and low light, and keep it moist. It usually bears 1 flower per inflorescence. The cultivar pictured is 'Jamboree' HCC/AOS.

■ **Raisin Expectations** (Raisin Jack × Maudiae) *p. 219*
Maudiae hybrids, also known as *Paphiopedilum callosum* types, are remarkably easy to grow. The deepest red varieties, or "vini-colors," approach the elusive black color. This hybrid usually has a single large flower per inflorescence. This is a 1994 cross. Grow it warm (60–65°F winter nights) in low light.

■ **St. Swithin** *(philippinense × rothschildianum) p. 219*
Multifloral *Paphiopedilum rothschildianum* hybrids such as this one are among the most prized; St. Swithin is a famous cross between two very closely related species. They need more light (southeast or south exposure) but are very slow growers. This one took 10 years from seedling to first bloom, finally producing an 18-in.-flower spray. It typically will bear 3–5 blooms per inflorescence. Grow it in warm temperatures (60–65°F winter nights).

Paraphalaenopsis
Pair-ah-fail-ay-ee-nop'siss
Dendrobium Group (Epidendrum Subfamily)
Epiphytic. Monopodial. No pseudobulbs

Description
Originally considered part of *Phalaenopsis,* these 4 somewhat gawky Borneo species were classified separately in 1963. Curiously, award and hybrid registrations still lump them under *Phalaenopsis,* even though none has ever been interbred with that genus, and they are in reality more closely allied with *Vanda.* The terete leaves, round in cross section, can reach $2^1/_2$ ft. long and often are pendulous. The large lavender-pink or greenish brown flowers usually bloom in summer on thick upright stems and are decidedly less graceful-looking than *Phalaenopsis.*

How to Grow
Grow *Paraphalaenopsis* in baskets, in hanging pots, or

mounted to accommodate the pendulous growth. Provide medium to low light on warm (60–65°F winter nights) windowsills of any exposure except north. Keep the plants moist. They can be reluctant growers.

■ **Asean** *(Boediardjo × denevei)* *p. 160*
All of the *Paraphalaenopsis* species are fairly rare. Hybrids such as this one are more apt to be seen in cultivation than are species. The greenish brown *Paraphalaenopsis denevei* is considered the best parent; it produced the deeply pigmented hybrid pictured. The inflorescence is often pendent and bears up to 15 flowers that last about 3 weeks.

Phaius (Phaius)

Fay'us
Epidendrum Group (Epidendrum Subfamily)
Terrestrial, epiphytic. Sympodial. Pseudobulbs

Description
The 45 species are native to lowland and montane Indo-Malaysian and Chinese forests. The plants have short or stemlike pseudobulbs that produce tall spikes of large tannish red-yellow and white successive blooms that last a long time. Flowers darken with age. They are often grown outdoors in gardens in mild climates. *Phaius* is from the Greek for "dusky," indicating the color tones in the flowers.

How to Grow
Phaius prefer low light and warm to intermediate temperatures (65–55°F winter nights). The tall size makes them best suited for a greenhouse or a sunroom, although they grow fine in a large picture window. Pot them in deep well-drained pots with semiterrestrial mix. They bloom best when fertilized regularly. Keep them moist but not soggy. Avoid splattering the leaves with water; they rot easily. For better blooming, divide and repot the plants frequently after they flower. *Phaius* can also be grown outdoors in frost-free climates in well-drained shaded spots. New *Phaius* plants can be rooted from the flower stalks after they have bloomed; cut them into 6-in. pieces, each bearing 2 nodes, and place on moist sand until new growth is seen, when they can be potted.

■ **hybrid** *(grandifolius × Gravesiae)* *p. 197*
Blooming in winter or spring, this hybrid is very similar to the well-known *Phaius tankervilleae*. The 10–20 flowers are fragrant and can last for months.

Phalaenopsis (Phal.)

Fail-en-op'siss
Dendrobium Group (Epidendrum Subfamily)
Epiphytic, lithophytic. Monopodial. No pseudobulbs

Description

Phalaenopsis, known as the Moth Orchid, is probably the most beloved orchid plant, and it is classically a beginner's first orchid. The generic name is from the Greek for "moth appearance," referring to the beautiful sprays of typically white blooms that resemble big moths in wide-winged flight. Actually, the "Moth Orchid" label really only befits those types with long sprays of many white blooms. *Phalaenopsis* can also have intensely colored, often waxy flowers, borne on short inflorescences. The *Phalaenopsis* color range includes white to white with colored lip, pink, yellow, green, and red, with spots, stripes, or barring, and many combinations thereof. The 44 species are found from the eastern Himalaya Mountains to Australia, with most native to the warm Philippine lowlands. The plant habit is pretty, with low-growing, elongated round leaves arising from a central crown. A well-grown plant can send up multiple inflorescences, and many species produce numerous flowers. Each bloom can last a month or more, and the plant can flower for 6 months at a time, often sending up new inflorescences and reblooming. The little "multifloral" types have tinier flowers, but they send up so many branching sprays that just one plant can seem like an entire orchid show. *Phalaenopsis* make excellent cut flowers, lasting 2 weeks in water. They have been extensively interbred and, together with the almost synonymous hybrid genus *Doritaenopsis*, constitute even more hybrids than *Paphiopedilum*. *Phalaenopsis* is also involved in some 50 new hybrid genera. See also *Doritaenopsis* (p. 274).

How to Grow

Phalaenopsis are very easy houseplants on low light windowsills (any exposure except north, or grow them under fluorescent lights). They like warm temperatures (60-65°F winter nights), and need a decided temperature drop between day and night of at least 10 degrees in late summer and fall in order to induce buds. Pot in a medium-fine mix (medium bark with perlite and chopped sphagnum moss often works well). Keep them moist, letting them dry only slightly between waterings. Fertilize often from spring to early fall. A classic complaint is that the buds "blast" and fall off before they open. To prevent this, keep the humidity from fluctuating widely when they are in bud and protect them from drafts. When the beginning flower inflorescence is about 4 in. high, tie it loosely to a tall, thin stake; tie it loosely again when it reaches 8 in. high, and then allow the spike to arch naturally for the best floral display. Avoid moving the pot while the flower inflorescence is developing, since that will result in the flowers twisting oddly in order to reorient to the light; water the pot in place instead. After bloom, if the end of the flower inflorescence is no longer green, cut it back to just above the second node from the bottom, which may encourage a secondary inflorescence. To facilitate longer bloom, keep the plant in lower light and cooler temperatures (55–60°F) while in flower.

■ *amboinensis* *p. 160*
The waxy blooms of this species from the Moluccas archipelago each last a long time, 2 months or more. It has been extensively used as a hybrid parent, often yielding yellow offspring, although flower color tends to fade with age, as it does in this species.

■ *aphrodite* *p. 161*
This dainty-flowered Philippine species is frequently at the origin of today's big white hybrids. It is sometimes called *Phalaenopsis amabilis,* although taxonomists now consider them closely related but separate species. When necessary, it can often tolerate cooler temperatures better than other *Phalaenopsis* can, to 55°F winter nights.

■ *equestris* *p. 161*
This Philippine/Taiwanese native is a compact "multifloral" *Phalaenopsis* that produces many little blooms on branching foot-long sprays. The oval leaves are commonly purplish underneath. The cultivar pictured, 'Bedford Fleur Delice' JC/AOS, is peloric, which means that the petals have attempted to become additional lips. It blooms in fall, although flowers can reappear almost any time of the year. Grow it in a very small pot.

■ **Class President (James Hausermann × Spica)** *p. 162*
Flowers of firm substance and concentric striping, such as in this excellent cross, harken back to the waxy Philippine species *lueddemanniana* and *fasciata.* The cultivar pictured is 'Golden Eagle' AM/AOS.

■ **Little Hal (Cassandra × Peppermint)** *p. 162*
Little multiflorals with lots of blooms on branching sprays are enormously popular. They are often produced from pink *equestris* and spotted *stuartiana* heritage, as in this well-known cross. The cultivar pictured is 'Diane' AM/AOS.

■ **Medford Star (Joseph Hampton × Celie)** *p. 163*
Big complex white *Phalaenopsis* can approach dinner-plate size flowers, arranged in gorgeous spacing along the inflorescence. To make sure the display orients properly to the light, don't move the pot while the inflorescence is developing.

■ **Miva Smartissimo (Entrechat × Elise de Valec)** *p. 163*
This 1988 hybrid shows the classic spotted breeding of the "French" *Phalaenopsis,* so called because of extensive hybridizing in France using *Phalaenopsis stuartiana.* Although pretty, the flowers tend to be floppy with thin substance.

■ **Sandra Livingston (Golden Gift × *venosa*)** *p. 164*
Unlike other yellow *Phalaenopsis, venosa* hybrids such as this one tend not to fade in color with age.

■ **Sierra Gold (Deventeriana × Mambo)** *p. 164*
The yellow *Phalaenopsis amboinensis* was present as grandparent on both sides to produce this vivid yellow color. Yellow *Phalaenopsis* can be slow growers and often need higher light (eastern or southern windowsill).

■ **Zuma Aussie Delight (Sweet Memory × *venosa*)** *p. 165*
This recent hybrid is bred with one of the few fragrant *Phalaenopsis, violacea,* in the heritage; its offspring can also be sweetly scented. The cultivar pictured is 'Zuma Canyon' AM/AOS.

■ **Zuma Urchin (Shu King × Debbie Wallace)** *p. 165*
This hybrid is an example of the very popular "white with colored lip" (WCL). It has just a hint of exquisite pink suffusion and veining.

■ **hybrid (Roy Fukumura × Ida Fukumura)** *p. 166*
Big pink hybrids are a perennial favorite. As in this hybrid, the pink in *Phalaenopsis* hybrids often stems from *Phalaenopsis schilleriana,* which also has mottled foliage.

■ ***stuartiana* hybrid (Kathleen Voelker × *stuartiana*)** *p. 166*
Stuartiana hybrids typically display spotted sepals and lip and branching habit, although flower substance can be thin and floppy; foliage is often mottled.

■ ***violacea* hybrid (George Vasquez × *violacea*)** *p. 167*
Breeding for red *Phalaenopsis* is an ongoing quest. *Violacea* hybrids can be fragrant, although flower count is frequently diminished, and plants tend to be slow-growing. Don't cut the spikes, however, since the blooms can appear successively at the ends for years.

Phragmipedium (Phrag.)

Frag-mi-pee'dee-um
Cypripedium Subfamily
Terrestrial, lithophytic, epiphytic. Sympodial. No pseudo-bulbs

Description

The long-tailed, mustache-faced Mandarin Orchids, also known as phrags, are allied to the *Paphiopedilum* lady's slippers, with which they have just begun to be interbred. The tails are actually long narrow petals, often beautifully twisted; pollinators may be able to crawl from the ground up the petals to the sexual portion of the flower. The dramatic flowers usually are successively produced on long spikes; each bloom lasts about a month, then drops off suddenly, still in pristine condition. The 16 very interesting species often grow on rocks along Central and South American streamsides, their roots seasonally immersed. The generic name is derived from the Greek for "divided shoe," in reference to the divided ovary and the slipper-shaped pouch.

How to Grow

Give *Phragmipedium* intermediate temperatures (55–60°F winter nights; avoid daytime temperatures above 90°F) and medium light on eastern or southern windowsills. Most will also bloom under fluorescent lights. *Phragmipedium* prefer small pots and a semiterrestrial mix such as one of seedling bark, chopped sphagnum moss, and charcoal. Fertilizer should be weak, and rainwater is a decided boon; keep plants fairly moist, somewhat more so than for *Paphiopedilum*, along with which they can grow quite well. Actively growing phrags often benefit when their pots are placed in trays of standing water; after growth is complete, allow plants to dry slightly between waterings. Let the plants grow into specimens rather than constantly dividing them; the resulting floral display can be astonishing. If bloom is reluctant, increase the water, light, and/or temperature. *Phragmipedium* cannot be propagated via meristem tissue culture, only by division or from seed.

■ *besseae* p. 220
Discovered in the 1980s, this highly coveted Colombian-Peruvian native is the only scarlet red *Phragmipedium*. Forms are very variable. Grow it cooler (48–55°F winter nights) and keep it constantly wet.

■ *longifolium* p. 220
This large terrestrial successively blooms one at a time over

a long period on a long inflorescence. This species likes a wide day/night temperature variation of at least 25°F (75°F days, 50°F nights, if possible).

■ *wallisi* *p. 221*
Native to Ecuador, this species has 3–6 very long-petaled flowers open at once. It is very similar to the more commonly available *Phragmipedium caudatum*. The cultivar pictured is 'Hamish Hog'.

■ Dominianum *(caricinum × caudatum)* *p. 221*
This extraordinary beauty is the oldest of all *Phragmipedium* hybrids, first made in 1870 yet still widely cultivated. It usually bears 4–5 blooms open at once per tall inflorescence.

■ Grande *(caudatum × longifolium)* *p. 222*
An old hybrid from 1881, the very long-petaled Grande easily grows to specimen size. Its multiflowered, successive-blooming inflorescence can reach 5 ft. Give it wide day/night temperature variation.

■ Mary Bess *(besseae × caricinum)* *p. 222*
A 1991 hybrid between cool-growing scarlet *besseae* and intermediate-growing lime green *caricinum,* this hybrid likes lots of water and intermediate to cool conditions (60–45°F winter nights). It carries several blooms open at once per inflorescence.

■ Schroederae *(caudatum × Sedenii)* *p. 223*
This is another early hybrid from 1882, with pink coloration that comes from the small-growing Colombian *schlimii* species in its heritage.

Pleione (Pln.)
Plye-oh'nee
Epidendrum Group (Epidendrum Subfamily)
Epiphytic, lithophytic. Sympodial. Deciduous cormlike pseudobulbs

Description
Pleione have become very popular only recently, as collectors discover the often fragrant, large, delightfully fringed blooms atop tiny plants. Native to seasonally dry, mid- to high-elevation forests in the Himalaya and Southeast Asia, the 15 species are sometimes called Indian Crocus. They are treated more like bulbs than typical orchid plants. The flowers ap-

pear either before the new growth or with it; 2–3 flowers bloom from the base of the new pseudobulbs, which carry 1–2 6-in. leaves. Each pseudobulb lasts but a single year. In Greek mythology, Pleione was the mother of seven daughters of Atlas, who were turned into the Pleiades constellation.

How to Grow
Plant the cormlike bulbs in a shallow pot of chopped sphagnum, with bulbs half covered and about 1 in. apart. While they are in growth, put them in medium light on windowsills of any exposure except north or in a greenhouse in intermediate to cool temperatures (50–45°F nights). Fertilize them only while the roots are growing, evidenced by flowers and new growth. The plants rest a bit after flowering. Water the plants carefully to avoid splashing the leaves, which spot easily. After their leaves fall, *Pleione* need a cool (35°F), absolutely dry rest in fall and winter. This 4–5-month true dormancy can take place in a refrigerator drawer; store the bulbs in their pot of sphagnum or in a paper bag of dry peat moss. In late January or February, remove the bulbs, clean them, repot and water them, place them back in light, and wait for flowering. Although most commonly encountered *Pleione* bloom in late winter or spring, the Indian species may be autumn flowerers; these are repotted right after bloom.

■ *pricei p. 201*
Sometimes this fine Tibetan species is considered a variety of *Pleione bulbocodioides* or *formosana*. The late winter or spring inflorescence appears with the new leaf. The fragrant blooms last several weeks.

Pleurothallis
Plur-oh-thal′liss
Epidendrum Group (Epidendrum Subfamily)
Epiphytic, lithophytic, terrestrial. Sympodial. No pseudobulbs

Description
In a recent recount and reorganization of all orchid species, *Pleurothallis* has become the genus with the largest number of species — 1120 — pushing the long-standing *Bulbophyllum* off the top of the chart. Most of the flowers, however, are so small that they require magnification to be enjoyed. Collectors are connoisseurs of these confusing American tropicals, which are often found in wet cloud forests. Plant habit is multistemmed and varies from minuscule to large. The generic name is Greek for "riblike leaf stalks."

How to Grow

Most *Pleurothallis* are easy given humid conditions, small pots or mounts, and low to medium greenhouse light or fluorescent lights. Water them well, keeping them moist, but let them dry out somewhat between waterings after the leaves are fully formed. They tend to grow year-round. Temperature needed depends on the elevation of the native habitat. If in doubt, start with intermediate conditions (55–60°F winter nights). Divide the tufted types if the central leaf portion begins to die out; they can take 2 years to reestablish after division.

■ *sanderana* *p. 185*
This is one of the showier species. It is easily grown into a specimen of many growths and flowers. Grow it intermediate (55–60°F winter nights). Blooms can last a month.

■ *truncata* *p. 186*
Flowers often lie across the leaf in this genus. Grow this species intermediate (55–60°F winter nights).

■ species *p. 185*
Pleurothallis are so little studied that is common to see them for sale simply labeled "species." Grow this one intermediate (55–60°F winter nights).

Polycycnis (Pcn.)

Pol-i-sik′niss
Cymbidium Group (Epidendrum Subfamily)
Epiphytic, terrestrial. Sympodial. Pseudobulbs

Description

The name is Greek for "many swans," an apt description of the intricate slender flowers on long hanging racemes. Found from Costa Rica to Brazil, the 15 mostly summer-blooming species inhabit mid-elevation embankments in wet forests. Plant size is usually medium, with ovoid unifoliate pseudobulbs.

How to Grow

To prevent rot, grow *Polycycnis* in a breezy, humid greenhouse in a spot that receives medium light. Intermediate to warm temperatures (55–65°F winter nights) are best. To accommodate the pendent flowers, place the plants either in baskets or on mounts. Water them copiously year-round, except when growth is complete, when watering can be slightly reduced. Keep water from sitting too long on the growths, which can rot.

■ *morganii* *p. 122*
As with most *Polycycnis,* the flowers of this species are exceedingly short-lived, fading within a week.

Polystachya (Pol.)
Pol-ee-stack'ee-ah
Epidendrum Group (Epidendrum Subfamily)
Epiphytic, lithophytic, (rarely) terrestrial. Sympodial. Pseudobulbs

Description
Racemes of many tiny upside-down flowers on small plants typify *Polystachya,* of which only a few of the 150 species are generally grown. Most are found in Africa, from low to high elevations, although they also appear in Asia and the tropical Americas. The plants can range from small to large. The generic name means "many ears of grain," which refers to either that type of appearance of the tufted stems of some species or the inflorescence in others.

How to Grow
Most are easy in medium to low light on any windowsill except north in small pots or mounts at intermediate to warm temperatures (55–65°F winter nights). Those with prominent pseudobulbs need to dry a bit between waterings. Most tolerate 40% humidity but prefer more.

■ *paniculata* *p. 209*
Definitely among the nicest *Polystachya,* this plant of Sierra Leone to Uganda has brightly colored, dense flowers on a branched inflorescence, purple-suffused leaves, and prominent pseudobulbs. It is one of the larger species. Allow it to dry slightly between waterings. Blooms last several weeks or more. Grow it intermediate (55–60°F winter nights).

Porroglossum
Por-roe-gloss'um
Epidendrum Group (Epidendrum Subfamily)
Epiphytic. Sympodial. No pseudobulbs

Description
The odd little fused-sepal flowers on tiny plants have a trap-

door lip that swings shut when touched, which is why the Greeks named it "distantly held tongue." Most of the 30 species inhabit mossy branches in mid-elevation Andean montane forests. The plant habit is a creeping rhizome; the few flowers are borne successively on racemes.

How to Grow

Keep *Porroglossum* moist in small pots in intermediate to cool temperatures (60–45°F winter nights). Pendent-flowered types are better in open mesh baskets. Give them low to medium greenhouse light, or grow them under fluorescent lights. Most grow easily.

■ *olivaceum* *p. 186*
This species is native to mountains of Ecuador and Colombia. It can be grown in a small pot.

Potinara (Pot.)

Pot-tin-ah'rah
Epidendrum Group (Epidendrum Subfamily)
Brassavola × *Cattleya* × *Laelia* × *Sophronitis*
Sympodial. Pseudobulbs

Description

The first in this four-generic hybrid genus of the Cattleya Alliance was produced in 1922. The large showy lip comes from the *Brassavola* parentage, the vivid color and round flowers from *Sophronitis,* color and many blooms from *Laelia,* and the large flower size from *Cattleya.* This complex mélange often yields frequent flowering, sometimes three times a year, with month-long blooms.

How to Grow

Medium windowsill light in any exposure except north and intermediate temperatures (55–60°F winter nights) are usually fine. Grow them in pots of medium-coarse mix (bark and perlite usually works well). Let them dry somewhat between waterings, and fertilize them regularly while they are in growth. If your plant is reluctant to bloom, try brighter light (southern windowsill) and cooler temperatures (to 50°F nights).

■ Beaufort Gold (*Brassolaeliocattleya* Waikiki Gold × *Sophrocattleya* Beaufort) *p. 92*
The small size of the *Sophrocattleya* parent keeps this 1989 hybrid compact. It does best on the cooler side (50–55°F win-

ter nights) and kept somewhat wetter. The cultivar pictured is 'South River' AM/AOS.

Promenaea (Prom.)

Pro-men-eye'ah
Cymbidium Group (Epidendrum Subfamily)
Epiphytic. Sympodial. Pseudobulbs

Description
Pretty, slightly cupped, waxy, medium-size blooms on often dwarf plants make the 14 species of *Promenaea* showy and worthwhile. These *Zygopetalum* relatives are native to moist forests of Brazil. There is usually only 1 flower per short inflorescence, normally blooming from the base of the small round pseudobulb. The leaves are gray-green. Flowers can last 6–8 weeks. Promeneia was a priestess at the mythical Greek oracle at Dodona.

How to Grow
Promenaea are easy. Grow them in small shallow pots or mounted in medium to low windowsill light of any exposure except north, or grow them under fluorescent lights. Give them intermediate to warm temperatures (55–65°F winter nights). They appreciate humidity trays. *Promenaea* like to be in the same mix for a long time, up to 10 years; they quickly grow into lovely specimens. Water them copiously in growth and fertilize regularly, but don't allow the soft growth to rot, which can happen easily. Keep them dry for several weeks after bloom. Plants are sometimes deciduous.

■ *xanthina* *p. 122*
This spring and summer bloomer from southern Brazil is very fragrant and long-lasting. It often grows up on top of itself in the same pot for years until no mix is left, at which time it can be repotted and set deeper.

Psychopsis

Sye-kop'siss
Cymbidium Group (Epidendrum Subfamily)
Epiphytic. Sympodial. Unifoliate pseudobulbs

Description
The Butterfly Orchids are a fabulously flowered, strikingly colored genus that helped start the Victorian rage for grow-

ing orchids. The 4 species are found in high tree canopies of wet forests from Costa Rica to Peru. The truly distinctive flowers are borne one at a time in succession on an elongating inflorescence, and *Psychopsis* can be in bloom for many months. Plants have unifoliate pseudobulbs and often mottled leaves. *Psychopsis* were removed from the genus *Oncidium* but are still treated as such for hybrid and award registration. The generic name is Greek for "butterfly appearance."

How to Grow

These easy plants can be grown in small pots or on mounts, in medium windowsill light of any exposure except north, and in intermediate to warm conditions (55–65°F winter nights). Repot them into fresh mix often. Water and fertilize well while in growth, and allow to dry somewhat between waterings.

■ *papilio* *p. 143*

This most popular species, which has won many awards, blooms successively at the end of a long inflorescence from May to September. The thick leaves are reddish with green blotches. It is native to the West Indies, Colombia, and Brazil, and is commonly called *Oncidium papilio*. Don't cut off the spikes after the flowers have faded, since they often bloom again throughout the year.

Renanthera (Ren.)

Ren-ann'the-rah
Dendrobium Group (Epidendrum Subfamily)
Epiphytic, lithophytic. Monopodial. No pseudobulbs

Description

The brilliant red and orange colors of these 15 tropical Southeast Asian species have given them the common name of Fire Orchids. *Renanthera* produce blooms generously on branched panicles; the dorsal sepal and petals are often narrow. Flowers last at least a month. Plant size is medium to large, with short leathery leaves, and some are vinelike. Because of their intense colors, they have been very popular in hybridizing some 60 new genera. The name of the genus is Greek for "kidney," for the shape of the pollinia.

How to Grow

All *Renanthera* are easy. Warm to intermediate temperatures (65–55°F winter nights) and high to medium southern windowsill exposures or greenhouse light are fine. Grow them in the smallest pots possible, with coarse mix; to "repot," pull out the old mix and simply add more when necessary. Water and fertilize *Renanthera* year-round. Plantlets may appear at the base of the plant and can be separately potted; such keiki offshoot production can be encouraged by keeping damp sphagnum moss around the base of the parent plant. The old stems get woody with age. Plants are either relatively compact or vinelike and rangy.

■ *imshootiana* p. 167
This vinelike Burmese northeast Indian species is considered one of the most endangered orchids and is fortunately available via seed as well as tissue propagation. The 18-in. inflorescence can carry 20 blooms. It prefers to stay a bit cooler and drier than most *Renanthera;* grow it intermediate (55–60°F winter nights) in medium eastern or southern light.

■ *monachica* p. 168
This Fire Orchid, found only in the Philippines, is vinelike. It prefers high light on a southern windowsill or in a greenhouse. Its 18-in. inflorescence boasts 30 spotted flowers at a time, yielding a truly spectacular display. The leaves have a purple tinge.

Restrepia (Rstp.)
Re-strep'ee-ah
Epidendrum Group (Epidendrum Subfamily)
Epiphytic. Sympodial. No pseudobulbs

Description
The 30 mostly Andean species might well be called the Clown Orchids for the mischievous elfin faces their little flowers typically suggest. The single flower often appears on the underside of the leaf, with the lateral sepals fused. The genus is named for 18th-century Colombian botanist José Restrepo.

How to Grow
Restrepia grow easily in moist, humid, intermediate to cool temperatures (58–45°F winter nights). Keep them continually damp in small pots and low greenhouse light or grow them under fluorescent lights. Many bloom intermittently more than once a year. *Restrepia* can be propagated by placing a leaf on damp sphagnum moss.

■ *striata* p. 187
The leaf stems of this striped-flower species are covered in a

papery sheath. Blooms can appear any time of the year, although November to March is most common.

Rhynchocentrum (Rhctm.)

Rink-oh-sen′trum
Dendrobium Group (Epidendrum Subfamily)
Ascocentrum × *Rhynchostylis*
Monopodial. No pseudobulbs

Description
Created in 1963, this perky-flowered hybrid genus generally yields brightly colored and marked upright racemes on medium-size plants.

How to Grow
Warm to intermediate temperatures (65–55°F winter nights) on southern or western windowsills with medium to high light are needed to flower *Rhynchocentrum.* Water and fertilize them well year-round. Grow the plants in baskets of coarse mix, repotting infrequently.

■ hybrid *(Rhynchostylis coelestis* × *Ascocentrum ampullaceum) p. 168*
Both parents of this hybrid are pictured elsewhere in the color plates (p.169 and p. 153). Flowers last 6 weeks, and can be fragrant.

Rhyncholaelia

Rink-oh-lay′lee-ah
Epidendrum Group (Epidendrum Subfamily)
Epiphytic. Sympodial. Thick pseudobulbs

Description
Native from Mexico to Honduras in lowland forests with a distinct dry season, the 2 species of *Rhyncholaelia* are beautiful and intensely fragrant. The plants have thick pseudobulbs that each carry one thick grayish green leaf and a solitary flower. Both species were originally classified as *Brassavola,* and, in fact, the fringed *digbyana* species has been responsible for the bulk of the big, fragrant, frilly-lipped Cattleya Alliance hybrids, especially the *Brassocattleya* and *Brassolaeliocattleya.* To avoid chaos, therefore, *Rhyncholaelia* are still considered *Brassavola* for hybrid and award registration. The generic name means "snouted *Laelia,*" referring to the seedpod.

How to Grow
Rhyncholaelia prefer higher light than *Cattleya* and do well in the high light of southern windowsills. They like intermediate temperatures (55–60°F winter nights). Pot them in coarse, well-drained mix (coarse bark and perlite is fine). Let them dry between waterings. Once they have grown into many pseudobulbs, which can take 6 years, they flower easily, but *Rhyncholaelia* may be reluctant bloomers until then. Buy mature plants for faster results.

■ *digbyana* *p. 92*
This spring- or summer-blooming, fringed-lip beauty has a wonderful night fragrance reminiscent of lemons. Each inflorescence has but 1 flower, which lasts 6 weeks.

■ *glauca* *p. 93*
This species blooms between January and March with powdery-covered flowers atop a foot-high compact plant. It has one of the loveliest of all orchid fragrances. It can be grown in a pot or mounted on a slab. Bloom lasts 6 weeks.

Rhynchostylis (Rhy.)
Rink-oh-stye′liss
Dendrobium Group (Epidendrum Subfamily)
Epiphytic. Monopodial. No pseudobulbs

Description
If bushy foxtails were pink, white, and violet, then these Foxtail Orchids would be very aptly named. An exquisite genus of three sometimes pendent species from India to Borneo and the Philippines, *Rhynchostylis* also boasts spicy fragrances during the day. Their generously produced, closely spaced flowers have been extensively hybridized into at least 45 new genera in the vandaceous alliance, and they are closely allied to *Vanda*. The name of the genus means "snouted style," referring to the beaked lip column.

How to Grow
Rhynchostylis is easy. Its tangle of thick coarse roots — many of which will wave in the air — grows best undisturbed in an empty hanging basket. Water it well and regularly year-round, except for after growth, when water can be slightly reduced. If it is not possible to water this frequently, grow it in a pot of medium bark and charcoal chunks, but it will need repotting every year. Grow the plant in the medium light of eastern, western, or southern windowsills (avoid direct sun) in

warm temperatures (60–65°F winter nights). Cool temperatures are the cause of most problems with this genus; the plant is then readily susceptible to fungal and bacterial infections that permanently scar the leaves. New plantlets may appear at the base of the plant and can be removed and potted separately. *Rhynchostylis* normally grow slowly.

■ *coelestis* *p. 169*
This Thailand Foxtail stands upright on a small plant that blooms in summer. It is one of the coveted "blue" orchids; an even rarer variety is pink and is highly sought by collectors. Grow it slightly cooler than most other *Rhynchostylis* (55–65°F). Blooms last 4–6 weeks.

■ *gigantea* *p. 169*
By far the most awarded *Rhynchostylis*, with an arching 15-in. inflorescence, this mostly summer bloomer has notable striped green leaves. It flowers best in good humidity. The species name means "gigantic," but although the leaves can reach 15 in. long, they extend out to the sides and the plant stays below a height of 10 in., making it suitable for limited windowsill space. Flowers last 6 weeks.

Rodricidium (Rdcm.)
Roh-dri-sid′ee-um
Cymbidium Group (Epidendrum Subfamily)
Oncidium × *Rodriguezia*
Sympodial. Pseudobulbs

Description
This 1957 hybrid genus is generally diminutive, since it usually incorporates brilliantly colored little equitant *Oncidium* with the fragrant, little *Rodriguezia*. The plants have very small pseudobulbs. These hybrids are much simpler to grow than the sometimes recalcitrant equitant *Oncidium,* since the *Rodriguezia* parent is relatively easy.

How to Grow
Grow *Rodricidium* on small loglike mounts or in small pots; the plants like to wander a bit. Place them in medium light of eastern, western, or southern windowsills, or in a greenhouse. *Rodricidium* do best in intermediate to warm temperatures (58–68°F winter nights). Make sure the roots stay well drained and well aired, but repot the plants infrequently, since the roots resent disturbance. Water the plants abundantly year-round, and provide extra humidity via humidity trays.

■ **Phyllis** (*Rodricidium* Beauty Spots × *Oncidium* Phyllis Hetfield) *p. 143*
These sprays of intensely marked little blooms are sometimes fragrant. The cultivar pictured is 'Robsan II' HCC/AOS. Grow it a bit warmer (62–70°F winter nights).

Rodriguezia (Rdza.)

Roh-dri-geez'ee-ah
Cymbidium Group (Epidendrum Subfamily)
Epiphytic. Sympodial. Small pseudobulbs

Description
Showy-lipped, fragrant, little rose to white flowers make these 40 species from Costa Rica to Peru decidedly worth collecting. Most grow in wet Brazilian cloud forests on guava trees, from sea level to 5,000 ft. The genus honors 18th-century Spanish botanist Don Manuel Rodriguez.

How to Grow
With unifoliate pseudobulbs that wander at intervals along a rhizome, most *Rodriguezia* do best mounted on totem twigs or in small shallow pots. Repot them infrequently, since *Rodriguezia* dislike being disturbed. Give them humid, intermediate temperatures (55–60°F winter nights) in the medium light of an eastern windowsill or in a greenhouse, with plenty of year-round water.

■ *decora p. 144*
The wiry rhizome of this Brazilian species should be grown mounted on a round 1½-in.-diameter branch, since the pseudobulbs are widely spaced at 4 in. apart. It produces 6–12 flowers on a branched 2-ft. inflorescence between October and December.

Sarcochilus (Sarco.)

Sar-koh-kye'lus
Dendrobium Group (Epidendrum Subfamily)
Epiphytic, lithophytic. Monopodial. Erect to pendulous stems

Description
Australia is home to all but 1 of these 14 showy, colorful, and often fragrant species of the vandaceous alliance. Plants can be small to large, with branching stems and fleshy leaves. They

commonly grow atop rocks. Inflorescences bear hordes of flowers. The generic name is from the Greek for "fleshy lip."

How to Grow
The need for humidity above 60% and good air movement means *Sarcochilus* generally do best in a greenhouse under medium light. *Sarcochilus* run the gamut of tropical, subtropical, and temperate zones, but most can be grown cool or intermediate (45–55°F winter nights). Mount the smaller types on cork and put larger ones in shallow pots or baskets filled with bark and rock. Water and fertilize them regularly throughout the year.

■ **Fitzhart** *(fitzgeraldii × hartmanii)* *p. 170*
This popular 1963 hybrid between two robust lithophytes grows easily into a potted cluster of many growths and flowers. Give it intermediate temperatures (55–60°F winter nights). Up to 15 flowers bloom freely on each of many branching inflorescences for 4 weeks in February and March.

Sarcoglottis
Sar-koh-glot'tiss
Spiranthes Subfamily
Terrestrial. Sympodial. Underground tuberous roots

Description
The pretty basal rosettes of the 40 mostly Brazilian species often have variegated leaves. The erect racemes of small to medium flowers are showy, typically appearing before the foliage, which emerges from tuberous roots. Some taxonomists classify this genus as *Spiranthes*. The generic name means "fleshy tongue."

How to Grow
Woodland compost in large deep pots is best for these terrestrials, which often grow into large clumps. Grow them in intermediate to warm temperatures (55–65°F winter nights) in the medium light of eastern, western, or southern windowsills, and keep them moist.

■ *metallica* *p. 226*
The variety in the photo is *variegata*, notable for its beautifully mottled foliage. Its tall raceme blooms for 4–6 weeks between January and March.

Scaphosepalum

Skaf-oh-see'pa-lum
Epidendrum Group (Epidendrum Subfamily)
Epiphytic. Sympodial. No pseudobulbs

Description

Successive upside-down small blooms on long zigzag racemes or scapes make this genus of 30 species very interesting. They are found mostly in cloud forests of Central America to Bolivia, growing on mossy trees. The plant habit is creeping or tufted, *Masdevallia*-like. The name of the genus is an amalgam from the Greek and Latin for "bowl-shaped sepal."

How to Grow

Most are easy. Keep them constantly moist on mounts or in small pots, and let them grow into specimens rather than dividing them into small plants. Give *Scaphosepalum* medium windowsill light of any exposure except north, or grow them under artificial light in intermediate to cool temperatures (60–45°F winter nights).

■ *decorum* p. 187
This species, as with many *Scaphosepalum*, seems to bloom forever, successively extending its long zigzag inflorescence at right angles and conjuring up yet another flower.

Sedirea

Se-deer'ee-ah
Dendrobium Group (Epidendrum Subfamily)
Epiphytic. Monopodial. No pseudobulbs

Description

The 2 medium-small Japanese/Chinese species were previously part of the vandaceous genus of *Aerides*, under which they are still classified for registration purposes. The pretty, waxy flowers open only halfway. In taxonomic humor, the name *Sedirea* is *Aerides* spelled backward.

How to Grow

Regular water is essential to keep these pseudobulbless plants from wilting, which they all too easily do. Grow them on eastern or southern windowsills in medium light and intermediate temperatures (55–60°F winter nights), in small pots or baskets.

■ *japonica* p. 170
This miniature species can have a dozen relatively large flow-

ers on each 7-in. spike, often with many spikes open at once. It blooms for at least a month between April and June. The flowers have a very fragrant, sweet scent.

Sigmatostalix (Sgmx.)

Sig-mat-oh-stay'licks
Cymbidium Group (Epidendrum Subfamily)
Epiphytic. Sympodial. Pseudobulbs

Description
The 35 diminutive species are found from Mexico to Brazil in wet forests of elevations from 1,600 to 6,500 ft. The neat plants have small, generally yellow flowers that can rebloom year after year off the same spike. They are related to *Oncidium*. The generic name means "S-shaped column."

How to Grow
In humid conditions, these do well on mounts. In drier spots, pot them in small pots, but keep them constantly moist, except for several weeks after the pseudobulbs finish their seasonal growth, when they need a slightly dry rest. Give *Sigmatostalix* medium windowsill light of eastern or southern exposure and intermediate to cool temperatures (60–45°F winter nights).

■ *sergii* *p. 144*
These fascinating little flowers bloom successively one at a time on a small neat plant. It does best mounted.

Sobralia (Sob.)

So-bral'ee-ah
Epidendrum Group (Epidendrum Subfamily)
Terrestrial, lithophytic, epiphytic. Sympodial. Canelike reed stems

Description
The 95 species are prized for their spectacular flowers, which are usually huge and shaped like beautiful *Cattleya*. Although the individual flowers last but a day or two, *Sobralia* bloom successively for months on reedlike, veined-leaf plants that can reach 8 ft. tall, although there are dwarf species. They are found in tropical America from Mexico to Brazil, often on the edges of wet forests from sea level to 6,500 ft. The genus honors Dr. Francisco Sobral, a Spanish botanist of the 18th century.

How to Grow
Sobralia prefer narrow, deep, well-crocked pots with semi-terrestrial (fine bark/perlite) mix. They like their roots pot-bound and left undisturbed. Grow them on eastern, southern, or western windowsills (a sunroom or greenhouse is best to accommodate the taller species) in medium bright light and intermediate to warm temperatures (55–65°F winter nights). Water and fertilize them weekly. In frost-free climates, they can be grown in well-drained garden beds. *Sobralia* must be mature to bloom well, which can take 5 years; buy mature plants, or be prepared to wait for flowers.

■ **species** *p. 209*
This unidentified "miniature" species was photographed in Ecuador at 4,500 ft. along the side of a wet forest road. It reaches only 4 ft. high.

Sophrocattleya (Sc.)
Sof-roe-kat'lee-yah
Epidendrum Group (Epidendrum Subfamily)
Cattleya × *Sophronitis*
Sympodial. Pseudobulbs

Description
Created in 1886, this hybrid genus of the Cattleya Alliance generally involves red *Sophronitis coccinea* in the parentage, which keeps plant size compact yet spawns relatively large, very colorful flowers. Many "mini-catts" (miniature *Cattleya* types) and "compact catts" (compact *Cattleya* types) are produced in this genus, which are then often used as building blocks for further hybridizing.

How to Grow
Keep *Sophrocattleya* relatively moist on eastern or southern windowsills with medium-bright light and intermediate temperatures (55–60°F winter nights). Pot in a medium-fine mix (medium bark, perlite, and chopped sphagnum often works well), and allow to dry only slightly between waterings. If your plant seems recalcitrant, growing slowly or not blooming, the problem is probably due to the sometimes difficult *Sophronitis* parentage; raise the humidity by placing the pots atop humidity trays and grouping plants together, drop the night temperatures to 50°F, and avoid daytime highs above 78°F.

■ **Beaufort** *(Sophronitis coccinea × Cattleya luteola)* *p. 93*
This is a very highly awarded and popular little cross between
two dwarf parent species, producing a mini-catt. Flowers can
be yellow like the *Cattleya* parent, and red or orange offspring are not uncommon. There are usually several blooms
per inflorescence; they last about a month. Give it 50–55°F
nights.

■ **Seagulls Beaulu Queen** *(Sophrocattleya* Beaufort × *Cattleya*
luteola) *p. 94*
This hybrid is the result of a "back cross," wherein one parent (in this case, *Sophrocattleya* Beaufort, described in the
preceding entry) is crossed with one of its own parents
(*Cattleya luteola*). The result is a mini-catt that intensifies
the easy-to-grow genetic heritage from the yellow *Cattleya*
luteola.

Sophrolaeliocattleya (Slc.)

Sof-roe-lay-lee-oh-kat′lee-yah
Epidendrum Group (Epidendrum Subfamily)
Cattleya × Laelia × Sophronitis
Sympodial. Pseudobulbs

Description
Notable for bright colors and a free-blooming habit on compact plants, this trigeneric Cattleya Alliance genus was created in 1892. *Sophrolaeliocattleya* can bloom almost any time
of the year, depending on its heritage. Flower color may vary
with the temperature; it will be more intense in cooler seasons.

How to Grow
Intermediate temperatures (55–60°F winter nights) and
medium-bright windowsills of eastern or southern exposure
are fine. Let the plants dry slightly between waterings. If your
plant grows slowly, drop the temperatures to 50–55°F nights
and raise the light.

■ **Coastal Sunrise** *(Laelia anceps × Sophrolaeliocattleya*
Helen Veliz) *p. 94*
Laelia anceps hybrids are generally not notable, but this 1987
cross is a decided exception. Flowers are beautifully arranged
on a long, well-held inflorescence and last a month. The cultivar pictured is 'Tropico' HCC/AOS.

■ **Hazel Boyd (California Apricot × Jewel Box)** *p. 95*
This famous easy-to-grow cross is the most awarded in the
genus, with brilliant colors (mostly in orange tones) and compact size. Many Hazel Boyd hybrids are "triploid," meaning
they carry an extra number of genes, giving them extraordinary plant vigor. Blooms last at least a month. The cultivar
pictured is 'Apricot Glow' AM/AOS.

■ **Jewel Box** (*Cattleya aurantiaca × Sophrolaeliocattleya*
Anzac) *p. 95*
This freely blooming hybrid from 1971 is still very popular.
It has produced many hybrids and won many awards. The
sprays of red flowers last at least a month.

■ **Precious Stones** (*Sophrolaelia* Psyche × *Cattleya aclandiae*)
p. 96
The spots in this compact hybrid come from its fragrant *Cattleya aclandiae* parent. The intense color is imparted from the
other parent. The result are waxy flowers that can last up to
6 weeks.

■ **hybrid (Bellicent × California Apricot)** *p. 96*
The full round flower shape on the diminutive plant achieved
here is a hybridizer's dream. Grow it intermediate to cool
(58–50°F winter nights). Flowers last about a month.

Sophronitis (Soph.)

Sof-roe-nye'tiss
Epidendrum Group (Epidendrum Subfamily)
Epiphytic, lithophytic. Sympodial. Pseudobulbs

Description
Dwarf plants with brilliant showy flowers highlight the 6
species that grow on mossy trees in wet, medium-elevation
forests of Brazil to Paraguay. The intense scarlet red found in
many Cattleya Alliance hybrids can often be traced back to
this genus. Flowers arise from the base of the pseudobulbs.
The generic name is the diminutive for "chaste," referring to
the modest size of the plants.

How to Grow
Sophronitis are sometimes difficult. They prefer more humidity and water than others in the Cattleya Alliance and absolutely must be well drained. Mount them on tree-fern slabs
or in small pots, and never allow them to dry out. They really resent potted mixes that have become old and stale; repot

before this happens, or the plants will go downhill quickly. Intermediate days (not above 75°F) with cool (48–50°F) nights often help greatly. Provide medium-bright light in a humid greenhouse or grow them under fluorescent lights in a humid basement. Give *Sophronitis* high air movement.

■ *cernua*   p. 97

Glossy and waxy-flowered, this little orange species is easier to grow than the more popularly known *Sophronitis coccinea,* tolerating warmer temperatures at night (55°F) and less humidity, making it possible to grow it on a southern windowsill if daytime temperatures don't go above 80°F. It can take almost full sun. Give it a short dry rest after growth. There are 2–5 blooms per inflorescence; they can last 6 weeks.

■ *coccinea*   p. 97

The most awarded and popular *Sophronitis* species usually has only 1 flower per inflorescence, but it increases in size the longer it stays open, usually about a month. Tetraploid varieties such as 'Neon Lights' are very vigorous because they have an extra set of genes and are much easier to grow. This species has been extensively hybridized for its color. Its finickiness is often best suited in a greenhouse. When grown well, it makes an astonishing specimen, with scarlet blooms covering the plant.

Spathoglottis (Spa.)

Spath-oh-glot'tiss
Epidendrum Group (Epidendrum Subfamily)
Terrestrial. Sympodial. Cormlike pseudobulbs, some deciduous

Description

Spadelike lips give the 30 species from India to China and Australia their generic name. Showy pink to yellow flowers bloom successively for months on tall spikes. *Spathoglottis* have become naturalized in Hawaii.

How to Grow

Cover the bottom one-fourth of the gladiolus-like corm in a chopped sphagnum mix in a well-drained shallow pot. Water it well and fertilize only while it is in active growth; reduce both after maturity until the new shoots appear. Some types are deciduous and bloom from bare pseudobulbs, needing to dry out after the leaves fall. Place *Spathoglottis* in the medium to high light of southern, eastern, or western windowsills in intermediate to warm conditions (55–65°F winter nights). In mild climates, grow them outdoors in light, highly organic garden soil in sun. *Spathoglottis* can bloom from seed in only 18 months; if you buy young seedlings, your reward is quick.

■ *vanoverberghii* *p. 198*
This high-elevation Philippine species blooms in late winter or spring from the bare pseudobulbs after its leaves fall. Grow it intermediate (55–60°F winter nights), and give the plant a dry rest after bloom. There are usually 4–6 flowers per inflorescence.

Stanhopea (Stan.)

Stan-hope′ee-ah
Cymbidium Group (Epidendrum Subfamily)
Epiphytic, lithophytic, terrestrial. Sympodial. Pseudobulbs

Description
Spectacular pendent, waxy blooms and heady scents from cinnamon to foul make the 55 species showstoppers, if only for the brief 2 days they are in bloom. Enthusiasts have *Stanhopea* parties to celebrate. The medium to large plants grow in wet forests from Mexico to Brazil, usually on trees but sometimes as terrestrials. The flowers emerge from the base of the ribbed pseudobulbs, generally in summer or fall. The genus is related to *Gongora* and honors the 4th Earl of Stanhope, an early-19th-century London medical botanist.

How to Grow
Stanhopea are easy if given abundant water; they should never dry out. Open mesh baskets allow the hanging inflorescence to burrow out naturally through the bottom of the container. Place the basket in the medium light of an eastern, southern, or western windowsill, or in a sunroom or greenhouse. Provide intermediate temperatures (55–60°F winter nights); daytime temperatures into the 90s are tolerated well. They like 40–60% humidity. Give *Stanhopea* a month-long cooler (50–55°F nights), drier rest after growth is complete. Divide them often after growth to keep them blooming well.

■ *wardii* *p. 123*
This popular epiphyte can have 3–8 large hanging blooms anytime from July to October. It is very fragrant, capable of scenting an entire greenhouse or room for the scant few days the flowers are open. The large plant is found from Nicaragua to Colombia and Venezuela. Grow it intermediate to warm (55–65°F winter nights). Flowers keep well frozen.

Stenorrhynchus

Ste-nor-rhin′kuss
Spiranthes Subfamily
Epiphytic, lithophytic, terrestrial. Sympodial. No pseudobulbs

Description

Two-foot-tall erect inflorescences of brightly colored flowers distinguish this tropical/temperate Central to South American genus of 13 species. *Stenorrhynchus* are sometimes found under the name *Spiranthes,* but they differ from that genus in not having a twisted flower spike. The genus is named from the Greek for "narrow snout," referring to the thin rostellum.

How to Grow

Give *Stenorrhynchus* medium light on any windowsill exposure except north, and intermediate to warm conditions (55–65°F winter nights). Pot them in sphagnum and oak leaves and keep the plants moist. Let them dry somewhat when their leaves wilt and die back.

■ *speciosum* *p. 226*
Found in mixed woods on sides of trees, this species bears a dense, rich red head atop a 2-ft.-long floral spike that appears once the basal rosette of leaves is grown. It blooms between December and March, often in flower for Christmas, and lasts at least a month.

Symphyglossum

Sim-fee-gloss′um
Cymbidium Group (Epidendrum Subfamily)
Epiphytic. Sympodial. Pseudobulbs

Description

Until 1919, the 5 showy species of this genus in the Oncidium Alliance were considered part of the genus *Cochlioda,* under which they are still registered for hybrids and awards. These wet-forest Andean natives from mid- to high elevations are small to medium-size and of neat habit. The generic name means "to grow the tongue together," because the lip is unusually united to the flower column.

How to Grow

Symphyglossum grow easily in the medium light of eastern or southern windowsills in intermediate to cool temperatures (58–48°F winter nights). Daytime temperatures should not exceed 75°F. Water year-round.

■ *sanguineum* p. 145
This exquisite bloomer can produce a 3½-ft. flower spike with more than a hundred 1-in. flowers that last 4–6 weeks. Although it typically blooms between March and September, with peak in May, *Symphyglossum sanguineum* can flower almost any time of the year. This species continues to be found as *Cochlioda sanguinea* for hybrid registrations.

Trichoglottis (Trgl.)

Trik-oh-glott′iss
Dendrobium Group (Epidendrum Subfamily)
Epiphytic. Monopodial (vinelike). No pseudobulbs

Description
Most of these 60 *Vanda*-like species are found in the warm Philippines and have waxy blooms on climbing or pendent leafy stems. The generic name is derived from the Greek for "hairy tongue," in reference to the bristly flower lips.

How to Grow
These long-stemmed climbers require support. Grow them in baskets or small hanging pots with a slab or trellis on which they can climb. Bright light in a big southern window or a sunroom works best. These warm-growing plants resent temperatures below 60°F. They grow well with *Vanda*. Give them lots of water and fertilizer year-round; 50% humidity is appreciated. Pieces of the upright stem with aerial roots can be cut off and repotted to propagate new plants.

■ *philippinensis* p. 171
Fragrant and tall, with 1 flower per inflorescence, this glossy-leaved species blooms for 4–6 weeks between July and October. It is native to low elevations of the Philippines. The highly awarded *brachiata* variety shown in the photo is dubbed the Black Orchid, although this is wishful thinking; it is decidedly more brown than black. Brenda Starr to the contrary, there is actually no such thing as a truly black orchid.

Trichopilia (Trpla.)

Trik-oh-pill′ee-ah
Cymbidium Group (Epidendrum Subfamily)
Epiphytic, lithophytic, terrestrial. Sympodial. Pseudobulbs

Description
Trumpet-shaped lips, often twisted sepals and petals, long-lasting corsage use, and super fragrance make these 30 species of the Oncidium Alliance, native from Mexico to Brazil, well worth growing. The small to medium-size compact plants grow with a creeping rhizome and neat pseudobulbs, each with a solitary thick leaf. The freely borne, *Cattleya*-like flowers last for 6 weeks and make long-lived corsages. *Trichopilia* means "hairy felt," so named for the fringe along the column.

How to Grow
Trichopilia are relatively easy to grow. Their native habitats are wet, so provide *Trichopilia* with abundant year-round water, except for a 2-week cooler, drier rest after growth. Grow them in pots or mounted, in intermediate to warm temperatures (55–65°F winter nights), in medium to low shaded windowsill light of any exposure except north. Divide often. *Trichopilia* is sensitive to fertilizer salts; apply very dilute organic fish emulsion instead of commercial chemical blends.

■ *fragrans* *p. 145*
This midsize epiphyte generally has 1–3 waxy blooms that arise from the base of the pseudobulb. It is in flower from April to June.

Vanda (V.)
Van'da
Dendrobium Group (Epidendrum Subfamily)
Epiphytic, lithophytic. Monopodial. No pseudobulbs

Description
Incredible crystalline color, including the rarest blues, combined with many large long-lasting flowers, wonderful fragrance, and easy culture, makes *Vanda* one of the most popular orchid genera. They are classic Florida houseplants in particular. The 45 generally large species are found in the Asiatic tropics, often in full sun in exposed spots. The generic name comes from the Sanskrit word for the species *Vanda tessellata*. *Vanda* has been involved in the creation of more intergeneric hybrids than any other genus, its parental heritage found in more than 75 new genera. See also *Euanthe*, p. 281, since one of *Vanda*'s major species, *sanderiana*, has been reclassified into its own genus, although hybrid registrations will still consider it as *Vanda*.

How to Grow

Often tall with a gawky tangle of heavy roots, *Vanda* does best in hanging baskets with a coarse, well-drained mix; many of the roots will insist on being aerial. Most *Vanda* grow easily in warm temperatures (60–70°F winter nights) and humid conditions on a very bright southern windowsill (avoid direct sun) or in a sunroom or greenhouse. Unfortunately, the high-light conditions for best bloom also cause the leaves to look a bit ratty. The plants like lots of water, which is generally needed daily; they prefer the same water and conditions from day to day and resent being neglected. Fertilize them well year-round for the most abundant bloom. When repotting is necessary, carefully place the basket into a larger one with or without new mix, and try not to break the roots. When your plant gets too tall, its stem can be lopped in half and its top repotted. Blue-toned *Vanda* usually need cooler temperatures (to 48°F winter nights) and higher humidity (60%), with a slight dry rest after growth.

■ *coerulea* *p. 171*
The Blue Orchid grows at higher elevations (2,600–5,500 ft.) than most other *Vanda* and therefore prefers intermediate to cool temperatures (58–48°F winter nights) and higher humidity (60%). Also give it a somewhat drier rest after its seasonal growth is done. *Vanda coerulea* is considered one of the most endangered orchids, and its trade is restricted; fortunately, it is readily available from laboratory propagation by seed and tissue culture. Each 18-in. branched inflorescence can bear up to 15 veined flowers that last 4–6 weeks.

■ **David Gardner (Robert's Delight × Bangkok Blue)** *p. 172*
A 1991 hybrid, this clearly shows the well-marked, two-toned *Euanthe sanderiana* influence. Its fragrant blooms last 4–6 weeks.

■ **Gordon Dillon (Madame Rattana × Bangkok Blue)** *p. 172*
The blue of *Vanda coerulea* dominates this highly awarded, gorgeous cross. Grow it intermediate to warm (55–62°F winter nights). The cultivar pictured is 'Pacific Blue'.

■ **Motes Resplendent (Kasem's Delight × Pimsai)** *p. 173*
Some of the most intense colors belong to *Vanda*, as seen in this glorious 1988 hybrid. Blooms last 4–6 weeks.

■ **Patricia Low (Josephine van Brero × Jennie Hashimoto)** *p. 173*
Orange coloration often harkens back to *Euanthe sanderiana*.

This hybrid usually has 6–10 blooms per inflorescence, which last 4–6 weeks. The cultivar pictured is 'Lorraine' AM/AOS.

Vuylstekeara (Vuyl.)

Vuyl-steek-uh-are′ah
Cymbidium Group (Epidendrum Subfamily)
Cochlioda × *Miltonia* × *Odontoglossum*
Sympodial. Pseudobulbs

Description
This trigeneric hybrid genus, created in Belgium in 1912, is another in the widely interbred Oncidium Alliance. *Cochlioda* imparts rich red coloration to the often intensely marked, arching racemes of flowers. The genus is named in honor of noted orchid hybridist C. Vuylsteke of Belgium, who was instrumental in developing many complex Oncidium Alliance hybrids.

How to Grow
Grow *Vuylstekeara* in small pots of medium-fine mix in intermediate to cool temperatures (58–45°F winter nights), avoiding daytime heat over 78°F. Medium light on a humid eastern windowsill or in a greenhouse is best. Water the plants well year-round. If your windowsill plant grows slowly, grow it more on the cool side and raise the humidity; it may need a greenhouse.

■ *Cambria (Vuylstekeara* **Rudra** × *Odontoglossum* **Clonius)** *p. 146*
This beauty is the most awarded hybrid in the genus, with 'Plush' FCC/AOS (shown in the photo) considered the finest cultivar. It is a truly splendid hybrid, with many-flowered inflorescences that can last at least 6 weeks.

Warmingia

War-ming′ee-ah
Cymbidium Group (Epidendrum Subfamily)
Epiphytic. Sympodial. Pseudobulbs

Description
Small plants with dense hanging racemes of translucent small white flowers distinguish the 4 species. *Warmingia* is native to wet forests from Ecuador to Brazil, from sea level to 3,300

ft. The inflorescence arises from the base of the unifoliate stemlike pseudobulb. The genus is named for its discoverer, Eugene Warming, a Danish botanist who founded the science of ecology.

How to Grow

Grow *Warmingia* on mounts or in small shallow pots in humid intermediate to warm temperatures, (55–65°F winter nights) with medium light of an eastern, western, or southern windowsill. Keep the plants moist, but water them carefully to avoid rot, which occurs easily on new growth.

■ *eugenii* *p. 146*
This showy little species is the most awarded and familiar. There can be 30 flowers on each pendent raceme. Plants are often grown into specimens bearing hundreds of blooms that last a few weeks between April and July.

Wilsonara (Wils.)

Wil-son-are'ah
Cymbidium Group (Epidendrum Subfamily)
Cochlioda × *Odontoglossum* × *Oncidium*
Sympodial. Pseudobulbs

Description

This trigeneric hybrid genus from 1916 is similar to another Oncidium Alliance hybrid genus, *Vuylstekeara.* It combines rich deep color from *Cochlioda,* vivid markings from *Odontoglossum,* and often yellow tones from *Oncidium.*

How to Grow

Most Wilsonara can be grown in small pots of medium-fine mix on eastern windowsills of medium light in intermediate temperatures (55–60°F winter nights). Daytime highs should never go above 80°F. Water them well year-round. If your plant grows slowly or not at all, drop the temperatures to 50–55°F at night, and raise the humidity by providing humidity trays and grouping plants closer together.

■ Eurydice (*Wilsonara* Jeanne Forter × *Odontocidium* Mackenzie Mountains) *p. 147*
Round full shape and orange tones on a long spray make this 1989 hybrid decidedly showy. The blooms can last 6 weeks.

■ **Hambürhen Stern** (*Oncidium tigrinum* × *Odontioda* Lippestern) *p. 147*
This 1976 cross has won many awards. It is especially free-flowering, and the 6-week blooms can be fragrant.

Zygopetalum (Z.)
Zye-go-pet′a-lum
Cymbidium Group (Epidendrum Subfamily)
Terrestrial, lithophytic, epiphytic. Sympodial. Deciduous pseudobulbs

Description
With big racemes of incredibly fragrant, long-lasting, multi-toned green, white, and brown blooms, the easy-to-grow *Zygopetalum* deserve even greater popularity. One plant can delightfully scent an entire room. The 15 species are handsome, glossy-leaved, medium-size plants from low- to mid-elevation South America. Many are terrestrial. The multiple blooms are often in flower for 8 weeks. They make excellent cut flowers and are used commercially for this purpose. The pseudobulbs are eventually deciduous. The generic name is derived from the Greek for "yoked petal," referring to the yoke-like growth at the base of the flower lip.

How to Grow
Large pots with semiterrestrial mix are needed to hold the jumble of thick roots. *Zygopetalum* are easy on humid, breezy, intermediate to warm (52–62°F winter nights) windowsills or in a greenhouse (hybrids with *Zygopetalum mackayi* will have the most warmth tolerance). Provide the medium-bright light of an eastern or southern exposure. Water and fertilize them year-round, except for a short rest after new growth.

■ *crinitum*   *p. 123*
This Brazilian species sends its 18-in.-long flower spike out horizontally, with 3–10 waxy blooms all attractively facing the same way. It is very fragrant and blooms between February and April.

Appendices

The American Orchid Society and Other Sources

The American Orchid Society (AOS) is a font of information and help for any orchidist, from beginner to the most advanced. The society's beautiful full-color monthly magazine, *Orchids* (formerly the *AOS Bulletin*), contains enormously useful articles and photographs. The AOS also publishes a journal for scientific researchers and academia, *Lindleyana*, and grants are made available for scientific studies. Member benefits include the monthly magazine; a 140-page AOS cultural handbook, *Growing Orchids;* and 10% discounts from the book division, which sells a wide variety of orchid books and also publishes some as well. Cultural information sheets are available free, and the AOS book and slide library is the best of its kind. An annual convention and many AOS-sanctioned regional meetings and orchid shows are held throughout the Americas.

A large full-time AOS staff, plus hundreds of devoted volunteers, works constantly to offer new services and innovative ideas, including videos on orchid culture. An Information Officer answers questions via telephone, mail, electronic mail and the Internet, with immediate access to orchid databases.

Nearly half of the AOS monthly magazine is made up of advertisements from the most active orchid firms. To see the vast array of orchids and related paraphernalia available, write away for as many orchid catalogs and lists as possible.

Catalogs vary. Some from big nurseries are in full color, with plant descriptions and cultural advice, while others have no pictures, just descriptions. Smaller places issue lists with names and prices, without much in the way of description. Catalogs with pictures are of great aid, but write for smaller lists as well, to get the best idea of prices and availability. Save helpful catalogs as reference tools, for the plants pictured may eventually be parents of plants purchased down the road.

The AOS also prints a directory of large and small commercial orchid growers, listing them by state, country, and specialties. The directory is handy to keep in the car, since any trip can be made to fit around a conveniently located greenhouse. Be a bit wary of general floral shops and places that don't specialize in orchids, for plants tend to be pricier, less robust, and of limited selection.

Visit orchid greenhouses in person to see the actual sizes of plants and flowers, as gorgeous catalog pictures may be of flowers an inch or less big, a fact not obvious from pictures. Seeing many types of flowers at once helps you to discover your personal taste. If you schedule your trips throughout the year, even once a month, and buy a plant in bloom at each trip, you can have a collection of orchids that blooms year-round in succession.

The most popular source of orchids for beginners is the orchid show. Often set in shopping malls, the shows are full of plants in flower and a host of orchid vendors ready to dispense cultural information, plants, books, and orchid supplies. Local orchid societies have representatives to recruit the interested novice. Orchid shows are great fun, well worth the few hours it may take to drive to one. Show schedules can be found in the AOS magazine or by calling the AOS. Two of the biggest shows in the country are the Greater New York Orchid Show in Manhattan and the Miami Orchid Show in Florida. Both are usually held in March or April.

Even if you're not the social hobby type, consider joining a local orchid society. Orchid "societies," despite the high-toned sound, are a fascinating blend of young and old, male and female, novice and advanced, doctors and mechanics, people with seemingly nothing else in common except a passion for orchids, which makes for a lively mix. Each monthly meeting highlights a show table of everyone's blooming plants, cultural workshops, question and answer times, and typically a guest speaker with slide show. Dues are minimal and generally include a monthly newsletter.

Society meetings are an excellent source of new plants, whether by door prizes, raffles, annual auctions and shows, or communal plant orders that yield big discounts or from commercial vendors who often bring plants to sell. Club members divide plants to give away, sell, or trade among themselves.

To find the nearest local society, contact the American Orchid Society, which has more than 550 affiliated local societies within the United States and around the world. The AOS will get you pointed toward sources for everything connected with orchids:

American Orchid Society
6000 South Olive Ave.
West Palm Beach, FL 33405
407-585-8666; FAX 407-585-0654

Orchid Potting Materials

Fir Bark
Deteriorating; organic. Holds 80% its weight in water. Water 1x/week. Repot every 1–2 years. Use 20-10-10 fertilizer. pH = 5.0.

Fir bark is the most widely utilized potting material, easy to use and obtain, a timber by-product from American evergreen firs. Deeply furrowed Douglas fir is preferred. Pieces are sized coarse, medium, and fine. The smaller the size, the more water is held and the faster the decay.

Fir bark is steam-treated and kiln-dried to remove resins, making it difficult to wet at first. Presoak it in warm water for 24 hours, until the pieces float. With use, decay begins; the mix turns to mush after 2 years. Beginners often err by waiting too long to repot a bark mix. Repotting annually staves off many problems.

Additives help keep the mix open. A common mix is fir bark, redwood bark or wool, peat, and perlite, in varying ratios, such as 7:1:1:1. Stone or expanded shale also helps ward off compacted decay.

Many people mistakenly believe that a high-nitrogen fertilizer is necessary for orchids no matter what the potting mix, but this is wrong. It's just for orchids in bark. Bark is broken down by a common wood-rotting fungus that also consumes a lot of nitrogen. Therefore bark-potted orchids need a high-nitrogen fertilizer, such as 20-10-10, to give extra nitrogen for the fungus.

Even though 30-10-10 has long been touted for orchids in bark, this too-high nitrogen ratio encourages growth of leaves at the expense of flowers and causes soft, fast growth prime for pest attack. Use 20-10-10 instead.

Tree fern (Hapuu, Punga)
Deteriorating; organic. Holds little water. Water 2x/week on average. Repot every 2 years. Use balanced fertilizer.

Tree fern is the second most popular main orchid potting medium and the second most popular slab for mount culture. Tree fern fibers look like thin, black, hard sticks and are the aerial rootlets from trunks of tree-height tropical ferns. Large pieces are used as slabs and baskets. Tree fern drains exceedingly well, and it resists fungal attack, even in extreme conditions. It provides some nutrients, although a 20-20-20 fertilizer is helpful.

Users generally add bark and/or charcoal to the mix and often use clay pots. Tree fern is generally not an additive, although sometimes it is used in fir bark.

Redwood Bark (Redwood Wool, Palco Wool)
Deteriorating; organic. Holds 50% its weight in water. Water 1x/week. Repot every 2½ years. Use 20-10-10 or 20-20-20 fertilizer. pH = 3.5.

Redwood bark is the thickly furrowed, fibrous reddish bark of the Californian sequoia tree. Unlike fir, redwood has no resins, has lower pH, and decays more slowly; less nitrogen is thus needed and 20-20-20 fertilizer is adequate.

Since redwood bark is expensive, it is used mostly as an additive, usually to fir bark, and is also available as a more absorptive fibrous "wool." Redwood bark is used more as a main ingredient in areas of high heat and light, such as Florida, where it outperforms fir. Charcoal is generally added.

Cork
Semideteriorating; organic. Holds little water. Water 2x/week. Repot every 3 years. Mounts last many years. Use 20-20-20 fertilizer with trace elements.

Cork is the most popular slab material for orchid mounts. Thick, lightweight bark from the Mediterranean cork oak is boiled and used as "nuggets" for potting orchids. Cork is inert, providing no nutrients. When cork is utilized as a main potting ingredient, charcoal is almost always added (60:40). Cork is sometimes used as an additive. Although its decay is slower than that of fir bark, cork is prone to millipede infestation, which turns it quickly to slush.

Sphagnum Moss
Deteriorating if dead; organic. Sphagnum moss holds 10 times its weight in water. Water 1–2x/week. Repot every 2½ years, annually if decayed. Use balanced fertilizer (slow-decay organics). pH = 3.5.

Sphagnum moss is the spongelike moss on peat bog surfaces. There are many species; longer-fibered, more resilient ones such as New Zealand moss are more desirable. Sphagnum is available dried (tan) or live (green), and it doesn't begin to decay unless it dies, when it becomes more like peat moss.

Sphagnum moss is used mostly as an additive to a general mix, often chopped, to retain moisture. It is especially good for ailing plants, possessing a unique antiseptic quality that inhibits fungi and other pathogens. A common complaint about sphagnum as a main ingredient is that orchids do not do well in it after a year. This is usually because it's packed too tightly in the pot; stuff sphagnum loosely, but evenly. Sphagnum disintegrates when chlorinated tap water is used; use rainwater or distilled water. Soak it before use.

A word of caution: Sphagnum can harbor fungi that cause difficult-to-eradicate infections through skin cuts and inhalation. Use rubber gloves and a dust mask when handling it.

Osmunda (Osmundine Fiber, Orchid Peat)

Deteriorating; organic. Holds 140% its weight in water. Repot after 3 years. Use balanced fertilizer. pH = 4.3.

Osmunda comes from the matted underground roots of the American *Osmunda* ferns. Roots are tough, fibrous, durable, and spongelike. There are two grades; the upper brownish part drains better and is preferred for epiphytes, while the darker, more decayed portion lends itself to terrestrials. A mix of the two is often sold. Another way to regulate drainage is by choosing which way the "grain" (fern root direction) lies when placed in a pot. Run it horizontally to retain more water; vertical lay of grain holds less. Osmunda is rarely combined with other materials.

Pack osmunda tightly into the pot (use a potting stick). If none of the old mix is rotten, move the plant and medium to a bigger pot, and add more. Osmunda provides nearly all nutrients needed by orchids, but nutrient content diminishes after a year of watering, and 20-20-20 is then necessary.

Peat Moss (Sphagnum Peat Moss, Peat, Moss Peat)
(See also "Soilless Mixes.")

Deteriorating; organic. Holds 7–10 times its weight in water. Water 1x/week. Repot every 2½ years. Use balanced fertilizer. pH = 3.5–5.0.

Sphagnum peat moss is the partially decayed, water-retentive debris formed when sphagnum moss dies and falls under bog water for centuries. Coarse peat is chunkier and more suitable for orchids than horticultural peat. It provides limited nutrients, decays rapidly, and needs frequent repotting.

Peat moss is an important secondary additive for better water retention, used in a quarter of all mixes, added mostly to a fir bark or charcoal mix. When used as a main ingredient, an equal amount of perlite is usually added.

Charcoal

Nondeteriorating; organic. Nonporous. Water 2x/week. Repot every 2 years. Use balanced fertilizer with trace elements.

Charcoal is a sturdy, light, chunky carbon material that comes from heated hardwood. Rarely used as a main ingredient, it is the second most popular additive to a mix (especially to cork or redwood bark), providing aeration and openness. Charcoal holds liquid and other dissolved substances only on its surface. It is therefore sometimes used on top of a medium to filter air and water passing through it. Within the medium, charcoal hangs onto salts unless flushed often with pure water. Charcoal provides no nutrients.

Perlite (Sponge Rock, Pahrock Coarse #3)
Nondeteriorating; inorganic. Nonporous. Use balanced fertilizer with trace elements. pH = usually neutral to 4.8.

Perlite is an everlasting, heat-processed volcanic ash mineral. Although "horticultural grade" perlite is most readily available, use the chunkier types ($\frac{1}{8}$ in. or more). It is the number-one additive to orchid mixes, especially for fir bark ones in a 25:75 ratio. It is basically a cost-effective inert filler, loosening the mix while improving water retention and buoyancy. A perlite/peat combination (50:50) also often performs well. Perlite is rarely added to tree fern, redwood bark, or cork and is seldom used as a main ingredient (mostly for angraecoids, sometimes with a little fir bark added).

Rockwool (Grodan, Pargro, Seagull's Landing Volcanic Fiber)
Nondeteriorating; inorganic. Porous. Water 2–3x/weekly. Repot only when plants outgrow pot. Use balanced fertilizer with trace elements. pH = 8.0.

Rockwool is rock of various composition (usually volcanic) melted and spun into fibers. Brands vary. There are two forms, water absorbent and water repellent (suggested mixes include 60:40 for cattleyas, 80:20 for *Phalaenopsis*). Rockwool holds lots of water and air at the same time.

Growing orchids in pure rockwool is virtually hydroponic. Fertilizing is critical, as are balanced pH and water quality. Results vary drastically between hobbyists. Plants often start out well, then go downhill when the nutrient balance is disrupted, a trace element runs out, or pH gets extreme.

Rockwool does not decay, so if roots are in good shape when they outgrow the pot, place the plant and rockwool intact into a larger pot, and add more. Do not stuff it tightly. It can be almost impossible to rewet if the top layer dries out.

Rockwool is better for most hobbyists as an additive. Adding 25% rockwool to a standard potting mix increases aeration threefold. A recommended mix is 25% rockwool, 25% perlite, and 50% fir bark. Rockwool in combination with organic materials gives many of its benefits without the need for a testing lab, and brings down its high pH.

Polystyrene Foam (Styrofoam™, Aerolite, Packing Peanuts)
Nondeteriorating; organic. Nonporous. pH = neutral.

Polystyrene foam is a light, white, durable solid plastic with closed foam pores. It is sometimes used as an alternative to perlite, especially when crumbled, to aerate and open a mix, typically at the pot bottom to improve drainage.

Other foams can be confused for polystyrene; porous types such as polyethylene and polyurethane absorb plant-damaging salts. Some foams are chemically treated, releasing toxins. Packing peanuts shaped like little binoculars are made of soluble cornstarch and dissolve into obstructive, disease-ridden sludge when used for potting orchids.

Rock Culture

Inorganic rock culture for orchids is often a more successful alternative to bark in decay-prone and/or overwatering situations. Stones, lava rock, and expanded shale pebbles are the three basic materials. When added to deteriorating mixes, they provide good air space. Use plastic pots for best results.

In rock culture, the medium does not decompose. Repotting is needed only when the pot gets too small. It does, however, mean growing virtually hydroponically; the grower must provide a complete, balanced fertilizer with trace elements, and water quality and pH also become important.

Soilless Mixes (Premier Pro-Mix BX, Metro-Mix, Fisions Sunshine Mix #4, "Mud")
Semideteriorating; organic/inorganic. Water 2x/week. Repot yearly. Use balanced fertilizer. pH = 5.5–6.0 (changes over time).

These various commercially available prepackaged mixes are usually some combination of sphagnum peat moss, vermiculite, sometimes perlite, and granular nutrients such as dolomitic limestone, superphosphate, calcium nitrate, and potassium nitrate. They can be tricky to learn to water properly, and they decay rapidly, and thus are better used for moisture-loving seedlings and *Phalaenopsis*, although soilless mixes in clay pots work well for orchids that need more drying (for example, *Cattleya*).

Sand (Builder's Sand, Sharp Sand)
Nondeteriorating; inorganic. Absorbs 20% its weight in water. pH = neutral to 4.3.

Sharp sand is the quartz or silica part of soil, found in gravel pits, not on beaches. The coarser the particle size, the better ($1/16$ in. or more). This is a good terrestrial mix additive for drainage and aeration. It is never used as a main ingredient.

Understanding Orchid Names and Hybrids

Possibly the most confusing aspect about orchids is in their names, which are often a combination of Latin terms and English words, with an assortment of obscure abbreviations and award designations. Standardized orchid nomenclature is also somewhat different than for many other types of plants and can be puzzling to even veteran plant growers.

Most simply put, orchids are either "species" or "hybrids." A species occurs naturally in the wild and usually only breeds there with others of the same species, mostly because orchids segregate themselves by different bloom times, different geographic regions, and different pollinators and pollination mechanisms. They do, however, often interbreed quite readily even between different allied genera once humans get in the picture with a pollinating toothpick. This readiness to interbreed makes orchid species different from most other plants and animals, one reason why scientists consider orchids a still actively evolving family.

Recognizing Species

It's easy to tell if a cultivated orchid is a species by looking at its nametag. The name of an orchid species always consists of two Latin terms. In scientific jargon, these two terms are known as "binomial nomenclature," or "two-name names."

The first Latin term is the name of the genus (a related group) to which the orchid belongs (such as *Cattleya, Phalaenopsis,* or *Dendrobium*). It always begins with a capital letter and is always italicized or underlined.

The second term is the name of the species within the genus. It too is always italicized or underlined, but it always begins with a lowercase letter. This second term is an adjective describing the genus, often a Latinized variant of the discoverer's name or a description of some feature of the plant or its flower. Therefore a tag with two Latin words, with the second one in lowercase letters, indicates that the plant is a species, something nature made all by itself.

What frequently is confusing to a novice is that the same

species names are often hooked to different generic names. For instance, there is *Cattleya violacea* as well as *Phalaenopsis violacea* (*violacea* referring to a violetlike color). The generic name distinguishes precisely which species is being discussed.

Sometimes a third Latin term is added to the genus and species, to indicate a variety (abbreviated var.), a further division of the species. A variety is a distinct population (not a freak individual) within the species that occurs naturally in the wild and displays definite characteristics that breed true when it is bred to another plant of that same variety. *Miltonia spectabilis* var. *moreliana,* which has much larger and darker-colored flowers than others of the species, is an example. (See photos, p. 131.)

Understanding Hybrids

Hybrid orchids are where humans enter the picture. Primary hybrids are made by hybridizing (or "crossing") two different orchid species together. This sometimes occurs in the wild between orchids in proximity, creating "natural" hybrids, but on a relative scale, usually it doesn't. Natural hybrids are often written with a "×" before or after the genus name, such as × *Phalaenopsis* Intermedia (*Phalaenopsis aphrodite* × *equestris*). There are even natural hybrids between different genera, such as × *Laeliocattleya* Elegans, which is *Laelia purpurata* × *Cattleya leopoldii.*

Hybrid names are not italicized. If, instead of two Latin terms on an orchid tag, there is the name (or initials) of the Latin genus and then a capitalized name following it, the plant is a hybrid orchid. The hybrid name is known as the grex. (The grex is often named after someone, and those that include the term "Mem." are named "in memoriam" of someone deceased.) Sometimes instead of the grex, there are names of two orchids, connected by a ×. These are the parents that have been crossed to create the hybrid. Sometimes the grex as well as the names of the parents will be on the tag, the parental names usually below or following the grex, in parentheses, separated by a ×.

The first artificial orchid hybrid to flower and be named was *Calanthe* Dominyi (*Calanthe furcata* × *masuca*), in 1856, made by (and named for) John Dominy, foreman of the orchid firm of Veitch & Sons in Chelsea, England. Dominy was the only orchid hybridizer in the world for the next twenty years, and he ushered in an entirely new orchid scenario.

More than 100,000 hybrid crosses have been registered to date, in a central registry begun in 1895 by the famous English orchid firm of Sander & Sons. The first *Sander's List of*

Orchid Hybrids, published in 1906, contained some 1,500 crosses, half of them in *Paphiopedilum* alone, which still remains the single most hybridized genus. By 1961 the number of total hybrids had risen to 35,000, when the Royal Horticultural Society (RHS) took over the by then onerous burden of maintaining registrations, a process which is now computerized. Whoever first makes and flowers a new hybrid cross is entitled to name and register it with the RHS.

The results of crosses are often further bred by orchidists, and hybridized again, and on and on, and generations later there are very complex crosses. Trying to trace on paper the family tree of a white *Phalaenopsis,* for example, is enough to drive anyone crazy, one reason computers have taken over. Much breeding is to create variety of flower color and form, to produce plants of manageable size, and to make plants that grow well in cultivated conditions.

Generally the simpler the hybrid's parentage (the closer to species), the easier it is to predict the outcome of the cross. Every hybrid cross yields variety, just as when parents have several children. The siblings typically look similar, unless the cross is very genetically mixed.

Intergeneric Hybrids

Often species from different but related genera are artificially bred together, incorporating a slew of different gene pools, resulting in plants that adapt to a wider range of environmental conditions.

There are 860 naturally occurring genera, but humankind has created some 550 new genera, for a total of over 1,400, a number that continues to increase. Only seven years after his first successful hybrid cross, John Dominy flowered the first hybrid between two genera, *Cattleya mossiae* × *Laelia crispa,* producing *Laeliocattleya* Exoniensis in 1863. The first trigeneric cross, *Sophrolaeliocattleya* Veitchi, appeared in 1892, a crossing of *Sophronitis grandiflora* × *Laeliocattleya* Schilleriana, and by 1922 the first four-genera hybrid genus, *Potinara* (*Brassavola* × *Cattleya* × *Laelia* × *Sophronitis*), had flowered. Today it is not unusual to find a genus comprising six different genera.

The related *Cattleya* groups were at the forefront of intergeneric breeding and continue to dominate the hybridizing scene to this day. Another alliance extensively interbred includes plants of the genera *Oncidium* and *Odontoglossum,* frequently bred with *Cochlioda, Miltonia, Miltoniopsis, Comparettia,* and others to create new intergenerics such as *Odontioda* and *Wilsonara.*

Generic Abbreviations

Orchid generic abbreviations are used more often than cumbersome full names, especially with multiple intergenerics such as *Sophrolaeliocattleya,* which is reduced to *Slc.,* the first initials of the three different genera in the crosses. Orchid abbreviations have been standardized to avoid confusion among the more than 1,400 genera that exist today. Abbreviations are listed in the Encyclopedia of Plants.

The Wonderful Uncertainty of Crosses

When orchids are crossed together, their seed sown and grown in laboratory conditions, the offspring are sold as a hybrid cross. Vendors may guess, but nobody knows exactly how a cross will turn out. Buying an unbloomed hybrid seedling is exciting, because when it blooms, it is a surprise, new to the world, the only one in existence. It may even be an award winner. The unbloomed status of a seedling is often mentioned by sellers. But such purchases may also yield relatively undesirable flowers. Perhaps 10 percent of the progeny of most crosses ends up better than the parents, with the other 90 percent the same or worse.

Sometimes a particularly stunning flower will result from a cross. This special plant will receive another name to distinguish it from its siblings. This "cultivar" name is given only to that plant and follows the rest of the name, set off by single quote marks. People may refer to "clonal" name instead of "cultivar," but essentially these terms mean the same thing, although there is a technical difference. (See "Mericlones and Divisions" below.)

Often a cross is "remade," using different plants than the original parents. The resulting offspring are named with the grex name originally registered. The plants do not have to be from the same seedpod in order to have the same grex name. Quality of different remakes of the same cross, therefore, can vary greatly.

Awarded Plants

The last notation on an orchid nametag may be some initials separated by a slash, such as AM/AOS or FCC/RHS, GM/13thWOC, or BM/JOGA, which indicates that the plant received an award from the American Orchid Society (AOS), the Royal Horticultural Society (RHS), the World Orchid Conference (WOC), the Japanese Orchid Growers Association (JOGA), or another orchid group. Awarded plants represent outstanding quality of some sort. They also cost more. If one or both parents of a cross have been awarded, this does not mean that the offspring also receive awards. Awards are not inherited. They must be individually earned.

The First Class Certificate (FCC/AOS) ranks as the highest AOS flower award appellation. Next is the Award of Merit (AM/AOS), and then the Highly Commended Certificate (HCC/AOS). All denote exceptional flower quality. Some 1,500 AOS awards are bestowed each year; but only about a dozen are FCCs. Gold, silver, and bronze medals (GM/SM/BM) are common awards from other orchid groups.

Although the bulk of awards honor exceptional form, color, and/or size of a particular flower, other AOS awards have been devised to recognize botanical rarity (CBR/AOS, Certificate of Botanical Recognition), exceptional horticultural aesthetic interest (CHM/AOS, Certificate of Horticultural Merit), and Judges' Commendations (JC/AOS) for unusual distinctions, all of which are awarded to the plant itself. An Award of Quality (AQ/AOS) can be awarded to an entire hybrid cross when it produces exceptional offspring, and an Award of Distinction (AD/AOS) is given to a cross demonstrating new directions in breeding.

There is also a coveted award given to a grower who demonstrates extraordinary culture of an orchid plant (CCM/AOS, Certificate of Cultural Merit).

There are more than two dozen official Judging Centers throughout the United States, each meeting monthly. Some are open to the public and afford fascinating insights as AOS judges debate the merits and demerits of a plant. Judging dates and times are published in the AOS magazine. All AOS awards are published in *Awards Quarterly* and available on CD-ROM.

Orchid shows also award ribbons, trophies, and medals. Since there are so many kinds of orchids, there are hundreds of categories for awards, which is why there will commonly be so many ribbons in exhibits. Cattleyas are not judged against phalaenopsis, but only against related orchids.

Obviously, genetics plays a large part in awards, but even flower awards are heavily dependent on how well the plant is grown. Two divisions of the same plant, in two different collections, can produce typical, unawardable flowers for one, yet in the hands of a truly gifted grower, the other may bloom so magnificently that an award is merited.

Mericlones and Divisions

Learning to read nametags and catalogs correctly means learning how to buy what you really want, avoiding mistakes. If a picture of a lovely yellow cattleya with a beautiful peach-pink throat stirs orchidmania, check the listing carefully. If that plant has a name followed by a cultivar name in single quotemarks, then in order to get exactly that plant, buy either a "mericlone" or a "division" of that specific plant.

A division is exactly that — a piece of the plant broken off and repotted. A mericlone (also called "meristem") is made by laboratory techniques that produce thousands of the same plant from a few actively growing stem-tip cells. When someone refers to the "clonal" name of a plant, instead of a "cultivar" name, technically this refers to the fact that the cultivar has been mericloned and that this plant is a clone of the original. The mericloning process is a relatively recent one, widely used for orchids only since the 1970s, and has made many orchids available at much lower prices. A mericlone usually is an exact copy of the original. However, occasionally mericlones aren't exact copies, due to so far inexplicable genetic aberrations during the laboratory process, a phenomenon known as somaclonal variation. Actual divisions of a plant are always true and thus cost more than a mericlone of the same plant.

Quite a few of the most popular genera of orchids are easily mericloned, such as *Cattleya*, *Cymbidium*, and *Phalaenopsis*, while others, such as *Paphiopedilum* and *Masdevallia*, cannot be physically mericloned, only propagated by division.

If a plant receives an award, all divisions or mericlones of that plant will also carry the award, since they are all the same plant.

If the big yellow flower with the peachy lip in the picture mentioned above is called *Brassolaeliocattleya* (*Blc.*) Malworth 'Orchidglade', then buy exactly that in order to get exactly that flower. If the plant is just listed as *Blc.* Malworth, without the 'Orchidglade' after the name, then what is for sale are sibling plants, bred from the same parental strain, and are not the exact plant in the picture. Siblings will turn out however they may, sometimes quite close to the pictured one but never exactly the same. If it doesn't really matter, order something from a cross rather than a mericlone. It will cost less. Mericlones can be very expensive, especially ones that have received awards.

Glossary

Alba White form of a flower.

AM Award of Merit. Second-highest flower-quality award given by the American Orchid Society for plants scoring 79.5–89.4 award points. An AM can also be bestowed by the Royal Horticultural Society (AM/RHS).

Angraecoid Term used to describe the monopodial orchids that belong to the African *Angraeceum* orchids and their close relatives.

AOS American Orchid Society.

Backbulb An old, often leafless, sympodial pseudobulb that is still alive and can be used for propagating a new plant.

Bare-root A method of shipping an orchid with its roots unpotted and bare of potting medium.

Bifoliate Having two leaves on a single pseudobulb.

Binomial nomenclature In Latin, literally a "two-name name," a two-word phrase that is the scientific way of naming living things, with the first term the genus and the second the species.

Bud Common term for a flower before it begins enlarging, although it is also applied to a tiny new growth or leaf.

Capsule The seedpod of an orchid, often containing thousands, even millions, of seeds.

CBR Certificate of Botanical Recognition. An AOS award given only once to an orchid species when it is first displayed in bloom.

CCM Certificate of Cultural Merit. An AOS award presented to the grower of a well-cultivated orchid plant.

Central growing point On a monopodial orchid, this is where the upright vegetative growth will begin.

CHM Certificate of Horticultural Merit. An AOS award given to a species of outstanding interest to growers.

CITES Convention on International Trade in Endangered Species. The multinational agreement that lists which plant and animal species are considered endangered and the rules by which their trade is governed.

Cleistogamous Term used to describe a flower that self-pollinates, often without even opening the flower fully; relatively rare in orchids.

Clone All the various vegetative manifestations (divisions, meristem propagations, and so forth) of a single orchid plant grown originally from a single seed; designated by single quotes around its name.

Column The fused sexual organ of an orchid flower, found atop the lip.

Community pot Many tiny seedlings planted together in a single container before they are individually repotted.

Compot Common term meaning "community pot."

Cool temperature For orchids, a minimum winter nighttime temperature of 45°F, with daytime temperatures 15–30°F higher.

Cross The progeny that result from transferring pollen from one plant to the flower of another; the act itself.

Crown The central part of the rosette of leaves in a monopodial orchid such as *Phalaenopsis*, from which new growth arises upward.

Cultivar In orchids, a specific plant grown from a single seed; designated by single quotes around its name.

Deciduous The term used to describe the loss of leaves or other growths upon maturity or at the end of a growing season, with regrowth after a dormant rest.

Diploid Having a normal number of two sets of chromosomes; also known as 2N.

Division Making new plants from old by cutting the rhizome of a sympodial orchid into pieces containing pseudobulbs and rhizome or by cutting off the top half of a stem of a vinelike orchid.

Dormancy A rest period during which no vegetative growth occurs, often following a growth period and/or the loss of leaves or other growths; may require cooler temperatures and less water.

Dorsal sepal In orchids, the uppermost "petal" of a flower.

Epiphytic Term used to describe any plant that grows above the ground and attaches to something else for support; nutrients are not taken from the supporting host but are derived instead from rain, air, and available debris.

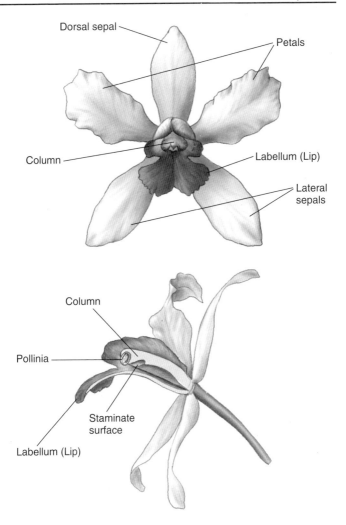

Dorsal sepal

Petals

Column

Labellum (Lip)

Lateral sepals

Column

Pollinia

Staminate surface

Labellum (Lip)

Equitant In orchids, having all the leaves arranged flat in one plane; specifically refers to a type of *Oncidium*.

FCC Highest flower-quality award given by the American Orchid Society for plants scoring 89.5–100 award points. An FCC can also be bestowed by the Royal Horticultural Society (FCC/RHS), which, in fact, originated the award.

Flask A clear container used for the laboratory germination of orchid seeds or for growing other laboratory micropropagated orchid seedlings.

Flask-grown Term used to describe an orchid grown via micropropagation techniques such as mericloning or stem propagation, and therefore a clone of some original specific plant, rather than grown from seed.

Floriferous Term used to describe a plant that flowers freely.

Flower spike A common term for any of the various types of the more properly termed flower inflorescence, whether bearing a solitary bloom atop a single stalk or in racemes or panicles of many flowers.

Footcandle A measure of light useful in determining intensity of light for growing orchids; the illumination produced by a candle at a distance of one foot.

Genera Plural of genus.

Genus A group of orchids that are classified together because of similar traits and an assumed common ancestry; there are some 860 naturally occurring orchid genera and an additional 550 manmade intergeneric ones.

Grex Term used to refer to the group of progeny of a specific cross.

Growths Any new shoots that emerge, whether they be pseudobulb, rhizome, leaf, stem, inflorescence, or root.

HCC Highly Commended Certificate. Lowest of the three flower-quality awards given by the American Orchid Society, for plants scoring 74.5–79.4 points.

High light For orchids, the brightest category of light-level needs, generally above 3,000 footcandles, and typically found only in sunrooms, in greenhouses, outdoors, in southern windows, or under high-intensity-discharge artificial lights.

Hybrid The resulting progeny from the union of two different species (known as a primary hybrid), or of a species and a hybrid, or of two hybrids (known as a complex hybrid).

Inflorescence The flowering portion of the orchid, in whatever of the various general arrangements, such as raceme, panicle, or solitary scape; often loosely referred to as the "spike."

Intergeneric Between two or more genera, usually referring to the hybridization that occurs therein.

Intermediate temperature For orchids, a minimum winter nighttime temperature of 55°F, with daytime temperatures 15–25°F higher.

JC (Judges' Commendation) Award given by the American Orchid Society for special plant and/or flower characteristics.

JOGA Japanese Orchid Growers Association. Term often found on orchid nametags, since this group also bestows awards (GM, or Gold Medal; SM, or Silver Metal; BM, or Bronze Metal).

Keiki A plantlet that develops from an orchid's flower inflorescence or cane.

Labellum The third petal of an orchid flower, modified by evolution into a lip often used as an attractive landing platform for pollinators.

Lateral sepal Term used to refer to the two lowermost sepals that extend to the sides, versus the topmost dorsal sepal.

Lip The orchid labellum.

Lithophytic Term used to describe any plant that grows attached to a rock; a subset of epiphytic life.

Low light For orchids, the lowest category of light-level needs, generally between 1,200 and 2,000 footcandles, and typically found on any windowsill (a bit back from the glass on brightest southern ones) or 8 inches under four fluorescent artificial tubes.

Medium The potting material or mix of materials that is being used inside an orchid pot; the medium may be organic or inorganic.

Medium light For orchids, the middle category of light-level needs, generally between 2,000 and 3,000 footcandles, and typically found on all windowsills except northern ones, or under high-intensity-discharge artificial lights.

Mericlone A generally exact copy of an original orchid plant made via the laboratory technique of meristem propagation; since it is a specific cultivar, it is designated by single quotes around its name.

Meristem Technically, the actively dividing cell tissue taken from root tips and from the tips of new growths or floral shoots; sometimes loosely used to refer to the mericlone plant that is produced from the laboratory propagation of meristem tissue.

Micropropagation Making new orchids by any of the laboratory techniques, including meristem tissue propagation and sterile seed culture.

Monopodial One of the two forms of orchid vegetative growth (the other is sympodial), wherein a single vegetative shoot grows continually upward, such as in the central rosette of *Phalaenopsis* and the more vinelike *Vanda*.

Multifloral Having more than one flower per inflorescence.

Natural hybrid A hybrid that occurs in the wild without the help of humans.

Node A distinct joint or notch on an inflorescence, stem, or pseudobulb from which a flower stem, leaves, or roots can emerge; a term often used to refer to the place on a *Phalaenopsis* inflorescence above which a cut can be made to induce a secondary bloom.

Nomenclature A system of naming; see "binomial nomenclature."

Nonresupinate In orchids, those plants whose flower lips are positioned uppermost relative to the inflorescence axis; the vast majority of orchid flowers are resupinate.

Panicle A type of flower inflorescence wherein the flowers are loosely arranged on a branching stem and open from the lowest or inner branches to the top.

Peloric In orchids, a term used to describe an unusual and often beautiful (sometimes grotesque) condition where all three petals (instead of just one) attempt to fashion themselves into lip colors and/or shapes.

Petal In orchids, one of the three inner segments of the flower that are positioned between the three sepals; one of the petals is modified into a lip.

Pod Term used to refer to the seedpod or capsule.

Pollinia Waxy pollen clumps or grains usually found in the anthers of most orchids; often yellow, distinct, and found under the pollen cap of the column.

Pseudobulb The thickened stem of a sympodial orchid arising from a rhizome that has so evolved for water-storage capacity but is not a true bulb.

Pseudobulbless Containing no pseudobulbs.

Raceme A simple type of flower inflorescence that looks like a long stem with flowers arising along it.

Reed-stem A type of growth wherein stems and pseudobulbs resemble reeds or canes, particularly in *Epidendrum* and *Dendrobium*.

Resupinate In orchids, those plants whose flower lips are positioned lowermost relative to the inflorescence axis; the vast majority of orchid flowers are resupinate.

Rhizome In orchids, a root-bearing stem that usually grows horizontally atop the substrate or potting mix, from which leafy growths such as pseudobulbs are sent up; sometimes called the rootstock.

RHS Royal Horticultural Society.

Scape A simple flower inflorescence that is topped by a solitary flower, such as in many *Paphiopedilum.*

Seed-grown Term used to describe an orchid grown from seed, usually in sterile laboratory conditions, rather than grown from meristem cloning techniques, and therefore a unique, original plant.

Seedling An unbloomed young orchid.

Seedpod The capsule bearing the seeds of an orchid.

Selfing Method of seed-propagating an orchid by placing its pollen on its own stigma; also known as self-fertilizing.

Semialba A white flower with a colored lip.

Semiterrestrial Term used to refer to orchids that grow near or on the ground in extremely loose, open substrate.

Sepal One of the three outer parts of an orchid flower, one of which is usually topmost and known as the dorsal, the other two lower sepals being known as the laterals.

Sib cross, sibling cross Method of seed propagation of an orchid wherein the pollen of one orchid is placed on the stigma of another orchid that was originally grown in the same seedpod as the first orchid, therefore a cross pollination of siblings.

Sibling An orchid that is related to another orchid by virtue of having been produced from the same seedpod.

Species A group of living things that appear to have common ancestry so closely related that their characteristics definitely separate them all from any other group; a further division of a genus.

Specimen Term usually used to refer to an orchid that has been allowed to grow to great size and floriferousness instead of being divided; also refers to the species that typifies a genus.

Spike Term often loosely used to refer to all flower inflorescences, but technically an unbranched flower stem with short-stalked or stalkless flowers.

Splash petal An orchid flower that modifies its petals by duplicating the coloring found on the lip; a type of peloric condition.

Stalk A part of the plant that supports something else.

Stamen The male, pollen-bearing organ of the flower.

Stem The leaf- and flower-bearing part of the plant.

Stem prop Loose term for "meristem propagation" or the plant that results from this technique.

Stigma Sticky area of the pistil of a flower that receives the pollen.

Sympodial One of the two forms of orchid growth (the other is monopodial), wherein each new growth arises from the rhizome of a previous growth, and each new growth is completely capable of bearing an inflorescence.

Systemic Term used to describe pesticides or fungicides that are taken up by plant leaves and growths and then work from within the plant.

Terete Type of orchid growth wherin the stem and/or leaves are circular in cross section.

Terrestrial In orchids, growing in the ground or in the loose substrate atop the ground.

Tetraploid Genetic aberration wherein the plant has twice as many chromosome sets as normal, often resulting in very vigorous, large plants and flowers.

Throat The inner portion of a tubular orchid lip.

Tissue culture Artificial propagation of plants via laboratory mericloning, also known as meristemming.

Unifoliate Bearing one leaf per growth.

Vandaceous Term used to describe any large monopodial orchid, particularly used for *Vanda* and its closely related orchids.

Variety A subdivision of a species that groups plants with a distinct form that is passed along to the progeny.

Vegetative propagation The creation of additional plants through division, encouragement of keiki formation, or any various meristematic techniques, but not via seed.

Velamen The thick layer of corklike, water-absorbing cells surrounding the roots of epiphytic orchids.

Warm temperature For orchids, a minimum winter nighttime temperature of 60°F, with daytime temperatures 15–25°F higher; very warm would be a night minimum of 65°F, with daytime maximum highs in the 90s.

Index

Numbers in **boldface** *type refer to pages on which color plates appear*